AF420734

THE SLOW LANE
and its
EVERYDAY WONDERS

Sandeep Dahiya

The Slow Lane

and its

Everyday Wonders

1

THERE is a dramatic and pulsating drive to build among the humans. Most of what we build is born of fears. Fear seems to be the predominant element of life on earth. Peace is a dream. We are always either fighting or preparing to fight. Therefore, the global military expenditure is 6.7 billion dollars per day. This huge amount of money is willingly spent, even eulogized under the jingoistic nationalistic banner. It's taken as a matter of pride. On the other hand, at the climate summit the major countries are fighting to muster up just 300 billion dollars for climate financing. It seems unimportant to us. Little do we realize that climate-induced ocean heating leading to a super-cyclone dents the economy by as much as the entire amount proposed for climate financing.

We are comfortable to kill each other on a dying planet. We are fundamentally inclined to lose our peace and feel restless. We get bored even with love and create disharmony and disputes. We even get bored with our freedoms as well as the mechanisms and institutions meant to ensure our individual and collective freedoms. When we get bored with freedom, we turn cynical and show apathy to the organized degradation of democratic process and institutions. Presently, the world seems to be bored with democracy. Democracy is gradually degrading over the world. Autocratic maneuvering is stealthily taking a firm grasp on the throat of democracy.

On the face value, democracy seems to follow the time-tested process, but behind the screen the indirect, subtle forgeries, lies, manipulations and misuse are eating into its soul. It's not that people can't see and feel it. They understand. They know that the spirit of democracy is being compromised like never before. But just like we get bored with love, we are receptive to the processes of democratic degradation. It's like we are ready for chaos and autocracy; a collectively depressed, anxious society getting addicted to autocracy.

While we smoothened and plastered our walls as the outward measures to cover the gaping holes inside our souls, the sparrows lost chances to build nests in niches, grooves, holes and crevices in walls, roofs and ceilings. The sparrows are now fighting to grab the abandoned wire-tail swallow mud-nest in the verandah. The mud-nest cup has a little space where they can put some grass sinews and lay eggs. The sparrows are cheeky, chirpy, petite, querulous ones. About a dozen couples are fighting to occupy the prime property. The moment a couple lands on the property, the others chase it away with angry, shrill notes. It's a big fight since morning—a little ounce of the same ghastly battlefields where one country is bombarding another to grab land and resources. They twirl, swirl, dive and shout to discourage each other from occupying the property. Finally, the most stubborn couple will win the rights. One angry couple even chased the poor flycatcher around the yard. They just banged into him the moment it perched anywhere. The sparrows in bad temper and the poor flycatcher has to pay; just like angry world leaders make the common people pay for their bursting tempers.

One can commit violence even using the naked sword of 'truth'—the so-called matter-of-fact truth. It's a bland, statistical, mechanical bit of information. A soulless entity. It's an arrow that's strung on the bow of 'honesty' to pierce, to hurt, to settle a score. Most of the so-called 'outspoken' and 'blunt' people, who assume that they are truthful, are in fact using the facts to hurt and settle scores with the people they don't like. They are no worshippers of truth.

The real truth is in spirit. Beyond technical accuracy, it has a soul. It possesses a sweet core. It's a feeling, lively entity. A really truthful person will not unleash a factually correct arrow to outscore some rival in a debate or argument. The facts that hurt someone can be retained and left unused. And if you need to use these facts at all, it should be with love, care and an intention to guide and bring positive change in someone's life, not just the plain intention of judging and showing someone in bad light and humiliate him/her.

So the intention behind what we say is the real decider of what is truthful in spirit. Even slightly modified facts that are meant to help someone, make her feel better, guide her on a nice path are far more 'truthful' than the naked, fanged facts that hurt someone and are basically used as weapons to pamper our ego.

As you stand lost in your thoughts, and you smell the fragrance of a rose. Know that it's smiling at you and sending a message through a fragrant whisper—that there is hope, love, sunshine and smile. The moment you are open like this to a thing of beauty, you realize that you had built a shell of your weakness and crawled into it for safety. The shell made of fears and insecurities. It's a big fort. It will make friends look like foes and foes like friends. It will block freedom, joy and sunlight from trickling in. But it will allow the agents of infirmities creep in. It wants to retain its prisoner. Because what jail is worth if not for the prisoner inside?

Infinity is possible in a cyclical way. The seasons change in a sequence. All the natural processes follow a cyclic path. Countless little cycles going on and on as part of the ultimate cosmic cycle. A human body is also a cyclical process involving millions of tiny cycles at the cellular level.

From birth to death, we are on the course of a cycle. But there is a linear force at every point on the curve of our life's cycle. The linearity of the intention to live, to survive, to retain this shape, to achieve something, to create something, to give some meaning to life, to realize dreams. This central linearity is the directive principle for all the smaller cycles to flow along a central path in the larger circle. In its absence the system breaks, giving free space to as many probabilities to take hold as it is possible. The closely defined system loses its shape and melts to a bigger shapelessness. For example, leave a new car unused in your yard for many years. The core linearity of its purpose—a vehicle for transport—is broken. All the little operational cycles that toe the line of the bigger machinery's cycle fall apart; the binding linearity ceases to operate, and random cycles open up, taking recourse to further little cycles in the absence of a central linear push.

The clearly defined linear push is the force that pushes point *a* to move to point *b* on the cyclical path. The linear push is what gives a thing, person, animal, bird or process a specific identity and purpose. If not claimed and bound by this central linearity, the different components of a system, thing or body are claimed by various small processes. Most of these are random and there is no coherence among them. That is *disintegration* from the point of view of the original shape of that thing, process or body. So an unused car will lose its identity over the years.

It will be pushed into shapelessness by the random forces operating out-of-bound from any linear push. In fact, the only *doing* force here seems to be the *undoing* force. So to keep evolving we have to always keep in mind the central linear idea—the one pushing all the cycles in themselves and along the curvature of the largest cycle of our overall existence—alive, kicking, fresh and invigorated.

Violence was a necessary evil in the survival game for our ancestors, the cave dwellers. To survive as one of the lesser animals (in physical terms) in the forests, the humankind used their mind and intelligence as a weapon to overcome the challenges of survival. And over thousands of years got primed to use their intelligence as basically a weapon in the game of violence necessitated by the urge to live, survive and thrive. To overcome the threats posed by the forest animals, the humankind's organized violence served as a platform for survival. But then it became our habit.

Violence has gone very deep in our cells. We have become a very violent species. As a result, our mind primarily comes as a weapon to us—to control, to manipulate, to exploit, to disempower others. The human species will burn in its own violence if this fundamental instinct to use mind as a weapon of violence is not changed. To beat the survival challenges as a weak forest-dwelling animal among more powerful beasts, violence was a 'regrettable necessity'. But to further rise from what we have now become, we will have to stop using mind as a weapon of violence. It cannot help us rise further. It'll only make us a powerful animal that will eat itself when there is nothing left to beat and eat on the earth.

The entire structure of using the mind as a means of violence (manifesting as a paranoid self-interest that pervades at individual and collective hierarchies based on identities ranging from individual, family, clan, caste, religion, nation and region) needs to be overhauled to further rise as a species. After chucking out all the enemies in the rest of the species, we are now creating virtual enemies on the basis of ever-unfolding self-interests, which in turn make us scared of losing out to the enemy out there on the other side of the identity that we have created for ourselves. For one species tamed in the forests, we have hatched 100 conceptualized species in our minds to give it more fodder to continue its violence.

Mind is a wonderful instrument. It can be primed for different nonviolent values like love, trust, care, kindness, consideration and cooperation. But the irony is that those who occupy the throne, and are in a position to start giving an institutionalized twist in that direction, are primarily structured to use mind as a weapon for manipulation and misguided control—the various types of violence in its myriad forms of the urge to be in control at any cost. It would be like expecting a serpent to cut down its own poison fangs.

The use of mind as an instrument of violence has too deep roots to be dug out. It seems an impossibility. Aren't we devising more and more means and reasons to unleash more, renewed violence against each other on the basis of nationality, caste, class, creed, religion, ethnicity? We are a haunted species—haunted with hunted by the fear of the enemy. The animals as the threats to our existence are gone. Now we are using our mind to manufacture more and more enemies. We are seeking enemies within the house in the form of soured family relations and domestic clashes. We are aiming sniper rifles against rivals, competitors and enemies in the neighborhood, offices, business sphere, even in the fields of art and culture. We are baying for the enemy's blood across the border, over the religious fence, beyond caste lines, beyond ethnicities.

It's plain raw fear blasting in a nuclear fission reaction. On and on. Acquiring atrophied mental shapes from the real physical threats of animals in the forests. The phantoms of the mind that haunt us always keep us insecure about our interests. We are tensed. We see danger everywhere. Everyone seems seeking to eat our share of the pie. But in seeking enemies everywhere, we have turned our own enemies.

The houseflies go gloatingly nibbling at your peace. You are helpless and watch wrathfully, nursing animosity. To rub salt on your wounds they land on your face, the representative of your worldly identity. That seems like vandalizing the holy altar of your existence by stomping their dirty feet on your facial skin. You turn taut with attention; muster up all determination to be at your quickest best. Then you take a ferocious swipe. You hurl all agility stored in your cells. But the houseflies are always quicker than the best of your shots. They escape unharmed. In fact, you run a high risk of pulling some muscle due to the sudden jerk to your limbs.

They doze past your furiously swatting newspaper or any other weapon you have at hand. They buzz away with elegant novelty in the art of escaping. And with a sneering, bantering buzz again land on your skin, to itch your frustration once again. This behavior is in close proximity with making a mockery of your sense of being a human, the supreme species on the earth. But over a period of time, you settle for mild reconciliation and finally sign armistice from your side.

Out of the thousands of strikes and swipes, effected with crouching hate and anger, I have hardly bruised even a wing in my confrontation with the houseflies. But this day it was a golden chance to strike with ravenous glee and kill two foes in one little strike, and undo all the humiliating hops of yore. But there are moments when such an act would sound full of revulsion and, more seriously, dishonorable.

A housefly pair is making love on my table. The fiery flakes of my revengeful self turn to cool showers of curiosity. I'm stopped from sledge-hammering this stupefying dream of these two tiny insects. At this tiny point in space-time fabric, a little episode of sensuous and voluptuous frequencies is unfolding with surrendering grace. I'm reading my morning newspaper. I turn pages. I move. I shift, snort, sigh, yawn and finally hum an uncouth Haryanvi *ragini* about a farmer's love, which is basically an animalistic lust.

I'm gloating over them like a shameless peeping tom. They are just a couple of feet away. They are oblivious to any kind of danger today. Aha, love's animated, flattering tones! All the force of fear and survival now focused on giving a pleasurable crescendo—to heave their species onwards from their end. I take my illegal prying into their private matter even further and start taking their pictures. My mobile is just inches away from them. It seems a bold couple. They aren't shy of getting filmed in their moments of deep intimacy.

Initiated by the male by striking or jumping into the female (like a typical male of any other species), their lovemaking can last 30-120 minutes. Well, it can give a big complex to most of the humans. Mating comes quite naturally to the species on earth. But to the human mind, it comes as a complex ritual.

The male houseflies use pheromones (produced by the females) to detect a female by colliding with them mid-air or ground striking. The drone tries to force open her wings. If she accepts his advances, she vibrates her wings to make a buzzing sound. Copulation begins, as it does now on my table. They must have had a very heavy breakfast prior to this as fly-mating takes a lot of energy and they need their bellies full before the ritual of procreation.

The drone fertilizes the female eggs. She then lays eggs in a filthy, warm, moist place. From my table she will go and fly to lay eggs on feces and filth a day after. The eggs will take a day to hatch. The larvae (maggots) will bury themselves in the filth and an adult fly will emerge from the pupa. In five to six batches over three or four days a housefly lays around 500 eggs in its lifetime of 15-30 days.

I have the choice to allow the rationality of mind—that these are carriers of diseases such as typhoid, tuberculosis and worms—to stifle the poetic romanticism of lovemaking insects, and squash them down with a newspaper strike. If I do this, I can easily close-up an entire branch of houseflies. It will wind up the new pathways for 500 new houseflies in a week, which would have ended up starting new chain reactions of 500 further houseflies from those previous ones, and onwards similarly. That means I would stop the evolution of millions of houseflies from this end. The rationality of the human mind would encourage one to stop at least one door to the proliferation of these germ-spreading insects.

But is there anything in nature that has not its benefits? Houseflies are waste decomposers and eat poo. A single tiny larva eats about a half gram of organic matter in a day. Beyond the side issues of disease transmission, hygiene and sanitation practices, mother nature produces them to decompose the natural and human-produced organic waste including feces and carcasses. There are houseflies because there is excess of organic matter that hasn't been suitably and properly managed. That opens the breeding potential for these opportunistic feeders. They lap up the putrefying sap with their sponging mouthparts.

Moreover, their pathogenic immunity can be studied to help us understand the causes and factors of immunity to help us devise similar medical defense guards for the humans also. So in the scheme of mother nature it's not clear whether stopping this particular point of evolution would be beneficiary or disadvantageous in the ultimate sense.

I think instead of trying to kill a pair of lovemaking houseflies, I should try to properly manage the organic waste around me, at least on my premises. That seems like a real solution—an effort to remove the cause instead of merely tempering with the effects. Helped by the self-approval of poetic romance, I strengthen my moral fortification and allow the fly couple their moments of surrender to the energetic throng of procreation. They are not concerned about my choice. They take their time, oblivious to my shuffling and flicking newspaper.

The drone then takes off after many prolonged minutes of joyride on the rollercoaster of creation. He has played his limited part in the process. The female has a bigger role to play. Her part has just started. She sniffles around for a couple of more minutes, preens her wings and takes off to look for a suitable filthy site to lay her eggs the next day.

I'm visiting Bhopal after two years of Corona mayhem. My sister stays there and the city with its cleaner air and more space usually entices me to extend my stays. Scores of *palash* (*dhak*) or 'flame of the forest' welcome you with their copious blooms. It's the flagship of spring in this part. It's considered to be the sacred *agni* tree with its vivid, stunning orange flowers. The attractive beacon has a beak-shaped keel petal, two wings by its side and a heart-shaped background petal pointing upwards giving the impression of rising flames.

The welcoming and sprawling campus of Barkatullah university, near my sister's place, is my evening time escape zone. It's a peaceful laidback campus, dry leaves rustling like the soft murmur of a poem in a Persian anthology. It's duly typified by the ancient-looking silent little block of Persian studies on the campus. But then you leapfrog into the future as well when you come across Advanced Research Center for Space and Earth Science under Department of Earth Sciences. I wonder what type of sophisticated tools must be there inside those unassuming old looking blocks. It's a modern world: remote sensing, geo-informatics, digital image processing of satellite data, mirror and prism stereoscopes, light tables, optical reflecting projector, optical pantograph, image analyzer. And when two buildings, one dealing with a medieval language and the other involving future technologies, stand nearby on the same campus, it's almost like Persian verses laced with space technology formulas between the lines. A senior research fellow to supervise the modern technical processes; just like a *hijab*-clad senior professor in the Persian studies department guiding the studying light among the dimly lit corridors of past. The space technology supervisor, her blond hair flashing almost yellow. She walks on the campus as an alien species. Silent, eyes on the ground, not expecting to come across anyone really familiar enough to engage in some talking. She loves walking through the not-so-dense parkland interspersed with scrub forest running along the asphalted path. For safety, she walks keeping the road in sight. The *hijab*-clad professor zooms past in her car, driving while on a call.

You can feel the changing winds. The Arabic and Persian studies department is a sad pale blue block. To put up a stark contrast, there is a swashbuckling new building, freshly minted, modernly designed. It's the department of Sanskrit Studies. Arabic and Persian saw their heydays. Before that it was Sanskrit that touched the pinnacle of glory. But by symbolically giving it respect and prestige, you can at least have a feeling of revivalism. The university's name is Barkatullah but to add to its secular credentials various academic blocks are named Chanakya, Vikramaditya, Shivaji. These signboards are vibrantly painted. There are winds of change for sure. Hindu revivalism, they say. Elsewhere in India the names of roads are getting changed, so are the names of cities. Mughal Garden is no longer Mughal Garden. As of now the word 'Mughal' connotes even bigger colonist government than that under the Britishers. The rulers will always have their say, in one form or the other. They will rake-up dirt. They will twist, mold, reshape things as per the suitability of their interests. So we have the modern kings who reshape the past to make it suitable for governance as per their beliefs and ideologies. As I walk musing over the winds of change, I come to realize that Mughals, Sultanate and Gujarat riots have been removed from senior secondary NCERT books. The present is being revamped on the rubble of the past.

The campus of Barkatullah University is a paradise for evening walkers like me; spacious, almost silent asphalted narrow roads tolerably travelling many hectares of near wilderness with unassuming academic blocks set up almost apologetically among the trees.

As is the case with any neighborhood, there are regular walkers, most of them obese elders trying to stay within the range of the bearing capacity of their frail bones. I remember a few elderly walkers from the last trip. I am glad to know that they are still there and have successfully warded off the corona waves. They seem to be doing fine. The first is a gentleman in his seventies. He comes in well-ironed shirt and trousers. The shirt officially tucked in. He walks slowly but talks a lot more energetically. He is always speaking on the mobile, maybe to a friend from the office days who has gone back to his native place. He takes a long, slow-paced walk and they gently unfold the current affairs going fast around their old legs. The other is a silent elderly woman, fat, bundled in a sari. She heaves herself to health every day. She walks with unassuming purpose by keeping her head tilted sideways. Maybe it helps as a propeller against her weight. To make me happy, both of them look exactly the way I remember from two years back. So walking definitely helps.

The other is an elderly couple. She wears tight three-quarter leggings and a frock to top it. She has broad manly shoulders. She looks bored with late-life household conundrum. He has extremely narrow shoulders and goes broadening below. His waistline quite ample from a plus-sized female barometer. If nature were a bit more lenient and caring, it would have given auntie's broad shoulders to uncle and fixed his enormous bottom on her, replacing her narrow hips.

I walk with the setting sunrays and then branch off into the more natural parts to the distant corners of the campus. A foot trail branches off from the asphalt road and sneaks over the dark soil bearing winter-beaten grass. It's not leveled up like a well-planned park. It still retains mother earth's very own open plan, a very fine undulation. The black soil bears a very short-cropped grassy grey hair and little sparse weeds. Lots of *sheesham* trees have been planted in the unkempt, free park. Planted in the same season, most of them lock similar in age and built— adolescent tree-boys having faint strains of mustachioed canopy.

One can walk in any direction even wearing bathroom slippers. But we are the children of beaten paths. We feel secure in following a trail of passage. There are feeble traceries of foot tracks across the grassy terrain deciding the little-little destinations and milestones. Maybe we have killed our spirit to just move around without looking for endpoints. Even on a perfectly walkable unpaved landscape, our feet feel a drag, an inhibition, an ambivalence, creating a discomfort that finally draws our steps to the beaten path. It's for this reason that walking on solitary trails brings a sense of freedom to the footloose revelers.

The setting is perfect for me. The scattered clouds present a shifting panorama of shapes and colors. Look into the shapes evolving and colors changing. At a cursory glance, it may appear meaningless. But look deeply and the mind will identify shapes. It will give ideas. In a way, it just is, but our mind will conjure up colorful things like elephants, gods, ships. Things on the ground are no different. They just are; mere shifting shapes. Our mind is what creates the newer and newer meanings, spinning spools of complexities.

A cluster of wild jasmine bush is my milestone to take to this solitary trail from the tar road. Wild jasmine flowers suffuse the evening with a heady aroma, egging one to seek more solitude to be in company with one's real self. The parkland bearing faded grass has a few stunted palms as well as tall date palms and tall thickets of bamboo bushes. A drongo is having a late evening feast on *palash* flowers as I pass by the tree. I usually walk to the clumps of bulrush, the waterside sedge, around a mossy waterhole on this black-soiled, faded grass-topped, *palash*-flamed panorama.

The sun is setting behind a cluster of palms, bamboos, *sheesham* and *palash*. A pale orange flame in the dark green bowl of the joint canopy—a lamp of sadness. What remains of the day bygone? What remains of the love lost? A distant whisper, a nearby murmur, a nostalgic tingling, some pain, a soft smile, a bruise, a hurt, some guilt, some blame. But above all, the dying pale rays sowing the seeds of a new bright day after the night.

Sweet-sour sadness to be topped with some wild berries. It's a clump of wild *karanda (carissa spinarum)*, a thorny, dense, multi-stemmed shrub with forked branches and ovate leathery green leaves. Its tiny flowers with five white narrow petals beckon me for sour-sweet solace. It's also called conkerberry or bush plum. It offers its ripe purple conkerberries and says these are edible. I usually accept its offerings in this solitude. But this time I have to be careful—watchful that beauty comes with its risks. Its milky sap and unripe fruits are harmful. I roll my tongue over the biter-sweet tart taste and absorb in the sweet-scented flowers. It's a heady smell, just like the smell of beauty usually is.

The trail leaves the faded beaten grass to enter a zone of wetland grass. A story says that little Moses was found in a bulrush boat. Its long, narrow eight or nine feet tall leaf stems provide sanctuary to a colony of black-breasted weaverbirds. It's the roosting time and they raise a high frequency din at the sundown as if discussing the day's events. You can hear this jingling music from a distance. There is *basa* (*ipomoea carnea*) or pink morning glory. It is also called *besharam*. I would prefer the last one for the fact of its shameless thuds and thwacks on our bums at the village school. It has a hardy, juicy stem that has enough hardness to burn the skin but sufficient suppleness to avoid serious bone injuries. Our teachers preferred it as their striking weapon. The favorite pipe-cane wielders of our school zoom in my memory as I appreciate the lovely heart-shaped purple blooms.

My brother-in-law has a vintage type Maruti 800. Its flashy red color can bring the best of cars to submissive blush. And when he obliges me and drives me to lovely places like Sanchi, Bhimbhetaka caves, Narmada *ghats* and massive uncompleted Bhojraja temple, I make it a point to encourage him: 'Instead of sitting as a passenger in someone's Lamborghini, drive your own Nano with pride.' He seems slightly disturbed. 'It's not a Nano. That is half of it,' he corrects me. As a big SUV sizzles past I really marvel at his capacity to look for little things to compare with his favorite car.

Sometimes I sneak into the little neighborhood market. A small world having little stores, medics, groceries, fruit and vegetable sellers, sweet makers and a confectioner. A *pan wallah* at one corner and a *chai wallah* at the other. A photocopier and stationer. Vineet Hair Dresser and Ananda Tailors at the end of the little passage at the back of the block. Have tea, chew a pan, smoke a cigarette on your cheat day, get glued to your phone sitting on a cushioned bench outside the hairdresser, look at the pretty ladies coming to the tailor to get their clothes fixed. The tailor's establishment is at the end, with its workshop area open to the passage. It's a little world in itself. You have young people waiting patiently for their hairdo turn. Smartphone is the new tool of meditation, of being in the moment. You have the cosmos on your fingertips. You are like a god having the power of witnessing what and how things are at the moment just by touching a few points on the screen. The elderly meanwhile seem itchy and restless while waiting for their turn. Time is a big element in their life as it moves towards the zero hour.

There is an old woman in my sister's neighborhood. I think she has stubbornly decided to hit the century mark. She is still around and looks same since I visited two years back. She still has enough motherhood to take care of her middle-aged son and attend to her toiletries. What else you need? She was diagnosed with blood cancer more than a decade ago. She but is an illiterate village woman whose son works here and she has joined him to share urban life for the last few years. Ignorance is bliss. She hasn't allowed someone's conceptual terminology of an imbalance in her energetic system as cancer to hijack her spirit. Lack of knowledge is blissful in such cases. It avoids the paranoia about a fatal diagnosis. Most often, the word 'cancer' kills more than the disease itself. An almost normal system suddenly surrenders the instinct of survival and one dies of shock basically. But the word has no big meaning for her. So here she is hopefully looking at the three-digit mark with good spirits.

Time flies. Three weeks fly in a jiffy. The spring is gone and we have early summer. In Bhopal summers are special, and very sweet. The streets in residential quarters have many mango trees. They fructify really well. In late March, the trees are laden with tiny clusters of flowers. Some already have little green unripe mangoes. A tree may reward you with a succulent drop, hopefully not on your head, as you walk in the street. But that will be during the peak of summers. As of now, I have to inhale and be content with the smell of mango flowers and little unripe green baby mangoes. I have to go back and rely on my sister's tales of ripe mangoes and their fruit feast.

It's early morning. Rani Kamla Pati railway station can rival with the capital airports of many developing countries. Sleek, semi-high-speed Vande Bharat train has been launched a couple of days back on April Fool's day by the honorable prime minister. It feels like you are going to board a plane while standing on the platform. This is the world of social updates. Most of the waiting passengers are taking proud selfies with the gently roaring engine.

Hordes of people line up at poor hamlets along the tracks to capture the fleeting glimpse of a vibrant, shiny India whizzing past their static, frozen poor fates. In the train many educated people audibly speak in English to do justice to the swanky new train. It's a high-end transport facility. In the first week, there is a feedback that it runs on time. Automatic sliding doors, airplane type seats, long and high glass windows, the staff moving with purpose. But then the toilets get bombarded with enthusiastic, misdirected squirts. An announcement has to be forced on the speakers requesting the passengers to aim well and flush the toilet after use—sorry misuse. We have a long way to go in the field of maintaining toilet decorum. Within a couple of hours of travel, the toilets are completely unusable for the women and children.

I have a curiosity and keen interest in watching the historical Chambal badlands from the train window. Pan Sing Tomar is my favorite movie. It's a complex topography around Chambal river. There are critically dissected ravines and undulating gullies. It's a maze of eroded clay-rich soils. The eroded landforms and scarce vegetation has spun many legends of rebels. All this topographic whirlpool is churned by perpetual vertical erosion by rivers and streams. It's particularly critical between Bhind and Morena. In these tiny sand hills, steep ridges, trenches and incised meanders many dacoits and rebels set up their own system to fight against what they deemed to be injustice. Those who wanted to fight on their own terms escaped into these badlands of fluvial erosion. The outlaws had their heydays in the messy tri-junction in Chambal valley among MP, UP and Rajasthan borders. The elements of social erosion flew along the puzzling ravines to set up their own fiefs primarily with a gun. There were plenty of *bagis* who considered themselves to be revolutionaries.

It's a quick travel and at noontime the train is safe home in Delhi. They have tried their level best to organize things at the New Delhi railway station. But no facelift is enough for the ever-increasing passenger footfall. They trample all facelifts within hours. And there you have it— the very same, stuffed, stomped, smelly railway station of old.

A massive chunk of sun breaks off unleashing a solar flare. A fiery slingshot of infernal tornado smashed into space. Solar flares affect our communication system. I hope it won't flare-up the already heated-up temperaments of the world leaders who are firing missiles and rockets with nefarious designs and conspiracies.

The solar flare seems to increase temperatures and separatist itch in the *khalistanis* in Punjab. They again raise the banner of revolt. These are the dark spin-offs of the ultra-nationalist ideology. You have been parroting 'Hindu *Rastra*, Hindu *Rastra*' too loudly of late. It creates ripple effects. It inspires—wrongly of course—others also to do the same. If you emphasize too much on an over-swiping *Hindutva*, coloring the entire country in one color, the minorities will justifiably feel threatened.

The extremist Hindu ideology itself is a reaction, an offshoot, to the blind religious zealotry of hard-line Muslim *maulvis* who have drilled a dangerous fact in the common Muslim psyche that their first identity is that of a Muslim before any other lesser identity like citizenship, designation, role, responsibility. So the bullyboys of Hinduism feel justified in raising a din in the name of their own religion also.

To begin with, in the contemporary scenario of extremist, communal violence, the hard-liners in Islam have wrongly inspired fiery sentiments among other religions. A few of the otherwise peace-loving *sanatan dharmis* have turned *trishul*-wielding mobsters. The main culprit is the fire of sectarianism. Catching the flame from Islamic zealots, it now burns in many Hindu hearts. In the same vein, the fiery Hindu hearts can't but help it from spreading to other sections. So they inspire resurgent *khalistanis* now.

As the shadows cast by the nationalistic sunrays—call it revived Hinduism—creep over the Indian diversities, we have the troublesome revival of *khalistan* movement. If you over-do it, so will others. You create justifications for others to do the same by your overblown actions. The *wrong* is far more effective in motivating the mobsters than the *right*.

Given the present government's trident-sharp rhetoric to link everything related to India as *Hindutva* in the entire historical and cultural context, the Muslims feel they are the victims of systematic discrimination at the level of state policies. It goes into doing the spadework or groundwork for separatism along communal lines. I smell a very distinct We *Vs* They odor like it must have been before 1947 leading to partition. Further, the din raised to the proportions of *pralya* whenever a Christian missionary converts a tribal in the forest will keep the Christians in the north-east hooked to the feeling of alienation.

India is too diversified to be colored in one ideological color. The shining nationalistic colorists may gain temporary benefits like forming governments but in the long run it will eat the foundation of India like termites eat wood. When Hindu youths go lynching over cows, of course the Sikh youths also get an itching to go on rampage along communal lines and carry Holy Guru Granth Sahib into the police stations challenging law and order.

The far rightist ideology colors the insanity of mobsters in patriotic hues. But then in India we have enough religions to catch the communal bug and bring down our castle. Let's talk of inclusivity. Let the elections be fought over the issues that concern the life of a common person. Let's put the blinding colors of the so-called *rastravadi* revolution on the sidelines and pick up simple tools of nation-making through real, effective developmental works.

All exclusivist principles draw their sustenance from an atrophied complex, the complex of superiority. If as a resurgent Hindu nationalist you feel justified in your exclusive ideology, don't you think others also feel the same way? Don't you think even a *khalistani* will try to justify his belief along the same lines? Or do you think your exclusivist right of narrow-mindedness is greater than theirs because *sanatan dharma* is older than Sikhism? From this principle of seniority in years, the religion of animism followed by the *Dravidian* tribals deep in the forests of south India has even bigger claim to hold the copyright over the faith of this geographical unit, because they were already functioning as a human society with its distinct culture when the Aryans arrived and laid the foundation of what we recognize today as Hindu dharma.

One ought to have transportable roots so that when the calamity strikes necessitating an exile, you can uproot yourself and move with your injured self to a new place. It's better than suffering and meeting a slow, painful death at the old place that has no option for you to lead even the most basic of a life.

Of course, you can't carry the earth around your roots with you. But its scent and feel in your heart and soul will be still enough to help you as you dig fresh earth at a strange place to fix your broken roots.

You can graft yourself and try to adjust to the new soil, new sun, new rain, new animals, new insects, new plants and grass, new people It's always good to give it a try; as long as there is some option—even if it's as little as carrying a part of your broken self and broken roots.

If you succeed in this self-grafting, this new you, built on the ruins of the old you, will save you from many a guilt of life. A self-reward it will be; bestowed in honor of having keep going—just for having crossed the desert to reach home; a far away oasis, strange and almost alien but still livable, where you can spread your roots to a decent degree.

We are pursuing a sense of oneness with something unknown, a vague sense of fulfillment. Almost an emptiness. And we make our own pictures of that which we suppose will fetch that sense of oneness. We have intangible glimpses of that something which drives us to try to fit in and taste rest, ease, oneness through aims, goals, desires, relationships, art, science, everything we do. That something which will eventually get us relieved of perpetual weariness and tension which make us feel that something is missing in life.

Either we have tasted this oneness before—there is a logical chance for it because otherwise why would we hanker so soulfully for something that hasn't been experienced earlier—or it never was, nor will ever be our fate to feel this oneness.

The second thing is more probable. And we are merely little particles in this stream of cosmic thrust; the aggressive, parasitic expansion; the powerful explosion in which the stronger elements chuck out the weaker ones—a black hole sucking a huge star into its empty innards; an eagle pouncing upon a soft rabbit to tear it apart—to make more and more complex structures and beings. From the perspective of timeless and spaceless infinity, it doesn't seem probable that there is one particular, permanent state of oneness.

2

THE birds seem to hold a nobler form of love. Wild free-will carried by their wings. The reflection of love on the screen of life seems tranquil, chirpy though, and wholesome. We on the other hand carry lots of false modesty on the grand old mule track of love. Our reasoning gets clouded with passion. Our emotions spin colossal tangle as we walk on the woodcutter trails in the forest of love.

Men are mostly snapping their jaws like sunning alligators trying to eat butterflies—to quench the insatiable hunger as well as provide amusement to the bored self. And women, beautifully enigmatic and amusing, scented breeze in their tresses, ravaging silence behind their gossips, they almost borrow happiness at a hard price in a male-dominated world. They have their pain and undulations while hanging between lucidity and illusion.

But the birds possess a nobler form of love, as I mentioned earlier. The wire-tail swallow couple, for example. They are the resident birds in the neighborhood. I see them flying around for most of the year. They are extra active during the monsoons. In the musty, humid air of July and August, they reflect extra dose of love, of being together, of caring and sharing. Despite their chipping quick notes, airy swirls and swift flapping of wings their love seems calm. Lyrical and real; very natural without any superfluous infusion.

Unlike young clandestine lovers in some town in a deeply conservative society, all sly and telling a lyrical lie, foul words stamped on perfumed paper with a luminous ink, the birds are free to spread their love on free wings.

The monsoon breeze is cooler. The swallows have a permanent nesting place on the verandah ceiling. They always modify the last year's mud nest. There is a cable going over the yard and I see them making love on it after fixing the house. It's never a hurried and pushed love like we humans. First they take their duties of setting up the nest and only then they allow themselves some pleasure. They seem so light—devoid of the extra weight of wisdom and knowledge. They are contended with the primitive trinket—mother nature's raw bouquet of life and living—and do full justice to it till death's slingshot brings them down.

There is a very lucid conviction in what and how they do it. But the mankind is different. Our love's character is furrowed by pain. We are caught in childish entanglements with dramatized perseverance. The funny authors of our own huge shame and tiny fame. We die every moment to sign in the gold book of life. The streets are vice-ridden and in disarray, crowded with distinguished, arrogant and prejudiced people. The scene revolting and ridiculous. Duplicities drizzling. Ingenuous villainies abounding. Mirrored doors stop this street clamor and try to retain the beautified and glorified private interiors holding little patches of succulent swamps. An effort to create a minute trace of picture-card peace. Gold thread embroidery on the muddy clothes mired in arduous morass. Cosmetics layered over enfeebled charms. Almost like an illicit dose of love—like a married man climbing into a widow's bed.

Beyond all this, I try to acknowledge and admit the possibility of real, natural love in the human world.

She, the wire-tail swallow lady, is plump now, carrying eggs. They are usually comfortable with my presence but sometimes play mischief and swiftly almost graze my just-shaven head, chipping away with a birdie joke maybe.

They do it now as I watch the labored journey of an earthworm in the yard. It started from a corner very early in the morning and after three hours I see it just a dozen feet from the destination, a little wet flowerbed with fresh mud. It seems a very adventurous earthworm. Luck, as they say, favors the brave. It has beaten many accidental possibilities in reaching this far in the journey. It's a lovely sight to witness such a fruitful homecoming. To add my helping share to its struggle, I decide to keep a watch till it reaches home to undo any risk because there are many a slip between the cup and lips.

A squirrel has shifted her base. It had its nest outside the wall among the clumps of trees. But there are snakes there, so possibly it's changing house to avoid encounter with the reptiles. So looking for a better lodge for its little ones it has made a nest of cloth strips, cotton and dry grass high among the branches of the *parijat* tree in the garden. There it comes bounding from under the gate's lower grills, its kid held in mouth. It almost bumps into my feet as I stand guard to see the earthworm safely home. It takes a sharp turn and looks worried from a distance. A mother shouldn't be stopped like this. So I move away and here it comes and climbs the tree to show their new place to the kid.

The tiny tailorbird is always in earnest, noisy and imperturbable. It keeps on letting out monitorial tweets about anything and everything. It sounds sharp and forbidding, a kind of sword-in-hand-fighter. The green guy with tautly drawn tail seems livid about the way things are managed in the world. On sultry monsoon noons its *cheeup-cheeup-cheeup* ruckus has alerted me many times about a reptilian encroachment in the yard. It is such a small bird but the wondrous hardihood of raillery and persuasive eloquence might force you to bow down to it and say, 'Hailed be thy cause Your Greatness!'

Oriental magpie robin is a very happy looking black and white bird. It has an exciting cavalcade of notes and sounds. A look at it gives you a feeling that it's a very cheerful bird. It's quite magisterial in looks; the prominent black and white gives the impression of a lawyer's attire. I have never heard it sad and sullen. During the monsoons its freely cantering verses of love are a treat to listen. Its positive spirit is wholeheartedly revealing, so much so that you feel good after listening to its songs.

The only other guy who can beat the magpie robin in lyrical positivity is the white-browed fantail flycatcher. The birdie chap resonates with fun with his mesmerizing dips and dives to catch fleas. He seems very free; beyond fear and its consequential rigidities. He flip-flops artistically and sings with voluminous range of notes. I have never felt him to be desperate; his is a relaxed foray, almost a play with the fleas even though they have to pay with their lives if they lose in the game. A fun-loving guy basically, he spreads his white-edged fantail while he modulates and varies his notes. The notes sound lovely. His best signature note is *ee-ee-oo-oo-aa-aa*, a distinct composition for love, which is basically a lively whistle of six notes. Well, sometimes he modifies it to make it of eight notes.

The peacocks look beautiful but their hoot is too candid and much acerbic. It pierces one's ears a bit ruefully. It's meticulously ebullient with high-pitched notes capable of dislodging the ball of wax in one's ears. They are the national bird so giving them more share of fame I would say their *peee-hooo* siren call sounds boldly virtuous shout of a rigorist.

The sparrows have chirpy effervescence. It carries the pleasant hustle and bustle of the birdie world. Their chorus is pretty coherent. It can raise one's spirit on a bleak dawn.

The crow has vivid but confounding notes for human ears—as if the guy is busy in sharpening his cleverness and use it against the humans. Many times his cawing almost scoffs at the listener.

The babblers hurl their *twein-twein-twein* domineeringly. They are always miffed at something and protest vociferously. If the *koel* is classical, they are plainly massical. They launch their *te-te-te* as if in pursuance of a long unsettled dispute.

The doves are mostly silence-wreathed but when they speak—except the laughing dove which seems to laugh even while she is crying—they carry distant or blurred notes of pain and suffering. They are for relaxing and complacency; don't carry the zipping enthusiasm usually seen among the birds.

I don't have the mesmerizing and bewitching whistling thrush around me. But the coucal, almost at the opposite end of the spectrum in tone and melody, sometimes comes from the farmside and gives a factory hooter kind of echoing call. It sounds an exuberant denial of the humans' sole right to shout.

Oriental white eyes raise barely audible little trills of anklet bells—an elegant softly jingling rhetoric if you care to listen to the complaints of such a little bird.

The red-vented bulbul's notes carry lots of emotive significance. Their name sounds lyrical and poetic but they are always mired in competing concerns with fellow birds of all species. When angry they become awfully confounding even to a human watching the show.

The wire-tail swallows let out finely crafted chip-chip sounds as they swiftly dart in airy spaciousness, picking up midges midair and even chipping a lice from your head if you dare to come near their mud nest.

There are genuine echoes of mother nature in their— the birds—calls. In a world cluttered with controversies, I listen to their calls. Their chattering is a treat during the peaceful, intimate pre-dawn air. Wherever or whoever you are, mentally bruised, homeless, dissident or outcast, listen to the call of birds. Even if your world is crumbling, listen to the birds. No words, no advice, no preaching—just the sound of mother nature. They are the threads to the silence of trees. The trees are the threads to stones. And the voiceless threads of mute stones are the passage to the womb of nothingness. But to begin with listen to the birds.

Lucky are the ones who get Mahadev's blessing to go on Amarnath pilgrimage.

Lord Shiva agreed to tell the tale of immortality to Ma Parvati. With sweet resignation to His wife's insistence, He, with an enigmatic smile, took care that there was no one apart from Mata Parvati to hear even a single world about the secret of His immortality. Gods have mystical sentries guarding the entry and the exit to the portals of real knowledge pointing to the ultimate, unqualified reality, the absolute truth. The gem of truth is hidden in the chest of illusions, the manifesting *maya*. That's why this remote cave, the holy shrine of Amarnath, was chosen for the purpose of telling the tale of immortality. It's a remote area in high Himalayas, the barren cliffs covered with snows for most of the year.

As the Lord told the tale in a pensive, loving and kind tone, perchance (or was it secretly planned by destiny acting independent even of the Gods' will) a pair of pigeons overheard the story and became immortal. The pilgrims get excited and feel validation of their faith if during their *darshan* in the holy cave they see white pigeons fluttering under the high, craggy roof of the cave.

The holy cave is located in a narrow gorge at the farther end of Lidder valley at an altitude of 4000 m. Since that mythical episode, beyond time's whence and thence, the ice lingam kept waxing and waning with the moon in complete solitude and isolation for many centuries. The cave is mentioned in ancient scriptures but was lost to humanity for many centuries. Finally, about 150 years ago a shepherd named Buta Malik discovered the cave. He was grazing his sheep and goats when he met a *sadhu*. The *sadhu* gave him a bag of coals. Back home when the shepherd opened the bag, he found gold coins instead of coal. He ran back to the place to find the *sadhu*. Buta Malik found the cave while he was looking for the *sadhu*. That's how the Muslim shepherd found himself face to face with the holy ice lingam and two more ice formations, which we now revere as Ma Parvati and Lord Ganesh. A *sadhu* appeared (believed to be Lord Shiva Himself) and asked the Muslim shepherd to make arrangement for annual pilgrimage to the cave. Unfortunately, these days there is a mischievous effort to separate Hindus and Muslims from each other's religious places.

Buta Malik's descendents took care of one of the holiest sites in India? Did that diminish its holy status? No. Then times changed and religious polarization became a major factor in Indian politics. In 2008, Shri Amarnath Shrine Board (SASB) did away with Malik family's management of Lord Shiva's shrine. There were three parties involved: the pundits of Mattan temple, the Mahant and the Malik family. The SASB offered 1.5 crore each to the parties to abandon their custodianship, so that SASB could be made the sole guardian. The two parties accepted the money but the Malik family refused the money. A gentleman of modest means from the family told the governor, who heads the SASB now, that mosques and temples can't be valued in terms of money. They maintain that they were never after the proceeds from the offerings; rather it gave them spiritual satisfaction in doing this *seva* work. They still keep a charity medical stall to give free medicines at the shrine. In remembrance of the old, more secular times, many *sadhus* visit the Malik family during their stay at the Nunwan base camp before taking the arduous journey.

It's a difficult trek, especially for the common plainsmen like me who are at the most below average amateur trekkers. Barren, stern mountains stare down at you with a foreboding look. You gasp for breath and take a grasp at your faith to help you struggle ahead. I have been lucky to visit the shrine thrice so far from the Baltal route, which is a short-cut but involves a very steep, risky climb. It might be difficult to look at the pilgrimage as one unit. We have been conditioned to deal with parts and fragments. So that's how one can proceed to make it easier. Baltal to Domail is 2 km. Walk with spring in your steps. Give your best and focus just on reaching Domail. From here on, brace yourself with a bigger challenge. Domail to Barari is 5 km. This is where you are supposed to be steady, almost warmed up, your lungs now inhaling the thinner put pure air with increased efficiency. Barari to Sangam gives you a 4 km of tougher challenge. Most of the walkers are now on the down-slope of strength and energy. So add your voice to the chants of Lord Shiva to give a kick to your lungs and legs. The 3 km final stretch from Sangam to the holy cave is the most arduous one. Each step a milestone on the path of faith. Here one leaves oneself to the Lord's mercy. This is the classical calculating way to rationalize the tough pilgrimage. One can mix it up with the poetic, romantic approach as well to make it more joyful.

Why not reach three days in advance before your scheduled registration date for the climb? Your lungs and legs will get acclimatized to the high altitude conditions. Roam around leisurely like you are at a funfair. It indeed is a big festive environment with tents, music, dance and free feisty *langar* food in plenty at the Baltal base camp. Go on small walks in the picturesque Baltal valley on the foothills of Zozila mountain pass. Enjoy the encouraging escalade of Amarganga on whose banks Baltal base camp is situated. Amarganga emerges from the glaciers around the holy cave. The joint flow of five streams from Panchtarni meets Amarganga at Sangam. Further on from Baltal another stream from Machoi glacier joins Amarganga to become Sindh river. The latter flows for 108 km to join Jhelum, which in turn rests in the lap of the Indian ocean. So enjoy the *langars*, dance to the devotional music and enjoy strolls through Baltal valley meadows, which further extend to Sonmurg's golden meadows few kilometers down the valley.

The more you observe, the more you learn and know, the wiser you become, the better life seems. There is more light under the sun of understanding.

Snow leopard is the flagship species here. They have become rare but you can visualize the silent snowy serenades of this solitary hunter on the slopes surrounding you. In the nearby meadows enjoy the violet or dark blue Himalayan bellflower and colorful dwarf rhododendrons. Inhale the freshness while walking through vibrant herbaceous community of *aster, jurinea, morina, anemone* and *primula*. See the stoic muse of the willows lining up along the shallow mountain streams. Peek into the lofty heights surrounding you and have a feel of the cold, imploringly impartial and majestically neutral game of mother nature where snow leopards and Tibetan wolves hunt mountain goat, goral, blue sheep, serow and Himalayan tahr. Open your face to the blue vault of open skies where avian predators like lammergeier, golden eagle and Himalayan griffon scan the predator radars for more colorful and agile preys like blood pheasant, western tragopan and Himalayan monal.

There are bouquets of beauty waiting to welcome you everywhere. Do your research on local flora, fauna, geography, culture and places. This knowledge and understanding gives a totally new meaning to your presence here. If you are an above-average observant of what passes on your path, just start soaking the unfoldment of mother nature in your journey from Srinagar itself. Pale yellow elderberry flowers hold a bouquet of their gentle smile by the roadside as you move from Srinagar to Baltal. Pines on the hillsides stand with grand elderly patience and fortitude. Say hello to the fresh, summer meadows blooming with roseroot, poppy, lousewort and aster flowers. Feel your ascension into higher mountains from the paradisiacal valley as the tree line gradually gives way to twisted, stunted rhodendron, juniper, stunted birch; green coniferous forests slowly surrendering to alpine shrubs and grasses between the tree line and the snow line. Keep going, following your faith, pampering the adventurous pilgrim in you, to reach the dark brown barren mass of sky-kissing rocks and cliffs wearing snowy tiara, finally to pay homage to the divine ice lingam, God. Feel the change in life forms from *chinar* and willows in Srinagar to the divine ice stalagmite formation as the drops of divinity from the cave roof fall for the benefit of devotees to form the representative of the majestic Lord.

Taushif, the taxi driver, is a happy man. An expert driver with quicksilver reflexes he would grasp narrowest chances to overtake on the heavily burdened narrow mountain road. At the dead-ends in traffic jams he flaunted an army taxi vendor card to get a special privilege to proceed. The long line of faith slowly crawling to the Lidder basin, a 40 km long and roughly 3 km wide escarpment surrounded by Pir Panjal and Zaskar ranges. And there the Lidder river fed by the glaciers at the looming heights flows to the tunes of mountainous serenity. Among all this snowy barren wilderness stands the holy cave made of limestone and gypsum. The people of faith from the plains make their way up panting for breath. The local Muslim *Bakarwal Gujjars* offer their services to the Hindu devotees.

We had to wait for a couple of days before we could start our trek from Baltal. Landslides in the upper reaches kept the pilgrimage suspended. The rains made the route to the holy cave very dangerous. Finally we found ourselves moving in the squelching mud while it was still dark early in the morning. By daylight the mass of pilgrims formed a bottleneck at the check post where one has to show the required papers. It comes a big reprieve to come out of that tight squeeze.

Our ageing bodies not up to the mark of taking up this difficult track and return in a single day, we got ponies as we struggled in the squelching mud on the narrow foot track. With three days of pilgrims stranded from both sides struggling to push and jostle ahead there was a thick wall of humans, ponies, horses and *palkis*. At a place the *palki* bearers slipped on the treacherous slope. They rolled down the stony slope like melons. Thanks God they didn't fall into the narrow gorge below.

It was taking too much time to move even a few yards. It was a frail pony I was perched upon. It was shivering even under my modest weight. The owner would wallop it cruelly from behind. I felt like a culprit torturing this poor, weak, possibly ailing pony. To avoid being the cause of its death, I got down, paid the owner full fare and started walking. I was lucky to even find some place to dismount. It was just a foot away from the edge of the dirt path overlooking a deep fall. I was even scared that the shivering weak pony might fall and roll down taking me with it. So kindness and fear were both equally involved in my decision to start walking on foot.

My friends had sturdy ponies bearing them and they were so stuck up among a mass of ponies that even to get down would be a serious challenge. I left them in their jammed, crammed security and comfort. It had been a gloomy, overcast, freezing day. It started drizzling on the way to the holy cave during the last phase of walk in the gorge.

It was something beyond tiredness. You get numb. You realize the significance of a single step. I walked past the makeshift tents bearing shops, night-stay accommodation and *bhandaras* hardly able to think anything or even feel. There were long lines of pilgrims stuck up on the wet steps leading to the holy cave. It started raining a bit more intensely and I simply allowed myself to be pushed by the crowd, letting myself to be moved by the energy of the humans squeezing from all sides. An early evening fell as I reached the holy place.

There I stood staring in awe at the majestic, tall ice lingam representing Bhagwan Mahadev. It felt like reaching home finally. The whitish glimpse of divinity as a *prasad* for all the troubles faced during the climb. We humans are habituated to link one's effort with the result or the outcome. We view them as inseparable. From this equation, what a beautiful outcome it was at the cost of all the trekking troubles! Such places are massive spiritual charging ports. We need not do anything special to get a sip of divinity there. All we need is just to be there, open ourselves and allow the high-frequency energies to give us a better alignment as per the natural laws. All that needs to be done for our evolution is done automatically, if we just stand there with acceptance, reverence and gratitude.

The pilgrims aren't allowed to carry their mobile phones during the pilgrimage, so there was no avenue to get in touch with my friends. As a gloomy, wet, cold night looked imminent, I started for the return journey. And finding it a very tough task to trek in the dark with the rain pouring, and having taken no rest, I hired a horse. I chose wisely this time. It was a robust one and hence costly. But the Lord wanted me to take the entire trouble of walking to bear the burden of my faith on myself. I got my test just 3 km down the trek. It was an impassable jam of ponies and horses jutted stomach to stomach on a narrow ledge. Just a big mass of animals, so thick that one couldn't see the land below. I had to draw up my legs in order to save them from getting crushed and lacerated by the saddles of others. Ponies from both sides blocked each other's path in a narrow pass. There was some fresh landslide somewhere. The army had forbidden the movement of ponies from that point onwards. It was a scary night, a freezing rain pouring, and cold wind howled on the narrow ledge where we were stranded.

The ponies would get jittery now and then and a stampede loomed large. If they got out of control, many pilgrims would find themselves in the gorge below. Getting down was the biggest challenge. There was hardly any place to land your feet and if you tried the ponies would squeeze you from all sides. So I struggled to get down and after almost half an hour of effort I was lucky to hang onto the inside cut of the ledge like a little monkey and crawled to the narrow path on which some of the pilgrims were already moving to take the footpath. The horse guy won't agree to part payment. 'I'm ready to wait all night and take you to the destination. It's your choice to get down, I'm not asking you to dismount,' he had a point. So I paid him the full amount and started my long, struggling walk to the base camp. There was hardly any energy left in me. I was tired to the core of my muscles. I literally crawled, chanting Lord's name and somehow managed to reach the rented tent in the wee hours.

My friends were more prudent. They stayed at a tent near the holy cave and made it comfortably the next day after a night's rest. As fate would have it, the next evening after our arrival there was a cloud burst near the holy cave and the rushing torrents of water claimed many lives.

When I dumped myself on the damp bedding under a thick musty quilt, the *Pandit ji* from Ujjain opened his eyes from the neighboring bedding in the tent. He was sharing the tent with us. He looked at me with genuine feminine compassion in his lovely eyes. I was too tired and fell asleep even before his loving, empathy-full look was over. He had started the trek on the same day and driven by his unquestionable faith in Lord Shiva had made it before anyone of us.

He was a loving man, spoke with extempore musicality of wit and humor or caustic remark as the situation demanded. He loved putting on different avatars. Sometimes a leopard skin print draped around his torso like a yogi; sometimes you found him in a sun hat and goggles in company with a swanky track suit and flashy sneakers like a celebrity from the entertainment industry. He was an impressive narrator of myths, *bhajans* and stories when the audience was receptive. But he could taunt and shut down the nonsense people with good effect. He possessed a beautiful feminine space in his sensitive loving heart. A sort of *shakti* looking for solace in her Shiva. He would hold my hand with a lover's affection and I felt pressure on my palm. I respected his feminine outreach in showing love and liking for someone. I maintained a straight face and responded at a neutral, respecting level. During the time when we were waiting for the trek to open, we had a friendly outing in the pastures around the base camp. He loved getting clicked and honoring his social media needs I tried my best to operate like a professional photographer. On our return journey, I saw him strolling with gentle ease at Srinagar airport as well. He was a head turner with his style, feminine elegance and charisma in his male body. We greeted him and hugged him like real friends.

Me and my friends had stayed at Srinagar for a day before the return flight to Delhi. I gave myself a treat in a *shikara* in the Dal lake. Naughty boatmen sold beer and cigarettes. With a bang the little boat would meet the *shikara* and beer cans and cigarettes changed hands and money passed on. I had two bottles of beer. And being a non-drinker who reserves this entertainment for few odd occasions not lasting more than two-three times in a year, I was on a high. I wanted to swim in the Dal lake with my clothes, mobile phone and purse. But my sober friends somehow held me back.

The next morning we hired an auto for taking us to visit Shankaracharya temple, Dilshad garden and Nishat bagh. The auto-driver was a kind fellow giving us full

hospitality like a caring host. He also offered salvation in
jannat: 'Hindus are very nice people. If a Hindu reads the
kalma, he will definitely go to *jannat* long before common
Muslims like us.'

Well, I know *kalma* but I somehow didn't recite it while
on the way to the airport. Who knows he would have
jumped with ecstasy on seeing a *kafir* getting salvaged by
his Muslim faith and it could have toppled the auto. So I
thought it better to end the journey on a happy note. We
were nearing the airport, so I thought it prudent to let
things remain normal.

'But we are already in *jannat*! Isn't Kashmir *jannat* on
earth?' I politely asked. He was thinking of some finer
argument but luckily we reached the airport and the
discussion was left incomplete.

The fall of Sheikh Hasina government in Bangladesh is
very worrisome for the Indian strategic interests; just like
the fall of Rajapakshe clan in Sri Lanka must have
bothered the Chinese communist government.

For a country like India, whose democracy is always on
the livewire, it's suitable to have democracies in its
neighboring countries. Bangladesh under Sheikh Hasina—
however milder version of democracy it might have
been—is always a better bet for India in comparison to
any other option.

She was firmly in the seat for the last fifteen years.
Despite all the diluting elements of a proper democracy—
like 'crackdown on the opposition, including the jailing of
leaders, stifling of dissent, and muzzling of media' (was she
too inspired by the strong, autocratic leaders who are
emerging world over of late?)—she has been the best shot
for the Indian interests. Her ouster acquires more
worrisome shades given the fact of unfriendly regimes in

Maldives, Nepal, Pakistan and the military junta in Myanmar.

When you are a proponent of strongman (or strongwoman) politics, there is a very fine line between what is tolerable and intolerable. Dissension builds up over a period of time and if you aren't prudent enough to keep safety valves for the seepage of extra effervescence—thus avoiding an explosion—you might become a villain suddenly. The fuel has accumulated over the years; now it needs just one trigger to ignite mass sentiments. There were people swimming in the private pools of the mighty Rajapakshes and now you have people taking away framed picture and paintings from Hasina's official residence.

She could have easily enjoyed her fifth term. What was the use of bringing job quota for the descendants of freedom fighters? One can give positive incentives in so many other ways instead of directly antagonizing the younger section of the population. It was foolish on her part; as farcical as would be the Indian government's job quota for the descendants of the founding members of the Hindu rightist organizations in the country. Instead of allowing the fire to spread while hundreds died in the protests she could have shown a clever side—staying adamant at all costs is being very foolish, even if it makes one feel strong—by revoking the said job reservation; like Modi did once during the farmer protests by taking back the unpopular farming laws. This is the only time I have seen him allowing some space to the voice of dissent; otherwise it has been a steel frame. But this one kind and considerate decision fetches much respect in my eyes for the powerful Indian ruler. It's fortunate that he did it because it saved India from a bigger fire. But the way female wrestlers were treated—and the oppressor facilitated—still rankles the soul of most of the people in the peasantry class. And the less we say about Manipur, the better it is. I know it's a far more complex situation over there than anyone of a common person like you or me can understand. But despite all the nitty-gritty, the country's premier can at least take some symbolic measures to put balm on the bleeding Manipuri wounds.

It's fortunate that the collective Indian psyche is far more mature and would respond—not react—through ballot paper during elections under similar circumstances, like it did during the recently held general elections. In the face of the talks of threat to the constitution in the country, the Indian voters' response has been to dilute the power structure by denying the BJP government an absolute majority in the general election. Despite the alleged misuse of agencies and partisan role played by the election commission—due to which many critics take the result with a pinch of salt and the opposition seems convinced that there are enough reasons to believe that election wasn't as fair as it's supposed to be in the world's largest democracy—the BJP lost its majority and hence the power to rule with an unsparing rod is diluted significantly. A coalition government is the best shot for the social harmony of the country at the moment.

What is it that undoes the position of a powerful authoritarian leader in a democracy? I think, it's the plain old overconfidence. An illusion that what has been passing for long will continue to do so. As the most powerful person in the country, you think that the alpha male type tactics are the only signs of strength and power. You think any adjustment of other's opinion is a sign of weakness.

About 700 farmers lost their lives during the cruel summer and winter months during the yearlong agitation. A kind leader—and kindness doesn't decrease the strength of a leader—would have met his farmer subjects. When the champion and elite female sporting icons were crying on the road for justice, a kinder ruler would have expressed his willingness to listen to them. Manipur is burning for more than a year. A kind ruler would have visited it during the times when his subjects need a healing touch. Just mere presence and soft words will do. He is after all our ruler and such kind symbolism puts balm on many wounds. All said, we are lucky that the Indian voters are far more mature and respond through ballot box only. And that's the strength of Indian democracy.

An earthworm is the mildest, most harmless version of a snake. Similarly, the common man is the mildest and the most harmless version of a politician. In both cases, the former ones crawl to survive and eat muddy crumbs for survival; while the latter ones are fanged, poisoned and slither around to hunt with impunity.

PS: Within the snakes and the politicians, there are different types. Some are vipers, cobras, kraits and mambas. The lethal ones. The others are rat snakes, sand boas and many other harmless crawlers who carry the fear and stigma of the lethal ones in the genre.

A person can be in perfectly celebratory mode only when he is totally balanced. I try to be balanced. I practice to remember it as many times as possible. But I have my fluctuations, especially with this unfoldment of the divine feminine (*kundalini*) within me. Ma *Shakti* knows exactly how to make one dance to Her fluctuating tunes till one is reshaped as per Her grace. I just flow with the tide, allowing myself to be touched by Her grace.

There are many religious people who are doing *tapasya* to become spiritually uplifted beings. But there are really spiritual persons in practice also, which is far more substantial than most of the people trying to be spiritual. My mother herself belonged to this category.

I have an opinion on women: they are lovely, undulating beings; cast in the mold of the divine feminine; like butterflies flying over a stone, the replica of the divine masculine. I have limited personal experience with women in terms of a strictly man-woman relationship. But I have personally heard and my friends shared their own as well as their friends' share on this issue. It gives me a large sample of females to make me arrive at this opinion. In any case, it's merely an opinion of someone who is himself a seeker on the path. So it's to be taken lightly, smiled at and discussed about.

On the question of whether men too are as fluctuating as females, my humble viewpoint is that even with all their dynamics, the men are still pretty solidly cast in one-dimensional mode. I don't think men are seeking too many different flavors in a woman. With a few exceptions, most of the men are looking for the same connect with a woman in terms of desire, his ego requirements and other typical physical expectations. I find them within a predictable set of needs and expectations regarding a woman.

I feel gratitude for having little-little privileges in life. All of us have our own challenges. I shouldn't be comparing people's challenges. That shouldn't be done. There is no common yardstick to do so. All of us have our unique privileges and challenges. Like anyone else I have both. But I cherish the little privileges I enjoy. I play down the challenges because I feel gratitude for whatever little privileges God has blessed me with. So gratitude is the key.

You may see some lucky people around you who don't have to slog like a mule to lead a comfortable life. They look blessed to you. But working to earn one's livelihood is no lesser blessing. It puts one on a testing stage, which is in fact a far bigger opportunity to know the Truth. It's a workshop basically. I'm sure you too have your own little privileges of a different nature. Work hard. Earn your privileges if you feel you fall short on them. Then ask God specifically in this regard—after giving it your full dose of pure karma—and you will have it. Believe me!

Imaginations are supposed to be colorful. If we take this liberty of imagining the best for us, then why not make it colorful. It refreshes the mood. Doesn't it?

I write a lot and I speak a lot as well when I'm with family or friends, almost like a chatterbox. But it's quite strange that I don't miss speaking to anyone when I'm alone for even a month. There are many times every year when I'm all alone for extended periods and hardly speak for almost a month. And it doesn't seem to make much of a difference. When all we siblings and our children are gathered at one place, I'm part of the group in chatting terms. And when all are busy and at their places, I straightaway get into my mode of seclusion involving reading and writing without missing anyone. I find it strange sometimes. But that's how it is. There doesn't seem to be any hangover of those pleasant gatherings and routine talks. I find both speaking and not-speaking relevant in their own contexts.

Most of my friends belong to the non-spiritual category, so there I have to be just like them. It makes them so happy that they never feel any carryover from my world of academics and spirituality. In fact, most of the people appreciate it that I just mix with them on their frequency. The nicest compliment I have received is: 'He meets an illiterate and poor person as if he himself is perfectly illiterate and even poorer than the person'. A wise village elder once said this about me. And I feel exactly like this. I just allow people to be what they are; try to be in their mold while I'm with them. It makes them comfortable with themselves.

My mother would always praise me for my simple ways about food. She would sometimes forget to put salt in the food and I would eat it without even knowing if something was missing. When she would eat later and come to know about the most crucial thing missing, she would laugh and tell me about it. Believe me, when I'm hungry eating a raw boiled potato or a spicy pizza are just the same. I swear on this. And I feel so good about it. It's a gift from nature. I know the basics of cooking and that enables me to prepare a few necessary things that only I would like to eat. People normally are very particular about so many things but to me a few basics matter. So salt, spice, ripe, overripe, cooked, undercooked, baked, over-baked, or the shape of chapatti hardly have any effect on me. I can relish whatever I make even if a street dog would not feel comfortable in enjoying it. So it's very simple regarding culinary matters. Simpler, the better. And there are so many ways one can survive upon. Like Sadhguru survived on a frugal meal for many years. It involved a fistful of raw peanuts soaked in water overnight and a banana. So one can have many variants of eatables either eaten naturally, boiled, fried or whatever. I had a discussion with Kaka *Maharaj* (who stays outside the village in a hut) and he told me that a devotee basically survives on *bhajan* or call it *sadhna*.

It was a lonely *tulsi* plant in a far corner of the brick-paved and cement-topped yard. A chance sprout; a little seed falling in an almost invisible hairline crack in the cemented yard. And there it grew; a stunted plant for the lack of space around it. A tough life; but it came helpful during the winter. While many big, luxuriant *tulsi* plants couldn't cope with harsh cold, it kept alive with its unassuming, low-profile self. The situational disadvantage, in terms of a cemented surrounding, provided an advantage also—a little projecting slab on the wall kept it safe from an open exposure to the frosty sky during the coldest months. It survived. Next spring, looking at this tiny fighter was a lovely sight; like basking in a roomful of light. The other day I gifted it with a neighbor. I put a flowerpot bearing a nice green flowering shrub near it. I hope they will turn friends. Their branches touch. I'm sure the lonely *tulsi* plant, away from the flowers beds, will surely feel happy about having a neighbor.

If you are feeling lonely despite the crowd or the sprawl of nature around you, it means you are just walking on the edge. A razor-sharp slice, the knife-edge. The narrowest path possible for anyone to walk. You are cut off from the companionship of both humans and nature. A sharp edge whereupon only your isolated self can walk. There is no space for anyone or anything to give you company.

It's primarily because you have rejected the offer of companionship by humans, books, trees, birds, animals, or some hobby, or any part of nature that gives company to someone in need. And as you walk on this edge, you cut your soles. It's painful. It develops a vicious circle. All your energies are focused on your cuts. It further insulates you from the friendly overtures of some wild flower, some tree, some bird, some smile, some lovely emotion. You are cut off from the fabric of life. A feeble thread; fragile to be broken and blown.

Jump off this self-lacerating edge. Walk on the ground where there are people, birds, trees, books and lovely hobbies waiting to be acknowledged by you. It's like coming back to the joint fabric of life. You can still stay aloof from the things and the people who don't suit your structure of life. You can even walk alone on this broad plain. It doesn't cut your feet. There are no edges of isolation.

By jumping off the sharp knife-edge, you have already accepted the little threads of coexistence, be it free air only. Now you are on the plain of many things even while being alone. You are not lonely. You are in solitude. In solitude you are equally near and far from everything around. It's a feeling of grand equanimity.

We, individually, are fragmented stories; almost incomplete stories somehow patched up together by various factors like family, friends, town, country, jobs, fears, joys, agonies, advantages, disadvantages. These fragments are always falling apart, trying to run their own course, to become complete stories in themselves. That's why we feel tension and restlessness.

We are merely bigger fragments made of smaller ones. The bigger fragment wants to pursue its own completion; the smaller ones their own. At different times, we are both larger and smaller than the sum total of all the fragments in us. It fluctuates. Our sum total. When we feel bigger, we look confident of going in a specific direction; when smaller, we are pulled apart by anxiety and uncertainty. A rambling house actually.

Many times the pieces fall apart and we rush to gather them in panic. With what we call our life, we maintain an invisible line around us, our boundary, the decider of our domain—our ego, our vulnerabilities. We are fighting to keep our fragments within this dominion. Because beyond that is the plain fear of falling apart beyond collection, getting destroyed, melting in oblivion.

We are born very supple and flexible. That's why we bounce back after a fall. Nature gives us that physical flexibility so that we can get up after a fall. And fall we have to many times to learn to walk. Then we grow up and physical rigidities set in. The same fall would now result in multiple fractures.

At the physical level, we can do a lot to stall and postpone this rigidity through exercise and proper nutrition. But there is another aspect of us where we can stay flexible like before. I mean the flexibility of mind. We can retain the suppleness of our mindset, attitude and belief system to allow it to be positively shifted along the alignment of the uncontrollable forces of nature and the shifting shades of time.

The suppleness of mind and attitude saves us from breaking relationships as well as our own spirit. It's essential to have this flexibility to continue growing and evolving as a person. An old man with a withering body having suppleness of mind is a nice combination.

3

THE monkeys leave me fuddled with vexation many times. The swaggering simian sense of mischief leaves this taciturn and tottering poet flummoxed beyond limits. They have to temper with normalcy all the time. The rest of the species are after food and mating. The monkeys know how to enjoy life beyond this realm. So they move assuredly, vivaciously with errant finesse. For example, beyond picking—sorry tearing—fruits from trees, they are aware that more fun can be drawn by spraying mugfuls of rascality among the branches and decimate the canopy. Looking at them I know exactly from where our rioting sense comes from.

I'm feeling the affable touch of early morning monsoon breeze, a sense of equanimity resonating in my being. It gives a meditative experience. I would say it's almost a walking meditation. Eh… *pah*… so much for the prancing merriment of the monkeys! It's a group of three young troublous wastrels—*goondas* even from the normal simian standards. Their chief jumps with a lacerating sense of criminality. My sonorous spell of ease is shattered. A big bough of *champa*, fully adorned with fragrant flowers, cracks and falls with a painful thud. The murderer is jubilant and jumps on the roof of my little car as if trying to squash it to junk like a nefarious press machine. Luckily, the car doesn't break like poor *champa*, so he is sniveling and sharply livid. I stare at him with copious loath. There I see him confidently cantering home, fleeing with glee. I'm wincing with impotent hate, the flowery big bough in my

47

hand. What egged him to this rascality, I wonder. I inhale the fragrance of *champa* flowers to douse the whirring oblivion of hate. In what delirium these desperados carry out such normalcy-slaying attacks?! *Pah…* ! I think they are excellently accustomed to the elements of chaos and disorder. So many times they've broken into the house and robbed fruits in broad daylight, leaving me feeling like a half-wit. After the raid they vanish all exultant and gay, while I stand morose and desolate.

Their flagrant digression into illegality hit a new high the other day. Any chance of India coming near winning a bronze at the Olympics embraces us with sparkling courtesy. I'm lost in the bronze medal match on the television. There he hits below the belt again, the head hoodlum; thus disfiguring morality forever. My cheering for the Indian player has come at a cost. He has smartly opened the door, opened the refrigerator, rummaged through it, without making the slightest sound, and not finding anything to its taste there enters the other room and opens the other refrigerator. He hits gold here. Our player has missed the bronze. I'm shocked, my words are frozen in the air. I'm stunned and surrounded by the walls of silence. It's a proof of the culture of violence challenging any sense of peace. The mangled, pulped mangoes are littered around, many just bitten once and thrown away, their pulp oozing out on the floor. It's a pulpy yellow mayhem. The shock waves hit me. He looks relaxed and unbothered. I let out a terrifying verbal innuendo. Hearing the echo of my own words, I lose self-esteem and dignity that still remained. He gallops away with glee, leaving the mess behind for me to clear. My confidence is crippled and maimed. What glorious freelancing of illicit fun! He stops to give me a horrid angry snarl from the wall and turns his lurid pink bottom towards my face and gallops away to further glory.

I have seen The Kingdom of the Planet of the Apes movie. And looking at the putrescent remnants of his

rascality, cleverness and smartness, I have no doubt that
what is shown in the movie will be reality some day. I look
on helplessly. He is industrious, in full earnest, mischief
egging him on forever. After the mango-slaying feast, he is
huffily trying to pry open the lid of a roof-top water tank. I
cannot just twiddle away time by impotently staring at
errant monkeys. I have better things to do. Already the
fleas from the entire neighborhood have arrived to enjoy
the funfair. I have to clean the mess. With throbbing,
pulsing verses of mute anger, I get down to the business—
to put the house in order so that he can slay it again and
bring disorder with his pink bottom.

Nesting birds are all ears and concentration. Be it
parching heat, torturing cold or piercing rain, they are
steadfastly manning the watch-post to first save their eggs
and later the hatchlings. The risk factors are always
bustling around.

An Indian robin bird couple is scowling with
indignation. They have almost successfully raised a chick.
It's maybe just a week away from full flight. Till then it has
to remain hidden among the tree branches while they feed
it. Of course, whoever happens to come near the tree is an
eye-sore to the parents. All impulsive and afire they are
snarling with *shrr-frr* angry notes on the curry-leaf tree in
the yard. It's their tree for the moment because their just-
out-of-nest tiny chick is huddled in a fork on a leafy
branch.

Presently the cause of their ruminations is a squirrel
that is trying to climb 'their' tree. Hurling their angry
monologues they are flying around her, trying to distract or
even give her an outright fall. When they are protecting
their chicks, even the softest and mutest birds become gut-
wrenching, freewheeling energy personified. I don't think

the squirrel can eat their little one. It can steal eggs of course. But her presence makes the parents all itchy with anger. Maybe it's the same squirrel that has just moved in with her little ones a few days ago. It must be on the way to her nest on the *parijat* comprising the same clump of trees in the yard.

To support the underdog is an aesthetic marvel for we humans. One gets a feel of being a visionary genius. In fact, a tailorbird is already sniveling from the side of the robins. I also add to their voice, stomp my feet and throw little dry twigs to scare away the squirrel. But to the insecure parents I'm no countryside gentleman. In their innocent alertness they almost graze against my shaven head. An aerial attack I would say. I leave the field. The chick is safely hidden at its leafy perch.

For many hours I see it exactly at the same place. It's an obedient chick following its parents' instructions. It of course increases its survival chances. That's the best thing to do till you don't have your own wings to fly. It will be good for the little one to do as its parents ask it to do. Then it can set out on a flirting furlough with life one fine day. It will have many moths, even years hopefully, to spend the strength of its youth's reserves. But till then a meek complaisance to the parental plans will be good. And that's what it does. It safely makes to the end of a very critical day, each second important, each hour adding strength to its tiny wings. I leave it safely tucked in its place as a humid twilight sets in.

As I write this and take a break to go out on the terrace, mother nature gives me a sight to add to this write-up. The wire-tail swallow couple has their chick out as well. The family is extended now. Three of them sitting on a wire, the parents on both sides of the chick. The parents all alert and anxious and the chick full of awe and wonder on this bigger stage outside the mud nest. It has dull grey head, which will grow to chocolate brown like its parents. The wings look very mild purple. These will grow to shiny metallic blue. Its tail will grow wires like its elders. But for that the parents will have to give their all to add enough strength and skills in its wings to fly freely. Mothers are extra possessive. As I look at them from a few feet away from the perch cable, she comes chipping and takes a swift turn around my nose, giving me a warning to stay away from her child.

It's a lovely sight to watch a fruitful nesting and the expansion of a birdie family. It's a bit more hopeful morning. The sun partially out. Yellow little butterflies fluttering among the flowers. The trees laden with fresh, young leaves. And the family of three, having crossed a milestone, looking to successfully cross over to the other.

Unlike the robin chick, the swallow youngster has to get its training under the open skies on the wires and cables in the locality because their toes don't allow a firm perch on the tree branches. I can just add my prayers for their cause. I can pray that the crows and the *shikra* (who is usually stalking the locality to fly away with any lazy bird or lizard) are busy somewhere else and won't come here as of now.

So the electricity department decides to install meters outside the houses to bring down the volume of electricity theft. New poles are being dug in the streets that will bear cables instead of the naked wires of earlier, which allowed the farmers to steal electricity at their will. Why do the farmers steal electricity from the wires and irrigation water from the canals? Because their income hasn't increased over the years. To somehow make the ends meet, they have to keep buffalos and cows and for that they need fodder cutters and flour machines. These consume lots of electricity. If the farmers pay fair and square, the electricity bill will itself cover the entire monthly budget available. So now when the department is taking strict measures and installing cables and fixing meters outside on the poles in the street, the farmers obviously are very worried. As the brand new sturdy-looking cables are drawn across the new poles, the farmers are already having nostalgic hiccups for the past when the naked wires smirked with a friendly mischief for taking out unmetered share from the flow. It helped them in making their ends meet.

I'm not promoting electricity theft. The best solution is to make agriculture feasible. There is a rumor that if you have an electricity pole near your roof, you might have a little chance of taking out unaccounted units by harnessing a little chink of possibility at a joint high up on the pole. It serves as the sole beacon of hope for the overstretched peasantry. So the farmers have gone berserk. Neighbors who shared a nice evening talk only yesterday have turned foes and are fighting to get the pole dug at their point of convenience. Brawls have compounded to assaults. In one such fight, a lame woman gave a flourishing display of guts to engage in a real fight—almost an unsullied and untouched spirit to take the matters to her hardened palm, the palm that has thwacked buffalos thousands of times. As her young son got into a scuffle, she lurched forward and very soon turned the scales in his favor. Giving plenty of airy spaciousness to the angry mother in her, she started slapping randomly. Her tongue also gave a suitable company to her hands as she hurled gems of obscenities. Thin and anemic in looks, she but showed disproportionate strength and stamina. Her ostensible moustache twitching with anger, by the time the heady round was over, many cheeks carried the print of her palm's authority.

It was disastrous for the poor laborers, as she rode roughshod over their already miserly fates. Most of them carried deep purple cheeks. Relentlessly grappling with anger, she then lunged forward to grab an iron pipe of very suitable length and weight to effect amazing punishment to human flesh. She needed this weapon to dispense justice on their bones after giving the cheeks their due share. They had to throw the weapon on a roof to avoid further blood. Who can understand the passionate nuances of motherhood? But the laborers surely can gauze its depth because they got unnecessarily beaten. So all in all it was a very busy, brawly day.

It's followed by an early twilight under an overcast sky, a very slight drizzle falling like robust mist to provide a seamless link between the night and the day. The monkey is in a position to strategically synergize his mischief to thrilling proportions. Beyond remotest concern of any type, he sits on a parapet wall on a roof, as if on lordly edifice, just five or six feet below the pole's top end. The earth is wet due to the rainy season. The soil is loose after being dug out and filled in hastily after putting the pole in the hole. Like we humans the simian world is also not stuck on the promotion ladder of mischief—like the rest of the species are. These two do things not just for necessity, they do majorly for vanity.

The monkey has an enlivening inspiration at the fag end of this rainy day. Imaginative pedagogy unfolding copiously. He stands on his hind-legs—like humans— holds the pole with his hands bearing highly active fingers and gives a serious shake to the pole's top end. The pole sways as the simian momentum spreads across the new cable lines. He then watches the slow swaying with a contended muse, a fine mist-like drizzle caressing his coat. He looks so relaxed as if sitting over a splendid coffee table book. He bears a wonder-tinted look. The pole is a toy to him. When the gentle swaying of the pole and the lines stops, he gets up again and pushes and pulls the pole to restart his toy once more.

It's the same thug who marauds our kitchen. I watch him from my yard. He is steeped in this fun for the last at least twenty minutes. It's fun for me as well, so I don't get catapulted into malice at his sight this time. All the villagers would welcome any chance of harm to these new poles. For obvious reasons—they have disturbed peace in the village. I'm enjoying the sight of it as much as he is enjoying the act. We might have a human-ape hybrid future—don't forget that movie where Moi and Noah tried to find a common ground for the humans and the apes. Getting sensitized to this reality, I offer him a banana that I won't eat without concern. It's not in perfect shape. I hold it for him using friendly words. But my glaring mask of dogmatism isn't enough. We have had very acrimonious brawls in recent past. He is happy with the pole-swaying game and doesn't spoil his fun for a quarter-rotten banana offered by an enemy.

Most of the people say it's a shrub, but I insist it's a tree—small though having slender woody stems and a thin main trunk. The fact is *jatropha integerrima* or *peregrina* is a flowering shrub. It's bigger than a plant and smaller than a tree. If you prune it well and keep it single trunked it grows 15-16 feet tall with a luxuriant round canopy having glossy elliptic or oval leaves. Mine is about 11 feet tall if I consider the highest shoot trying to touch the sky with its flowery head. Had I kept it single-stemmed it could have gone to 15 feet and then I won't have to defend its tree status with arguments. My *peregrina* has several slender trunks that inhibit its vertical growth. But vertical loss is horizontal gain. It has a domed canopy broader than the tall guys of its species. Most importantly, the slender side stems have plenty of leaves and flowers that keep their crimson smiles year around.

The little tree is always smiling with its clusters of star-shaped crimson flowers, a bright and flashy smile. Irrespective of the wars and political intrigues, there it's with its bright smile most of the year. The flowers sharply silhouetted against, like lofty overseers, the humanoid background where everyone is trying to reach the majestic zenith with taut bosoms, whipping up mad frenzy. It's a world where the majority is bustling, but some are relaxed and languid—like yours truly—and the latter enjoy the charm of these lovely flowers. As people prance for profiteering, huffing and puffing with their progressively worsening mood, here I'm safely holed and peacefully cornered to enjoy the bouquet of beauty offered by this little tree. Your royal majesties, you can convulse with pain for penury gain, here I enjoy the free booty of mother nature.

The scientists say that its parts are toxic. Its milky sap can cause skin inflation and rashes. Its seeds are also toxic in nature. The smoke of its leaves is also said to be harmful to our lungs. I'm happy that this little tree knows how to hit back. It does so with its numerous flowery smiles. In any case, it's merely our human-centric view. I'm happy that it gives us a knee-kick in terms of utility. Beyond our consumerist whinnying—although it has various medicinal usages—the beauty stands proud and nonchalant. Its essence has something sweet because usually its flowers are laden with honeybees. But the honeybees are vanishing at an alarming rate. While each cluster had several of them till a couple of years back, now there is just one for several clusters. Maybe there is a tiny ball of honeycomb still surviving somewhere. That sweetens my hope a little.

It's dreary and dismal in a horribly vindictive world. My fading enthusiasm is revived this sultry morning. The crimson blooms are extra happy today. There is a swarm of small grass yellow butterflies (*eurema briggita*) fluttering with exciting feminine artifice. Aha, the bounding quintessence of life! All perplexities melt. It's a very comforting sight. They flutter jovially. Spirituous sallies in the little dense rain-fed dome. There are a few honeybees as well who sometimes butt into the butterflies. But no hard feelings like we have in the form of road rages.

I'm lost in this beautiful spectacle. Suddenly my reverie is broken by the frisky, twittering *tik-tikking* by the resident squirrel, the one who had arrived with her little ones a few days ago. A brown-yellow stripped feral cat is a great hunter. To the mother squirrel her little ones are the star of her eyes. A small-time writer like me has poetic sentiments. But to the cat, it's simply food. I see the cat running away with its breakfast tucked in its mouth. Mother squirrel is inconsolable. I see the curled tail of the stolen baby sticking out of the cat's mouth. It's slightly bigger than the previous occasion when I saw it tucked in its mother's mouth, its bushy tail curled sideways, mother cautiously carrying it to a new house she had prepared among the top branches of the *parijat* tree in the yard. Now it was again tucked up in a different mouth. The tail curled exactly like earlier.

My pitying reverie is suddenly broken. The wire-tail swallow couple almost chip away lice from my head, if there is any among the one-week old crop on my top. I think the elder chick is flying with them now and needs semi-care. They must be guarding the small chick, the latter hatch, because they have objections even against a poet marveling at the butterflies and sympathizing with a grieving squirrel.

It's May and wheat harvesting is proceeding under the tyrannical fits of a blazing sun. The summers are getting hotter each passing season; the springs arrive with lesser flowers; the autumns have less windfalls simply because trees are vanishing; and the winters are losing their chilly pinch. We seem to have internecine conflict with mother nature, the same mother that gives us birth and nurtures us. The interminable monotony of growth models unrivalled; the capricious ingenuity to further dent mother nature. The economic models are basically the schemes of profligacy in which the rich are getting richer and the poor turn poorer. According to a survey, just forty wealthiest Indians hold wealth equal to that owned by 700 million people collectively. India might be gearing for five-trillion economy but this hardly matters to the millions of poor Indians. There are white-collar crimes that further tilt the scale in the favor of the moneyed class. Everything related to the poor people is getting into a pell-mell situation. So there are vertical towers of soft, upstanding class and horizontal slum-spreads of hard, downstanding people. But these 'soft' and 'hard' categories are just apparent surface realities. In deep reality, the poor people are very brittle, they crumble and scatter; the rich possess the hardness of wealth to give them a steel armor. But there is one occasion when the rich and the poor stand in the same queue, carrying the same worth—the election day.

The Government of India runs Pradhan Mantri Garib Kalyan Anna Yojana (PM-GKAY), a kind of mass charity or *bhiksha* to make the beggary masses *atmanirbhar* by providing food grains to migrant, poor laborers and below poverty line families. Well, how will you make a beggar self-standing by giving him 5 kg food grains per month is quite a mystery to me. It also provides subsidized food grains at 2-3 rupees per kg from fair price shops under National Food Security Act. These are provided to Below Poverty Line Families (BPL) and Priority Households (PHH) who are issued a special ration card to help them avail this paltry grocery to keep the fire going in their kitchen.

I need Rashe Ram's services for a task. I call him. I'm relieved that his number is working and his tiny handset is intact. His voice comes with overwhelming despondency from the remotest desolate corner. He sounds drained out, sounds indifferent and complaisant. He is cutting wheat so that they can store wheat for the season. I'm surprised to hear this. These days the daily wage laborers in the village avoid taking this soul-sapping brutal work with sickle because they get free and subsidized ration and use the spared energies for other wage tasks. The two brothers (both unmarried) and their widowed mother are cutting wheat furrows to get enough wheat in storage that would last a year. The youngest brother works at a needle factory at a paltry monthly income. It saves him from the sun and rain at least, he says. His wife rests at home and freshens up to launch reinvigorated tirade once the workers arrive home. That seems to be her task, which she takes very seriously as is proved by her shrill harangue that subdues all other lesser noises in the neighborhood. All in all, it's a poor family, very poor I should say.

'You don't get free and subsidized ration?' I'm scandalized. 'No!' the gentle giant demurely replies. The bizarreness of it strikes me. I have seen rich landowners (from the village standards at least) taking away bundles of free ration, most of them on bikes, and some even in cars (can you believe it?) so that at least their buffalos may eat that ration. My head spins as I realize that their cattle are eating a human's share.

Morality, law and ethics are scrunched under boots by those who can manipulate the system at their level. They simply fix with the village head to get a free ration card even though they don't fulfill even a single eligibility condition. Law is crunchy and crispy. It gives a nice grating, surrendering sound under thick boots of the strong. But it easily pierces the naked foot soles of the poor. So the local gentry has a heyday on the date of free distribution. Plunder, pillage, desecration, savagery, debauchery of the strong and the mighty—seeping from the top lions to the neighborhood bullies. I have a vision of poor Rashe Ram and his family—mute like a flayed sheep. They are undoubtedly the most eligible family for a free ration card in the village. And they don't have it, while literally everyone from car-owning richies to the bike-owning filthies is having this almost ubiquitous item. You just wish for it; and there you have it.

To be eligible for it the annual family income should be less than 1,80,000 rupees. Theirs won't reach even one lakh from all sources even if we add the sum of their mother's own housework at the most exorbitant pay scale of a housemaid. The household is headed by a widow (another prominent eligibility condition); they have no assured means of subsistence or social support; two brothers are uneducated and single with no socio-economic support; they are far lower down the caste hierarchy; they are landless agricultural laborers, earning livelihood on a daily basis in the informal sector (which isn't regular in the strict sense and work comes randomly not amounting to more than half of the month, the rest of the time they are idle). It's an ideal below poverty line family deserving a free ration card—more than anyone else in the entire village—but they are left out. The system can be—usually is—merciless. I'm hit by piercing remorse and torturing anguish. My cloister morals nudge at my overwhelming poetic lassitude. I can feel how it feels to be denied your right.

I ask them to bring their documents. 'And don't forget to carry the registered mobile number for the Family ID!' I emphasize. The government has futuristic conceptualization—digitalization. Every household must have a Family ID linked to a registered mobile number. His brother—a lanky, stoic fellow whom I have never seen speaking—stands in front of me with chronic somnolence. He has their documents in a green polythene bag, faded, jaded, frayed and holed. Poverty has a peculiar inertia. It will seep into torn polybags and prevent the fresh ones from replacing them even if these are available for free. I take out the documents. They carry the dog-eared smell and myth of poverty. Poverty gives spankings. It mollifies all confidence and courage with comic candor. One stands guiltily as if just by being poor he has committed a crime.

I drive the bike with virtuous and upright air. The lanky boy pillion rides with his documents, almost weightless and invisible, shaped by the grating struggle of hard labor on construction sites and agriculture farms. We reach the SARAL Kendra at the village's other end that facilitates such tasks. I broach the subject to the young man operating it. He belongs to the village itself and runs his operations from a room in the village *chaupal*. Karne (real name Karan but who bothers about the real name of a poor man) stands in a corner with a mournful autumnal air. He wants to be invisible. I share the poverty-shaped bleeding reminiscences of this poor family. 'And still they don't get free ration and I see even people with cars carrying away free ration like loot!' I'm at a loss of words.

The guy is slightly acquiescing but cold and taciturn to begin with. 'Give me the registered mobile number for their Family ID,' he says with professional air. The number is the key to the digital portal. No number, no entry to the digital world. Karne shares the number with lots of effort at mustering courage. As a poor man you hardly believe yourself to be a full human. You think you are sub-human and that makes you guilty and at loss of all normal sense of dignity. The man tries to log into their account. 'Share the OTP!' he demands suddenly and sternly. Karne is all focus on the tiny basic handset. No OTP. I fear the number is dead for not being recharged for a long time. No balance. The SARAL Kendra guy looks exasperated and peers at me as if to say what a dunderhead you have fetched here. I'm not the one to bungle even the slightest chance here— at least in this episode. My smartphone is the saving grace for both me and Karne. I take a chance and recharge their number. It buzzes back to life. Money is more important than even air these days. Dead phones come alive with money fed online. There is an OTP. Good news. I'm elated. Our efforts are bearing fruit. 'Thank God the number wasn't closed forever!' I'm full of gratitude to the almighty.

'In the Family ID records their annual income is shown to be three lakh rupees,' he drops the bombshell. 'This is the biggest digital lie!' I lose my breath and fumble with words. Karne's head must be swimming with shock after hearing this mountainous sum. They don't earn even a third of it. He is sympathetic to my vexation. 'See there are about 800 free ration cards in the village and not more than five or seven are eligible in reality,' he is very honest about it. It's easy business. The village head doesn't want to antagonize anyone applying even if he has a big house, car, tractor, AC or large landholding. The personnel from the Block Development Office usually don't come to inspect the applicant's socio-economic status. Signatures of the village head, a member of the village council, the local government school principal and another committee member do the job. In fact the kind boy running the village SARAL Kendra himself puts the signatures of all these people to further facilitate the process and allow governmental charity to reach each and every home. In this scenario, whoever applies gets a free ration card and you have a big crowd on the day of free distribution.

Here my dollops of witticism won't help me. I have no problem regarding ineligible people getting free ration. It's a far bigger game—country level—so let the mighty lions handle it. They know it and if they are comfortable with it, I have no reasons to object. My only issue is that a truly deserving poor family should also get its due in the scheme. 'Get an affidavit in his mother's name declaring her status and income,' he instructs the logical course of action. I feel mettlesome in spirit on this particular day. So there we go to the town to get the affidavit typed on a stamp paper. The notary is a full-of-mischief chatty guy. As his assistant types the affidavit he is giving most ingenuous schemes to a man whose wife has gone to her parents after getting beaten and he also getting thrashed by her brothers as retaliation. He is giving very crooked plans to use the law for the man's benefit. Then he looks keenly at a cowering Karne and throws an advisory gem, 'He looks mentally retarded, we can write this as well.' For the first time I see some reaction on Karne's face but he keeps silent. 'He is at least mentally sounder than you,' I'm about to say but let it go.

We return to the village with the new affidavit safely tucked among the old smelly papers. The affidavit needs his mother's thumb impression. But we cannot locate her. We scan all the poor localities to find her, thinking she must have gone to some woman friend in one of the poor neighborhoods. We turn the cap inside out but to no avail. Maybe she went to some agriculture farm or to cut wood, we conclude. I leave the paper with him, giving him a gel pen with loads of clearest instruction how to lace the thumb with ink and put the impression on the designated place. Inspired by the mischievous notary even I doubt Karne's mental faculties, so emphasize each point multiple times. Even he turn restless. But all my fears are allayed when he comes back after an hour with the task done to a reasonable accuracy. A milestone crossed, we have the income affidavit. The task will be smooth now, I'm sure. We again go to the SARAL guy so that he can upload the document and further process the application.

There is a fragrant ruffling of the sense of justice in me as he hits the keys and peers into the screen. Then there are traces of discomfiture on his face. 'Seems like they have already applied for the correction of income figure in the Family ID. But they didn't upload the supporting document,' he brandishes the fresh affidavit. 'So you can upload it now,' I gently request him, acknowledging the silver-headed staff of authority in his hand. He shakes his head firmly, 'No it's showing the status as pending and we cannot restart the process for this particular application number. The system doesn't show any upload option.' So the system is already the master of its will, I silently rue and think about my misgivings about artificial intelligence. 'Who guided you to apply for the revision of income figure without submitting the income self-declaration in the form of this simple affidavit?' he sternly asks Karne, waving the useless piece of paper for which we had gone speeding like formula race drivers to the town. The poor guy looks as if he is standing in the dock in a court facing some criminal charges. I come to his rescue, 'It must have been done by his youngest brother. He is fifth pass and knows a, b, c, d,' I save Karne. 'Yes, he spoils everything,' the ever-taciturn Karne breaks silence. I'm sure his anger is targeted at his sister-in-law who harangues them profusely. I hope they won't have a fight at home, accusing each other for depriving the family of free ration.

The guy respects my focus in this episode and is at least sympathetic to my cause if not the wellbeing of Karne and his family. He gives a call to the Block Development Officer based at the town. She trusts him in all the income verification matters. As long as he is there she need not bother about unnecessary hassles of the landed farmers sticking to the point of declaring themselves below poverty line to get some free ration for their cattle. So usually she simply asks this boy to get all the signatures done without verifications and all the applicants get free rations—the relatively poor ones for their kitchen and the better placed for their buffalos. It's not that this particular pair of SARAL Kendra guy and the BDO are committing a scandal here. It's the norm, almost a law. The government knows it and they are comfortable about it. The more the benefits reaching to all the people, the more the chances of votes.

They hold a talk over phone. I listen still holding onto the threads of hope. She knows the case. She even remembers the widow's name. With a sullen face the boy disconnects the call and tells the story.

If an application for the revision of income figure stays pending without uploading the self-declared income affidavit, the BDO visits the family house to verify the socio-economic status of the applicant. So she had come for the inspection. She knew that they deserve this more than anyone else in the village. People with *havelis* are getting the benefits, she knew it all. But on this rare real physical inspection her hands were bound by the law. It's a *pucca* house, a tiny *pucca* house with a concrete slab roof. And to be eligible for a free ration card one must have a *kacha* house apart from all other eligibility criteria. 'But all the houses in the village are *pucca* and even palace dwellers are getting free ration for their cows because they have *kacha* houses on paper,' I grumble. 'But in the eyes of law they are *kacha* houses because there was no onsite inspection of the property and in the report they are poor households even if ACs are humming inside and cars are parked in front. But this house is *pucca* house as the report says,' he enunciates the law to me the ignorant.

He is genuinely sympathetic and tells that these guys are just unlucky because on the day of inspection he was away and the BDO *sahiba* had to personally visit the site for inspection. Had he been present in the village that day she would have simply asked him over phone without coming and he would have given a nod like the rest of the villagers. To him all are neighborhood peasants and he cannot be cruel to anyone's application. 'After all, it's the farmers' own grain that comes back to them,' he has a point. 'The government loots us in so many ways, so if this little bit comes back we welcome it. In any case it's ours to begin with,' he elaborates. I understand his point and tell the entire story behind this so-called *pucca* house. 'See, let me explain this *pucca* house story. Till ten years back they stayed in a 30-yard hovel with their horse and bales of fodder. The horse even bit Rashe, his elder brother, on the jaw and he still carries that slurred speech due to the resultant defect. Karne himself was kicked on his back as an infant. I remember him crawling till the age of four. I suspected the kick has deformed his spine and he would crawl throughout his life. Thank God, he got to his feet! Then their lame father died in a road accident. The rich car owner paid them ten lakh rupees for the out-of-court settlement. Out of this, two lakh were pocketed by the smart lawyer who managed this settlement. The rest they used in buying a 30-yard plot and build this so-called tiny *pucca* house. But that doesn't mean they aren't the poorest in the village and they fulfill every condition to get a free ration card. Their mother is a widow. They don't have any landed property apart from this house. They don't have regular income. They just work as casual farm hands or construction site workers for a fortnight at the most every month because work doesn't come regularly. Sometimes they are all without any job throughout the month,' I baulk out their poor story, its each line seeped in poverty.

He is sympathetic and feels sorry for the episode. He calls the BDO madam again and tells her the entire story. She also is very sorry for their bad luck to have a tiny *pucca* house that turns them ineligible for free ration card, while swanky marble-walled houses get free ration. She then suggests a solution. She cannot prepare a report today and nullify it tomorrow. 'There is just one solution. Can you please ask the village head to give it in written that he granted money to help them build this tiny *pucca* house? If he gives it written that the village council donated funds to help them then I can afford to effectively nullify my earlier report,' she tells the SARAL Kendra guy. It's also confided from her end that there is no other way. So we are scuttling around to find the village head who is on an outstation visit. I have serious, practical doubts that he will write this declaration. The house is a decade old and he is just one year into the job. Even he has his position to safeguard.

My frozen pessimism begins to thaw under the onslaught of cruel May heat. It oozes out and makes me swim in the current of its comic tragedy. I tell them that their only chance is to visit the village head as and when possible, with their widow mother in tow, and keep beseeching for help to raise the prospects, which they diligently do two-three times every month. I sometimes meet one of the brothers on the way to their work site and ask for any update in the matter. 'Yes we go there sometimes and *sarpanch sahab* says yes he will look into the matter.' Hard work is a big bulwark against such sensitivities of life. They are busy in the rut of life beyond the concepts of justice or injustice. But sometimes I feel the dull rumbling of sadness for their failed cause.

Some parts are extremely fragile in us, our Achilles heel. Stay guarded about them. That's where we need family, friends and partners to help us defend these weakest fronts.

Similarly, some parts are extremely hard in us. The sharp edges. We have to mind them to avoid those near us getting pinched and cut by them. Or we can use these hard edges to defend the weak, soft spots of our near and dear ones.

The rest part of us comprises plain normal, the lukewarm good-bad of life, the normal pitch on which we usually play. This is actually our living room where we spend most of our time.

As long as we are mindful of each other's hard and soft spots, we can have a very lively time in the normal big part of ourselves.

4

BEING an avid Bond fan, I once thought of writing him a letter—a real handwritten one posted through the traditional mail. Just the typical Ruskin Bond image sitting and looking from his window for inspiration is enough to lighten my being. He has written for fifty years from the same spot. What stability! I usually go to bed after reading some pages from his collections. It makes the world feel so simple beyond all complexities. Long time back I almost met him. Well, that is a good story in itself. Recently I thought of acting on my resolution of writing him a letter—a real handwritten one—and post it with one of my books. I'm scarcely confident about my handwriting but here I wrote carefully like a secondary school boy. The letter was never posted. The other day I saw it in the sheaf of papers and thinking of doing it some justice I reproduce it here:

Dear Bond Sahib,

Hope your cutely funny bone is still strong enough to help you keep going on the literary path. We need it. I'm an old man—into my fifth decade—pretending to be a child in my excitement while writing to one of my favorite authors.

I have seen you once in real life. In fact we had a short talk. It was in the autumn of 2006 or 2007. I climbed up the hill to reach your place, Ivy Cottage. And what a timing it was in terms of my arrival! There you were at your favorite window, restfully looking into the misty distances in the valley below. I'm an uncouth person—almost. I startled you by hollering some crazy fan lines from the road below. I hardly knew what I was shouting in childish nervous excitement. But I remember I had also piped, 'Thanks for giving us so much

Well guys, the unsent incomplete letter carries a strange sad charm. Isn't it?

Recently I thought of giving it a try to meet Bond Sahib. I plan to stay at Mussoorie for a couple of days and try my luck.

I'm walking on the Mall Road looking for a suitable accommodation. Something catches my attention. A glimmer of hope. It's a small hotel named 'Write Star'. Very attractive name so I go in. Something in celebration of writers, a rarity. And a writer looking to spend a night would obviously go to a hotel named as such. The boy at the reception has watery eyes and a guilty startled look, possibly due to being new to the job. I enter the tiniest lobby, hailing their naming sense in hyperbolic terms. But my enthusiasm startles him even more. After he uses all his brain to make a sense of my congratulating eulogy for their name, he manages to say, 'Yes sir, **Bright Star** is a good name.'

Well, he thought they are named Bright Star! My mood dampened and I came out and started to walk up the Mall Road. I intended to stay very near to Bond Sahib's residence, popularly known as Ivy cottage, to maximize my chances of spotting him.

It was a literary pilgrimage from Library Chowk to Ivy cottage, Landour on Lal Tibba hill. As I said I made it a goal to at least see the literary prince of the famous hill station, if not meet him personally. He is ninety and deserves to spend his time in the way he deems fit. So I thought of basing myself at some modest hotel in Landour Bazaar, a little down the hill from his residence. Packed like a mule I walked almost 6 km uphill, panting and exhausted. When was meeting with famous writers easy?

There I stood on the narrow road by the famous cottage whose window overlooking the Doon valley has opened so many pages of simple, beautiful stories, notes and sketches. From the frustrating chaos, Ruskin Bond, with his famous ease and poise in life, draws our simple, charming, funny, witty strands to spin lovingly flowing threads of simple words, which he uses to weave beautiful stories. He makes life look so easy and tolerable. In fact reading him at bedtime is almost healing in nature. It calms down your nerves. After a hard day his words have provided balmy support during cold, dreary nights. I feel like thanking him personally.

His house has changed a lot since the last time I remember it. It's gratifying to see a writer's economic fate taking a healthy shape. Ivy cottage looks very impressive now with new front tiling and fresh paint. I think they have added another floor. It looks a safe and happy place, solid and equipped to shelter and protect an old writer and his adopted family. It has a solid roofing now, in contrast to the corrugated tin roof that had given in on a stormy night, pouring water into his study. Now there were more impressive windows looking into the misty valley below.

Right in front of his house I had a brief talk a man whom I found sitting by the road on the bend. He turned out to be a *kabadi wala*. He tells me that he gets an opportunity to go to his study to collect old newspapers and other paper waste that he might consider to discard. He tells me that Ruskin *sahab* is still in possession of sharp wits and can walk enough to attend to his private needs.

The narrow, steep staircase ascending right from the road seems inviting. But as you crawl up to the small landing and look at the main door, a quite, respectful message on a plaque softly whispers to you to protect his privacy by not buzzing the doorbell. I hardly stand a chance of getting admitted. Then a group of about ten young men, fresh-faced collegiates, appeared on the scene. As the college boys enquired about meeting him, I sensed my chance of sneaking with them. He is children's and young boys' and girls' favorite author. I think maybe he will oblige these young flowers. So I encouraged them to queue up on the stairs and somehow pluck out a chance to go inside. I positioned myself in the middle of the line so as to troop in with the young students.

They were well-behaved boys, lovers of books; not the ones who arrive here on thundering bikes with flashy girlfriends sticking to their backs and then go on to loosen the bed hinges in cheap hotels, spurting stains on the bed sheets, filling the waste bins with used condoms. I think in entire Mussoorie that day these were the ten odd boys, well behaved and lovers of books who came to meet Ruskin Bond. I am sure all of them will do well in their lives.

'Please don't ring the bell'—we are staring at the request. The polite author is still better in not putting a warning sign such as 'Beware of dogs!' They are decent boys. Reading the plaque none of them dares to break the rule and press the doorbell. We were whispering encouragement to each other to give a slight knock at the door instead. That won't break the rule written on the plate. Then their maid came upstairs, squeezing through the crowded stairs. She was visibly irritated. Who would take the extra trouble of attending almost a dozen uninvited guests? She went inside carrying our request to at least see him from a little distance and just pass greetings.

She returned after a moment and told us that Mr. Bond was away. He was at Dehradun for his grandson's birthday and would be available at Cambridge school on Saturday. We were knocking at his door on a Sunday—long way off the mark. But the boys had their fan moments, a very diluted one though. I talked to them as the self-published author of about 20 books. Since they were already in that fan mode, they readily accepted my writer status. We held a little discussion about the pleasure of reading. I gave them tips about writing and shared my favorite books and authors with them. They even took a selfie with me.

Ruskin Bond's house on Lal Tibba hill is a great literary landmark at the crest of the queen of hills, Mussoorie. Having read many of his books, I could easily identify the places that have inspired his stories. So wandering through Landour bazaar, clock tower, church, post office, camel back road and cemetery gave me a surreal feeling of being in his tales personally for the next two days. It's sad that I couldn't see him at least. Although his maid says he is in Dehradun, but maybe he was chuckling from behind the door while he passed this innocent lie. But it was nice to have a feel of the places that have inspired the stories of one of India's greatest and most admired living writers. Well, as I said, 18 years ago he had dodged me when I had caught him sitting in his famous window. It was a smaller world then. Mussoorie was far less crowed. His house looked pretty ordinary. And when I harked his attention he mischievously said, 'Come sometime when I'm free.' Well there is always another time and I'm hopeful.

A bright morning always has been the stuff of legend—even on sultry, humid monsoon days when the sun seems to accentuate the musty torture. The morning sun cuts through the humid air, the sunrays seep through the humidity as if checking the proliferation of poetic anachronism pervading in this little yard. The peregrina flowers are abloom with narrative vigor. Tiny crimson clusters playing cultural cameos for a brief time. The lemon green butterflies are busy among the flowers as if holding musical dialogue with them. The small crimson flowers hold their jam, soup and syrup on the breakfasting table. Happy breakfasting you little chits of flying colors!

Poets are merchants of dreams. I copiously inhale my profits from the sight. Beyond the stony walls of the gawky and showy world, I marvel at the unrestrained seduction of the butterflies by the flowers offering their nectar with graceful candor. Then my eyes go to the ground and meet a sight—sad and sweet. A tiny classical tragedy spun by death and its heartless desertions. My emotion is sweetly sorrowful. I pick it up. A dead butterfly. It's not deeply disquieting as death usually is when beheld from such close quarters because the colors of a dead butterfly are still peppered with sweet life-giving allusions. Your eyes become luminous when you hold a butterfly even if it's a dead one.

Life and death are always engaged in melancholic-joyful, lengthy-short, haunting-uplifting, bitter-sweet tussle of duality. A butterfly carries its colors with such astonishing simplicity! I hold the fresh butterfly corpse bearing the trademark of colorful flirtations with life. The rest of her ilk are busy among the flowers with elegant gaiety, unmindful that one of them lost the air in her wings and fell down. I'm sure it was a painless journey for the winged beauty. As I hold it in my hand, I catch the sight of a bright blue kite stranded in the top branches of a prickly *keekar*. Monsoon storms have mercilessly chaffed at its once flying self. The kite also flew with charming airy anecdotes, scurrying off in different directions, challenging the power of the holding cord. Aflame with desire for freedom, it swayed with suppleness and airy assiduity. Well, it had its mundane magic and handful of revelry.

Life is only about playing for big (or small) stakes. It's our choice basically. Some have easygoing disposition, others are loquacious with an ever-faltering composure. The butterfly corpse is still endearing and demure with its feminine colorful liveliness. I give it a leaf burial.

The sky is full of dragonflies. They feast upon midges and mosquitoes. The bee-eaters and swallows scoop up the dragonflies. Relentless tragedies side-by-side to vibrant ecstasies. And the sepia-tinted trilling call of a bee-eater is a treat to my ears. How will this vocal beauty emerge if not for this game of life and death? Though steeped in commonness and stashed in ordinariness, everything is magically so-so special. And like snuffy scholars we have to seek and shape that beauty with our eyes, our heart, our sensitivities.

'We have seen a big black snake just near your gate!' many people have warned me. I can understand their spasmodic delirium at the sight of a snake even if it's non-poisonous. I take their information with a pinch of salt. I expect it to be a harmless rat snake. A dangerous krait won't usually be seen in broad daylight because it's a nocturnal guy. Moreover, it's smaller than the ones they point out with their arms stretched out to meet many feet. This one they say is huge, so they confuse it with a cobra. But a cobra will always announce its presence with warning hisses and a taut hood. So my choice filters down to the harmless rat snake. And I'm proven right. My sister comes raising a war cry against the snakes, 'It's there…didn't I tell you!' I rush to the spot and find a big rat snake inspecting our toilet in the yard corner. Its size scares the people. Still on precaution, I thump a stick near it. It doesn't raise a warning hood, confirming what I think of it—a rat snake not a cobra. I just beat the ground near it. It slithers out and enters a little section of the covered drain in the yard formed under the steps leading to the toilet. It sneaks into the tiny culvert. My sister is jittery with fear, so I push a stick into the narrow inlet and prod it out from the other end. It slithers away with its curvy, crawling majesty.

A rat snake is very fast. It just vanishes from your sight in a moment. I think it will return at night. It is most welcome to stay hidden during the day and thus not scare the family females. But I know the benefits of its presence. I haven't seen even a single mouse in months with this resident reptile around. And no frogs as well. During the monsoons there would be so many frogs in the yard that they would even challenge my right of an evening stroll after the meals. They would keep bumping against my feet during the pensive walks. They even leave a sticky substance on collision with you. It isn't good for one's skin. No frogs, no mice—welcome my snake friend!

But one frog is very clever. It entered the house while very young. It's an old country house where a frog can hide with safety. It's grown up now. I hear its adolescent croak at the dinner time from some hidden corner. It feeds upon fleas and other insects so need not go out and risk its life. O yes, forgot to mention it. I saw a cute little baby monitor lizard in the store. It isn't *gavera*, linked to the myth of a poisonous reptile, as they say, which can kill a person. It has harmful bacteria only in its saliva. I am not too bothered about it. I hope it will go out when it comes of age.

We have been turning on our heels in antipathy—he moving away with a snarl and me with mouthfuls of cuss words holding something in my hand to ward off any potential attack from his side. But the profoundly irresistible dislike for him has melted a bit after his dusk-time play with the newly dug pole. The next time when I see him I offer a good banana. His imperial majesty looks suspiciously. In any case he will steal, I think, so it's better to offer one myself and gather some good points in his books. The supreme monarch of the simian kingdom in the village is aware of the risks of fruit traps by the humans. Huddled in utter detachedness to my ceasefire offer, he simply looks away. I'm again on the verge of faltering, capitulate and cave into anger about his not accepting my gift. But somehow I retain my composure and leave the banana on the compound wall. He arrives casually after some time—as if he didn't know about the

74

banana and merely found it on the way. What attitude! He sniffed at it with extra-dilated nostrils. Vah, the royal connoisseur of the olfactory art! He accepted it in an off-hand manner as if his highness has done me a favor by doing so. I'm relieved that I have bought peace for just one banana—no broken branches, no angry snarls, no foul words, no mangoes mangled on the floor.

A couple of days later I see a lady monkey with her infant. Driven by the far-flung memories of encounters with monkeys, my initial impulse is to scare her away using hard words, stomping of feet, brandishing a stick and a lynching tongue well in toe. She makes a sound which only a mother can, a kind of request to hold my temper because her little one is there. Her red face peering at me from a space in the roof railing. I hold back my reaction and immoderately throw a guava on the roof. Immediately I see him emerging from his secret watch post. He claims the peace booty. So he was watching me! I hold another guava for the mother monkey, but two monkey lads—teenagers, his sons from the previous season of love—smartly gallop and one of them claims it. Meantime, he gives me an avid scrutiny from a distance. *Ahaa* the art of autumnal armistice in the monsoon season! It scoops a handful of pleasure and peace for both parties.

He sits solemn and recalcitrant while his brood is enjoying within limits. A miracle! His old wife, the one with the infant, has her tail missing. There are two young boys and one young second wife. I'm not in a querulous mood today; as a result neither are they. All of us play our parts in conflicts. If both sides don't add their share, peace prevails. He sits like a monarch—with astute magnanimity. His lads fidget and dolt around, crawl on a cable to reach a tree outside the yard and pluck leaves and buds to eat. I laugh at their antics and natural laughter makes one amiable and solicitous. All this is harmony-augmenting stuff. Today I have not given them a fright; they haven't reacted on their part. I know he is stealing glances at me while I'm suffused with the wonderful sight of his tailless wife showering maternal affection on her baby. She is relaxed and lies belly down, legs dangling on both sides of the parapet wall, her tailless pink bottom gleaming under the monsoonal sky, her chin supported on the wall, the baby playing in front of her face; tranquilly and lugubriously she braces it behind the ears to find out any lice. This is all-surpassing love and affection.

There are no stony stares and distrustful eyes, no scandalous alertness, no sly ingenuity, no tenacious passions, no gratifying deceit. Just a normal world with pulsating excursion. A soft and supple world that can easily turn treacherous and ferocious if we don't hold our respective parts of peace. They are enjoying on the terrace. Today I don't make them feel that they are marauding thugs; don't snivel and dribble with cuss words. He has a despondent and limpid grimace on his face. I have to go to my den on the terrace. I'm moving up the open staircase with a book and the day's newspaper in my hand. As I reach the landing, I see him moving along the railings just three-four feet away. There are no glowering looks on either side, just traces of timidity. He just double checks by sniffing in the direction of the book and moves away slowly and sits on the wall, his back to me, assured that I don't mean any harm.

His brood is playing but surprisingly they haven't raised the usual ruckus. I think like Moi and Noah tried to come to terms with each other's presence in the ape movie, we both also should try to come to terms with the reality of our respective existence. I have to understand that he simply is a father fighting for his family. Theirs is a big fight for survival in the concrete jungles. I can't expect them to be well behaved all the time. But are we ourselves as such? So I can try to buy peace like I did this time with a banana, two guavas and a behavior missing reprimanding words.

All of us should try to buy peace. It's not costly; hate, anger and wars are very costly on the other hand. They burn relationships and countries. Let the bigger issues be decided by big authorities. I shall prioritize buying peace with the monkeys in lieu of some fruits. I mean with this group at least. They keep moving across the localities. But for the fresh truants I reserve my right to act, behave and jump in the usual ways when they will arrive to slay peace. And I'm sure they will.

They emerge from the prodigality of entanglements, like mushroom sprouts from the savage and fertile humus in the human soul. Destiny chuckles with perfidious pleasure as it pushes them onto the stage—faceless, no defined character role, just fuddle-muddle-headed lousy slow-creepers among the smart stampede of noticeable boots. Most of them are pushed by abhorrent native circumstances. And they somehow float into relatively better parts, their existence as trivial as slut, scum and scamp. They move tactlessly, all of them bearing the marks of ravaging thunderbolts back home—civil wars, genocide, hunger, poverty, natural calamity, systematic targeting and the likes. All of them sharing the same pool of ineffaceable memories of pain and suffering. Destiny holds them tight. They are mere harnessed horses pulling at the traces and pathetically biting at the bits as if to douse their hunger with it only.

They come from different regions and religions but look the same—poor scum of the society. Snatchily squelching in the survival sludge, they chatter in various unknown dialects. But it's the same language, the same script of poverty. It's the same sobbing choir. They might be *Rohingyas*, Bangladeshis, Nepalese or anyone from the poorest parts of India. They share their very own unique nationality of disadvantages, oppression and exploitation. They simply barge in to survive, to stay alive. They aren't welcome but they smartly swim in the stench of sewage drains, rapaciously picking up the discards like these are tasty, pickled raw vegetable slices. They pick up and eat and accept anything at which even the poorest local won't even look. They do this so that they are seen to survive without giving competition to anyone. They pick up what even the native rag pickers won't touch.

They know that capacious ears get pricked up to catch their presence. They stoop so low that no one feels slighted by their presence. Their glum disposition would enable you to see through them like you would through a pig. Thoroughly gnawed and devoured, they scamper stealthily like big rats in the sewage lines. Then sometimes malice and temptation catches a few of them, inflicting a cold-blooded derangement to the logical part—a small section where some sense still exists despite such horrible emotional trauma—in their poverty-knotted brain. In chocking resentment, depressed and downcast, the horribly miserable being slays someone's good fate. Some crime is committed.

Usually the current days carry a severe air. And why won't the days be heavy, laden with stress and anxiety? The modern culture suffers from the suffocating paroxysm of whooping cough—the cough of staying busy at all costs and milk every second for economic gains. But most of what we do as a species would sound as a practical joke from the perspective of those who seek the dimension of ease and just being.

A terribly humid, sultry, worn out and bedraggled day is downing its shutters here in my small yard and its little garden. Its pain and yearning melting away as it moves to the twilight, which is maybe just twenty minutes away. This is late August and after many rainy, cloudy days the sky cleared this afternoon with a feeling that we will have a few days of sunshine. A strange stability sets in; things settling down like a journeyman coming home after listlessly wandering in life without anchorage. The sky is full of dragonflies feasting upon midges and mosquitoes. They themselves are sometimes shot down by the swallows, *neelkanths* and bee-eaters. Some boys tattle and prattle on the roofs, their kites almost hung at a point in the humid air. These are slow but sweatily stupefying proceedings.

Most of the butterflies have retired for the day. Just a few of them still dance among the peregrina clusters. As I watch, a grass green butterfly that I thought was sleeping on a leaf nattily floated down like an old leaf. An imperceptible death. I pick it up. It's fresh and beautiful but its ounce of life has flown away on an eternal journey. It's a sad sight to hold a dead butterfly. I leave it among the flowers.

Two juvenile butterflies—siblings, friends, lovers?—are wise beyond their age. They retire early under a big *tulsi* leaf hung horizontally in a musty safe corner. Good night, have a lovely sleep you girls!

The next day is sunny and the peregrina blooms have dozens of dancing butterflies right from the start. But I find those two still asleep. Then one of them got awake a bit after seven and joined the revelry among the blooms. The other was lazier. It got up around eight to have its flying, fluttering fun.

The monsoon has been vigorous this season, pouring down with fluffed obduracy. The earth stands expatiated, its pining thirst slackened down, softly yielding to the countless kisses. A greener world looks hopeful despite the wars and political intrigues. Kaka *Maharaj* has been pushing and prodding the realm of spirituality for the last four decades. He is nearing 78 years in age now. The coarse sheets of materiality slowly shedding; he has a sagely countenance now. Meanwhile I have been plowing the field of paperwork and books. But we somehow manage an effective communication—me with my theoretical knowledge and he with experiential one.

'Now for the next three years I will stand in the pond water for *tapasya*!' he declared a few months back. I let out a low-toned defiant muttering against such austerity in old age. We had a discussion on this and I'm able to convince him to settle for *maun vrata*, the vow of silence, now and then. Since then he has kept the fast of silence for a month on average and speaks only when someone like me makes it impossible for him to keep his vow of silence.

This time I visit him after more than a month. He has a rope swing dangling from a banyan branch and supporting his old torso on it he meditates on his guru. I find him very drained out this time. He slowly writes on the page of a pocket diary I have gifted him for the purpose. He is having fever for the last one week. He can't feel his feet from the knees down. He can't feel the presence of his head and face above the neck. Then finding the diary and gesticulations insufficient to convey all he has to say he drawls and forces out vocal sounds. 'In any case writing and trying sign language is as good as speaking,' he says in a feeble voice, his vocal cords waking up after a month of vacation and sleep. Then in measured tones he explains the matter. The story goes like this.

He saw a very strange and unique wild mushroom in the overgrown bushes and grass around his hut. A few insects were feasting upon it. 'If these tiny ones don't die after eating it, I'm a human after all,' he thought. The mushroom was snatched away from the beetles in one quick swipe. Actually that's how the ancient people must have discovered the medicinal herbs. It was something very nastily potent. Once it entered his system, stroke by stroke and pigment by pigment it almost turned his intestines inside out. 'I'm thoroughly washed and rinsed from inside. I don't think anything remained inside,' he elaborated the after effects of that unknown wild mushroom. I'm glad that he has taken the bout of torrential diarrhea caused by some poisonous fungi as stomach cleansing. Of course it has caused some infection in his stomach which resulted in a fever. No wonder he is in bad shape. But he is very happy about discovering a detoxification treatment to cleanse the system.

'I shall show it to you! And I will give it to someone looking to cleanse his stomach,' he looks forward to spread the effects of that unknown fungi for the cause of humanity. I choke with fear. I tell him the story of Buddha's nirvana. How a low caste devotee unknowingly picked up poisonous wild mushrooms and cooked them with devotional love for the visiting mahatma. The Buddha ate it despite knowing its poisonous nature. He didn't want to belittle the hospitality shown by the poor man.

I try to dissuade him from risking his life by doing such experiments with unknown substances. He waves me off dismissively. 'It has its purpose otherwise my guru won't allow me to touch it,' he is perfect in his faith. I also have some vague idea about the mysterious purpose it must have served in his system on his path.

Whatever is the intensity of ailment he never takes tablets or mainstream treatment. He starts laughing at the mention of the word 'doctor'. He would be the last person to allow an MBBS to come near him even if he is dying. Well, he shows me his magical discovery. He has stored it in a utensil for some lucky person to be cleansed inside out. It's tart black. Stinking. My head spins, '*Maharaj*, for God's sake don't give it to anyone. It will be plain murder. You somehow survived,' I blabber with panic. Looking at me so serious and out of wits he somehow gets the message. I walk with him to the hand-pump to ensure that the last bit is cleaned and washed. I wish the insects good luck as he cleans and throws the black substance on the grass nearby. I'm sure it would count as a chemical attack on the insect kingdom.

Musty evenings, a decoction of sweat and sultry mawkishness. This is the season of mating. A peacock hooting, scattering the suggestive fragrance of its desire to be caught by some coquettish brunette of its species. Creation is fortuitously bound to chance winds at this level. Sometimes it fruitlessly sails through the sky; sometimes it hits home and the dance of desire starts, the fantail spread to handover its thoroughbred royal blue hues to the next generation.

The yard bricks have moss, the air musty, the day grey and old. It gives a very ancient feeling. A little bit before the twilight hits, I light my lamp of devotion under a holy pair—*tulsi* and *shami* plants. My little altar is under the peregrina tree. The latter has ample leafy garments thanks to the rainy season. It's aflame with crimson clusters of flowers—a representative of the smoldering sensuality riding the humid layer. Little grass-green butterflies flutter among the flowers through the day. The flowers are aplenty and hundreds of them drizzle over the place of my clay lamp after fulfilling their blooming duty. And so do a few butterflies that fall with the flowers never to rise again.

It's a sad sight to see dead butterflies among the fallen flowers around the evening twilight. You smell the musty odor of death. But flowers and butterflies—even when dead—have enough colors in them to still hold the beacon of life. They somehow thwart the overflowing silence of death. And there I light my lamp of faith among old dead flowers and forever sleeping butterflies. A flicker of hope and faith, fallen flowers and butterfly corpses, musty moments hung with sultry detachment, the day slowly dying to finish its journey at the twilight, a humid night taking birth, a lone butterfly still dancing among the flowers owning the entire tree to herself, the birds retiring to roost for the night and a poetic man witnessing this slowly shifting picture on the canvas of mother existence.

Happiness is primarily an acceptance of one's situation in life. It might not come to you even in a palace if you don't really settle inside the walls and within your skin. You are a cranky host, so it will avoid you. And it will definitely come to visit your slum hut if it finds you an unashamed, guilt free, kind host. As an old, poor charwoman, whom Somerset Maugham meets after many years in 1949, when there had been lots of developmental works in the meanwhile, says to him: 'They have cleaned up the slums and the dirt, and all the happiness and joy has gone with it.'

There were killings, slaughter and genocide. Holocaust. From its fire a dagger was born. The Desert Dagger. Forged in the sandy, fiery furnace of killings, torture and annihilation. Enemies rasping at its edges from all sides to annihilate it. But that merely sharpens the edges. The Desert Dagger has a pointed tip, the pinnacle of all the sharp, serrated edges around it—survival. It has the soul of steel. It has one soul, one goal, one dream, one people— survival. It knows how to reshape its pain into hope and then turn hope into cutting-edge technology—sharp, precise, surgical, unsparing.

The Desert Dagger cuts and writes its destiny on the book of life having sandy pages. It's a mighty pen held in one hand. It knows what it has to write—the book of survival, the manual of survival at any cost. Where do the Desert Dagger's soul, spirit and matter come from? It comes from the memories of the millions who perished in gas chambers. It comes from the teary, rosy dreams in the hearts—the dreams of the survival of a race. It comes from the razor sharp logic in the mind—the logic of fight when surrounded from all sides and kill before getting killed.

Give Indians first a cheated fake result. Even the commonest of us have enough brains to discuss and chalk out the true success story of a fake result. We will then spin the success hypothesis to validate the false. You just need to cheat us and then leave it on us to prove with our shrewd acumen that it was no cheating, it was rather a masterstroke to achieve true, honest success. Well done Kumar sir! You did your job, now we do ours.

Pre-script: This one is inspired by my conversation with one of the best devotees of Ma Ganga I have come across.

Who wouldn't like to stay longer on the banks of Ma Ganga? But She would like Her children to be active in the world as well. To me Her maternal touch is like *prasad*. Even the little bit of it gives a feeling of getting satiated and fulfilled that buckets of normal food won't give.

Frankly speaking dear friends, I feel blessed and happy whatever time She allows me near Her for my learning and growth. Don't you see those who are born on Her banks and stay there since birth are even more common and worldly than those born in cities far away? I mean most of them are. Because to them Her presence is like food, not *prasad*. They take it for granted. The people like you, me and countless others who get Her presence like *prasad* now and then are really blessed. She calls us at intervals, gives lessons and new realizations, sends us away to find the meaning of life, come back again, evolve a bit more by Her touch and go back again—a real *prasad* in small bits. But to those who stay with Her all the time She is mere food, in abundance, and thus taken for granted. So bow down and be grateful for the loving *prasad* She has given you.

We go to the temples but not all of us stay in a temple to feel blessed. We can carry the spark of divinity that we get from the temple. To me She is a living temple. And whatever chance She gives to have Her *darshan* is *prasad*. I know She would love me to do my worldly role, which I do with a very balanced approach. I just told my view dear friends. I'm not saying everyone should feel like that.

Maybe She sends us away when She feels that *prasad* ought not to become food. Separation with an assured coming together: the loveliest subtle twine that binds the deity and the devotee. Subtle and effective, just like silence is the best language.

Loitering on the banks of Ma Ganga I see the real beauty of India. The faith, *seva bhav*, love. A few *sadhus* and animal welfare volunteers have come together to treat the injured horn of a bull. Coming from a farming family I have seen such scenes in my village. When pinned down like this by the humans, the poor cattle think they are getting slaughtered. I remember that fear in the rolled eyes of the pinned down buffalo or bull. Those strong puffs of breath spurting saliva and slime on the muzzle. But here the bull is somehow relaxed. Its eyes aren't popping out with the fear of death. This I feel is due to the touch of the *sadhus*. There is an assurance of safety, love and care. Their presence makes the bull behave well even in the face of such a painful, scary experience. Its eyes are normal. Its muzzle isn't oozing with slime, which a cattle normally does with strong puffs of breathing under such circumstances. The bull seems assured of safety. The touch of loving *sadhus* mixed with the touch of caring animal lovers from an animal welfare foundation. It's in safe hands. The injured horn is dressed. And the volunteers move away slowly releasing the rope, leaving only the *sadhus* near the bull as it gets up. The young bull gets onto its feet with wonderful calm. The *sadhus* pat it lovingly. 'You are a good boy. Now don't fight too much over girlfriends,' says the young doctor. The onlookers laugh. The *sadhus* guide it to a relatively open space.

It's a world of bitter-sweet experiences. For hundreds of sweet ones on the banks of Ma Ganga, one can't help coming across a sour one. And that forms the basis of this muttering from Rishikesh.

When I'm at Rishikesh I simply go footloose. I just keep walking most of the time, soaking the smell, sight, touch, taste and listen all that is on offer at the pilgrimage town.

Seeing we walking with such careless demeanor, a woman ascetic with a brass *kamandal* tried to plunder money. She approached like a realized mother, all made up of course as a mendicant friar and asked for money. To begin with, she asked for food for the five of them. 'We

86

are five *matajis*, so 20 rupees for the food for each of us,' she says. These are *navaratra* days, so I give her 100 rupees without bargaining. She probably thinks that I'm a sitting duck for cheating. Meanwhile she took a thief's peek into my modest wallet as I took out the money to give to her. I want to move but she puts her hand on my head, trying possibly to play some psychotic energy game or magical trick or some sort of hypnotic maneuver so that she could plunder more money. With the blessings of Ma Ganga, I have enough energies in my head. She starts shivering. 'Please take out two notes from your wallet. I take a vow in the name of Ma Ganga that I will give them back,' she says. Before I realize she is tying a *mauli dhaga* on my wrist asking, 'Are you married?' I'm not interested in her queries about my matrimonial status.

I don't have a change in my wallet but since she has taken a vow in the name of Ganga Ma while standing on Her banks, I give her two 500 rupees notes expecting her to return them. The moment the notes land in her claws she folds them in her fist. The way she holds them makes it sure that they are in her greedy talons not to be returned. Now I realize the tales of the thugs who take money and play the magic trick of making it disappear with the clap of a hand.

I remember an incidence from early youth in the village. A street magician took 100 rupees from my friend and with a clap the money vanished. He had a lovely python and a flute to add to the charm of his street show. Now the 100 rupees of those times created a big issue. So we manhandled him, his *pagri* fell. One guy was just ready to break his flute on his head. That's when the poor magician realized that the Jatland isn't suitable for magic tricks. And the money comes out of his *gullak*. He holds the python's mouth, pries it open, puts his hand in and draws out the money. Imagine the smartness. Magic money goes into the python's mouth!

'We will go to *kedar* with the money,' the female thief in saffron says. To me it's not about money. It's about taking a false vow in Ma Ganga's name. I don't know what Ganga Ma thinks of me but I feel I'm Her ardent devotee. I shame the woman for being a liar, looting money in the name of Ma Ganga. I get really angry and in no nonsense terms ask her to return the money as promised. Somehow she hasn't been able to make the money vanish. Good that she hasn't a python with her. Somehow her trick of making the money vanish fails. Ma Ganga's blessings!

She gives back one note, with a look as if I'm plundering her. I am firmly against such a sham *sadhvi*, so I point my finger at her and asked her to return the other note as well. She is trying to make me feel ashamed for getting angry, for losing control of myself just about money. Why should I be? I'm not a saffron-clad saint to be ashamed of my well-deserved anger on cheats. With a broken heart she hands back the other note all crushed due to the pressure of her talons. 'I was just checking your heart for its grasp on money,' she says as if I have failed her testing of my desire for worldly things like 500 rupees notes.

Then she tries to give me a *rudraksh* bead. I tell her I that don't need anything from her. Neither her blessings, nor her bead. I don't want at least from those who tell lies in the name of taking vow of Ganga Ma. Had it been a male *sadhu* I would have snatched away even the hundred rupees. But these I leave with her as a grace mark for her being a woman.

But Ma Ganga knows how to spin her lovely magic and change mutterings into musings.

I'm walking sullenly about cheats on the banks of Ma Ganga. But She is such a kind mother. She knows how to uplift the spirit of Her child. I'm walking in the crowd and suddenly see the autistic girl on whom I wrote a story a few years back. I see her with her parents on the banks of Ma Ganga. The last time, a mere child, she looked so unjustifiably deprived of her slice of joy among all that festival aura and with tears in my eyes I prayed so sincerely for her during my entire stay at that time. I wrote a long story of blessings on her. She is a woman now! I had prayed for the faith and health of her parents so that they would help her in her journey for as long as possible because nobody can take care of a special child like her parents. And there I see them carrying her in a wheel chair in the busy bazaar. She looks healthy and beautiful; a lovely young woman now. Her parents appear in good spirits and look healthy, happily carrying their responsibility.

Imagine out of the thousands of pilgrims, Ma Ganga blesses me with their sight to let me know that She remembers my prayers for this family.

There are *sadhus* in front of an ashram in Rishikesh that serves food daily in the morning. There are cows also. The *sadhus* are having the routine sweet-sour chit chat while having food. The cows are chewing cud, contended. There are drops of dung around. Then a cute roly-poly *baba* arrives, his presence silent and peaceful. He has a unique attire: a piece of sackcloth tied like ancient Romans across his torso, a woolen cap on the head and a small towel on the bare shoulder. His left hand isn't visible. To be frank, I'm not sure about its status. It might be missing; it might be tied along his stomach in hard penance to take this worldly *yatra* with a single hand. I give fifty-fifty chances to both probabilities.

He has a lovely way of walking, a kind of spirited ease of a child. A trace of smile doesn't leave his face even for a single moment. He is a *mauni baba*, the one who takes a vow of silence, so by default his tongue is restful, which in turn avoids unnecessary fuel to the chattering mind. There he comes and starts picking the cow dung with the joyful ease of a child playing on the beach. He uses his free hand to pick up cow dung and drop it into the garden across the street. The street is soon clean. In fact his lovely walk to and fro works like a cosmic broom to clean the air itself.

There are *gau rakshaks* who take to violence in the name of holy cows. I would say most of them are people with violent tendencies and take shelter under mother cow's name to hide their violence. *Gau mata* doesn't need *rakshaks*, she needs *sevaks* like this kind and loving *baba*.

The *baba* then cleans his hand under a tap, caresses the cows with the feel of a boy touching something precious. That's when the wagging tongues between the Hindu *babas* and a Buddhist monk start the fireworks and before the tongues could handover the work to fists, the joyful *mauni baba* comes in between and dispels the heat just with his smile, silent nods and gentle wave of hand. It's a divine feeling just to *be* in the presence of someone who is at ease with himself.

As I walk in the busy little bazaar street on the banks of Ma Ganga, a *sadhu* and his dog meet my attention. The *sadhu's* one hand supports the dog's head like a soft pillow. With the other hand he is fanning the dog to sleep. The people get amused and laugh, thinking him to be a crazy *baba*. To be frank I also think so initially. But when I return after a couple of hours, he is still fanning the dog to sleep with the same loving care. I think there must be something wrong with the dog otherwise why would it lie so still and calm with closed eyes in broad daylight with hundreds of feet tapping the narrow street. So I sit down to chat with the *baba*. 'Maybe the dog is sick,' I ask. He laughs and points to a big food bowl, 'No Badal ate too much and who won't sleep with cool fan air and a palm to support?' The dog's name is Badal. 'Badal also is Bhagwan's avatar.

If you can't love a dog, how will you love humans, and if you can't love humans, how will you love God,' he elaborates his simple spiritual equation. He was offered to Joona Akhara by his parents at an early age. I ask him does he miss his parents sometimes. He cracks a big laugh, 'What a question! He is the biggest *mai baap*!' he brandishes his bright pink plastic hand fan towards Lord Shiva's statue kindly looking at us from the top of a gateway. I feel embarrassed. Yes he is under the protection of the biggest *baap*!

Bhola Rikiyasan is the sole Buddhist monk among hundreds of Hindu mendicants at the pilgrimage town. He stands out quite naturally with his separate religious identity. The other day he said to the group of saffron-clad *sadhus* around him that all of you are not at peace and that's why you people are wandering around. An argument started, turned into a brawl and soon it would have changed to a fist fight, from the side of Hindu friars of course who looked very spirited to defend their dharma. A Hindu *mauni baba* negotiated peace with his loving presence.

Rikiyasan is from Gaya. He was a Shiva devotee for 26 years, felt stuck up on the path and converted to Buddhism six years back. Maybe that's the reason the Hindu *babas* dislike him. Religious conversion is a serious issue in India. But look at the great syncretic tradition of India, he still has Bhola, Shiva's name, in his official name. Well, he is 75 years old—I have to check his ID to confirm it because he doesn't look three-quarters of a century old from any angle.

'One meal a day and meditation to calm the mind are the reasons for it,' he says. He looks at peace and joyful about life. I see a thick wad of money in his wallet as he stuffs ten rupees just offered to him by a man. 'Just ten rupee notes. Won't count for much!' he laughs. 'I'm collecting money for making a little Buddha shrine at my village,' he justifies his collection. Well, all of us are after money for our reasons and I have talked to hundreds of *sadhus* in this regard. Most of them are after money to make ashrams and temples. The householders are after it for building houses and buying cars. I hardly see any qualitative difference between the two.

A couple of days ago he was bitten by a dog in the wee hours as he was walking in the street after taking a bath in Ma Ganga. A few hours after the painful bite I found him standing desolate at his corner with his brass begging bowl. He had tied a strip of cloth on the wound. The cloth was all bloody. It was a big bite. I hope his Hindu *baba* adversaries didn't set a dog after him. I go to the small charity hospital run by a prominent ashram to seek help for him. They inform me that there is no anti-rabies vaccination available at their place. To get it one has to go to the government hospital a few kilometers away on the opposite bank.

I come back and tell him to walk to Ram Jhoola—it's just 50 meters from where he is sitting—and take an auto to go to the hospital. He says he will prefer to walk towards the other bridge, Janaki bridge, almost a kilometer down the stream because if he goes from here the auto would charge 50 rupees and from there it will be only 10 rupees. But he can hardly walk. I understand that he would delay his treatment because he is in pain and can barely walk. And one needs vaccination at the earliest after the bite.

I wonder, why would he still bother so much about money even in such a situation. Well, I think *baba* or no *baba*, money is a big issue in the world. And like ordinary householders, the *babas* have every right to think that it's their hard-earned money because they have to stand throughout the day to get alms.

Since he needs vaccination so I hire a scooty to take him to the government hospital, requesting the scooty guy to take him to the concerned block and guide him through the process. By this time he is in much pain and looks all ready to shed this miserable body. 'I would be good if I die. It seems this poor body needs to be shed!' he looks depressed, sad and sullen. I say an encouraging bye as the rental scooty takes him away through the crowd.

The next day I find him all freshened up with three anti-rabies injections, one on his left *chuttar* (as he puts it with a feeling of insult and pain) and one each on both arms. But the urge to live and be joyful and meditate has returned. He looks contended and at peace with life. I advise him to carry a stick. Maybe that can help him in religious debates and brawls with Hindu *babas* as well.

I'm walking to the famous *jhilmil gufa* in the hills above Rishikesh. In order to take a shortcut I end up taking a long-cut as it usually happens. The hill forests are mischievous. The tiny foot trails are green leafy mazes where they will try to keep you busy in solving the puzzle. Then a *baba* arrives from some other trail. I ask him about the caves where sage Gorakhnath did *tapasya* for many years. Incidentally he is also going to the caves.

He is one of the most friendly *babas* I have seen. It's surprising given the fact that he is a *naga sadhu*, the warrior ascetics who worship lord Shiva. Within a few minutes we are talking like good friends.

Baba Shambhu Giri is from Jalna, Maharashtra. He was a sickly child in a poor family. They couldn't afford to get treatment for him. So his helpless parents offered him to the holy fireplace at the ashram of a *naga baba*. The *baba* took care of him from the age of five, treated him with herbal medicines, and initiated him into the order. He turned out to be a healthy, robust *sadhu*. Then his guru left his body, leaving the ashram and its 41 acres of agricultural land under the disciple's care.

'I'm a farming *naga baba*. I don't believe in asking for alms. I do farming on the ashram land,' he shows me his tough farming hands. The *nagas* have fought many times in wars to upkeep dharma. 'Only a person from a warrior clan, the martial castes like Maratha, Jat, Sikh and Rajput, can become a *naga*,' he says with pride as he walks with force in his steps like a soldier sage.

I am surprised to know about the level of their opposition to the Brahmins. I will avoid the details of that discussion because my Brahmin friends will get angry about this. I'm from a Jat family and to be frank at the level of community we too have lots of things to say against Brahmins, just like Brahmins have against us.

He is happy to learn that I'm also from a martial caste. We Indians can't help getting into the casteist talk even when we are in the hill forests and happen to be a *naga* baba and a spiritual seeker. So we have our share of bitching against the Brahmins. The details should always be avoided. The summary I can say is that *naga baba* told me that Brahmins come from the lineage of *daityas* and in Maharashtra about 75% of the people avoid getting a Brahmin for officiating at a *havan* on auspicious occasions like marriages and other *pujas*. So that should give you the level of our partisan talk. Caste becomes a major factor even in talks between two strangers in a forest. No wonder caste decides who rules the country.

'The ashram land provides enough money. Then there is charity which we *sadhus* get so easily just sitting on our bums whether we deserve it or not. I use the money to manage the ashram, getting poor girls married and other charity work. And once a year I come out on my wanderings like this,' he is very honest about what he thinks and feels, be it money or caste. I like his honesty about most of the things. He just says what he thinks inside. No pretensions.

Suddenly he gets excited like a boy and goes to a bush nearby. '*Bichhu buti*, scorpion plant, I got myself bitten by it yesterday. It's very discomfiting and painful but I won't get any disease for the next six months,' he tells me. Who won't wish to have free, natural immunity against all diseases for six months? I ask him to get me bitten by the *buti* in the right proportions. He is hesitant. Then agrees. He holds a little shoot softly and gently allowing one tip to touch on the back of my palm. He removes it before it barely touches the skin, like a father would be careful not to harm his child. No effect. I pester him for a bit higher dose. So this time the touch is bigger, and still bigger on successive trials. I don't wince with pain. I don't get my free immunity shot. Both of us are disappointed. 'This is no *bichhu buti*. It's some fake plant imitating a famous one,' we conclude.

Most of the *sadhus* have a free passage to the places of other *sadhus*. An ash-smeared *naga baba* is performing a *havan* for a seemingly rich man. It's a large fireplace, the big *trishuls* are blackened with smoke and look ferocious. We sit in front of our host, he with friendly ease and me with apprehension because I have heard about their inflammable tempers when disturbed. But my *naga baba* friend is a shield against getting shoved away with the tip of a *trishul*. The ash-smeared *naga* is calm, focused on his rituals. He nods to our greeting and without stopping the process, gives us soaked grams and raisins as *prasad*. To be frank I take almost as much as would fill my cupped palms together. I am hungry and eat *prasad* like dinner. The *naga baba* watches me with a strange muse. So I have my food and my friend *baba* has *prasad*.

We take leave from the *baba* and move onto our path. Then he suddenly points to a place where he faced a leopard during the Corona period. The world of humans had retreated and the animals came out. 'It was standing there and snarled. I knew it could injure me if it didn't run away. Had I turned my back to it, it would have reached me in three bounding strides. So I stood upfront and took up a stone. Never look away from a predator and never show your back. And hit it on the nose if it approaches you. By the grace of God, the leopard backed away and vanished in the forest,' he shares the story.

Then the *baba's chappal* gets broken. I am wearing shoes. I feel guilty in walking in shoes while the *baba* has a broken *chappal*. But surprisingly he walks as if it's not broken at all. Once in the gufa he tells me all the stories related to the place. We have tea in front of Baba Gorakhnath's fireplace. They smoke weed. The cave's resident *sadhus* are good hosts. Again the matter of caste comes up. 'Brahmins and householders aren't allowed to touch the holy ash in the fireplace,' the Gorakhnath order *sadhu* tells me. The casteist bugs in me are getting fattened today. I nod with glee, almost happy, even joyful about the fact that Brahmins don't hold monopoly to our faith. They maybe manage more of the ritualistic part of it. So we have to accept the fact that casteism is deeply entrenched in our Indian soul. It decides things from caves to presidential palaces. They *babas* are on a meditative high on weed, my head spins just with the smoke.

I stand up and walk to another small cave on the side of the big cave. And here I come across the most mischievous *bala yogi*, a *naga* boy *sadhu*. He doesn't speak, just hums like a black bee. Continuously. I marvel that he is actually a black bee hovering over the divine flower to sip the nectar of self realization.

My *naga* friend will stay here today but I have to walk back. So Baba Shambhu Giri introduces other caves to me like Hanuman gufa and Ganesh gufa. The kind baba then guides me to the trail that would take me to Neelkanth from where I could easily walk back to Rishikesh. I take out 500 rupees before taking leave. He isn't interested in it. He has enough he already told me. '*Maharaj*, your *chappal*

96

got broken while sharing this lovely journey with me, so it's my duty to give a replacement,' I request in all sincerity. He agrees. 'Ok, if you say so. I will buy a nice pair of *chappals* in your name,' he laughs. We take leave.

I had a bamboo stick with me as a companion on the way up. But I forgot it at the place where we had sat down to eat *prasad* at the *naga baba's* place on the way up. Now I miss the sturdy stick as I wade through a steep, faint trail among lots of bushes in the forest. And when I reach the place where he had pointed out the leopard I miss my stick even more. What will I do with a stick in the face of a leopard? Well, at least I would try to hit it on the foe's nose as suggested by the *baba* and get a solace that I die fighting. But there is no leopard and I quickly move on the feeble trails to get to the main path.

The squirrel stays among the larger clump of trees outside the yard wall. Now and then it flits in to have a view of the little clump of garden trees—*parijat*, *bhelpatra*, guava, *karipatta*, *champa*. A cloth line is strung between the yard wall and this small group of trees in the middle of the courtyard.

Usually the squirrel runs in from below the lower grills of the main iron gate. But of late I see it crawling over the cloth line to reach the trees. Then one day I find the reason for this difficult crawl. It nibbles at the seam threads of my clothes hung for drying.

Actually it's making a new house among the *parijat's* top branches. It's resourceful enough to pick out fluffy threads—the construction material for its new house—available near the site. After that, when I see it crawling over the line, I run to the capacity of my bones, shake the rope vigorously to make it fall down. It jumps in panic.

But it's a stubborn squirrel or maybe knows that a poet has a severe limitation in carrying on such behavior. So despite my frantic efforts to cut down its supply lines from this end, it continues with its crawling mission.

Tariff war is a suitable replacement for the actual bloodshed on battlefields. We have been at war on many fronts since thousands of years. It has gone deep into our genes. So if a war it has to be, let it be a tariff war. We carry lots of hate, fear, suspicion, ego, the urge to dominate. All these seek an outlet. It leaks like lava from narrow fissures and avoids a big blast which occurs after a long cycle. So this tariff war is a nice, new vent that opens for the inner lava to come out of the guts of powerful leaders. It would postpone a bloody explosion. So businessman Trump might delay actual blood and gore which President Trump might not have achieved. By the way, hey you AI guys, why don't you devise virtual wars that can be played by the mightily angry rulers to vent out their hot lava? I would love it if the bloody reality is replaced by a virtual one.

5

THE hills unfold in all sublimity as nature goes for unpaved walks. All around there is an illustrious and august affluence of her smiles, shoots, saplings, flowers, fruits, plants and trees. Foggy and pleasantly confusing trails beckon the wanderlust souls. Fleeting streamlets coolly rushing on with an assured music on their lips and spontaneous foresight in head. We try to catch up with our roads and boundaries and strive to own our share from one air, one earth, one sky, one water, one fire.

The serpentine road from Tiuni to a little hamlet near Arakot 30 km away represents this administrative and ownership tussle between Himachal Pradesh and Uttarakhand. It's a narrow road along Pabbar river flowing with the spirit of a young lass to merge with Tons near Tiuni. The road serving almost as the border between Himachal Pradesh (left) and Uttarakhand (right).

Pandranu they tell me is in Himachal. But if you cross the iron bridge over the rapidly rushing Pabbar river and reach the other bank you are in Uttarakhand. I am staying at a lone house overlooking the Pabbar river. The owner family has gone to the higher hills because it's apple harvest season. They have an ancient house at the native village surrounded by their apple orchards. During the day as I cross the bridge and go to the small market having a few shops by the road, I'm actually crossing boundaries many times in a day.

The common peacock butterfly (*Paplio biamor*), all bright and shiny, is a beautiful flier full of colors: bluish green, blue, green; a solitary fast flier in lovely fluorescent peacock colors. It's bigger in size in comparison to the butterflies at my native place. It can even afford to flutter its colors in the windy swirls over the spating Pabbar river. So when it flutters here near the place where I'm staying, it's the state butterfly of Uttarakhand. But when it flutters to the other side of the road, it turns an ordinary butterfly and loses its status of a state butterfly.

Near the market, down the road is a small auction *mandi* for the apple farmers. It's a busy place in the morning. The pick-up trucks arriving laden with apple crates and card boxes. The main commission agent is a wily, smart middlemen between the farmers and the traders from the plains. Nearby, in the same open compound, is a tiny tin-shed snack point run by two glamorous ladies. They have tattooed limbs, wear very tight leggings and T-shirts, flaunt bleached brown hair and display flashy lipsticks. A phone number is prominently displayed on the signboard in front of the establishment. So you have many people taking extra tea or maggi even while they aren't hungry. The porters naughtily wink that there is some side business as well.

Rajesh, the owner of the house where I'm staying, is a small man with slightly bandy legs that gives him an elderly grace as he walks. He is busy in his orchards high up in the hills. The crow flight might not be that much but to reach there one has to travel about 22 km, first on the main narrow tarred road, then cross the bridge over the river and then move up the barely motorable mud track up the hill to his native village and orchards. He and his Nepalese workers work very hard. They have even fixed rudimentary spans (wire trolleys). It's a basic contrivance made of massive logs, planks and wires to convey apples from the higher reaches. From there the produce is laden on pick-up jeeps. These travel about 40 km on the narrow, winding hill roads. The apple boxes are then loaded on cargo trucks plying on broader, better roads to be ferried to the plains.

Rajesh has a dominating wife and maybe to keep her happy he has a framed photo of his in-laws with his little brother-in-law standing between them. I mistook it to be his parents photo because people usually keep their own photos. He was embarrassed when I pointed this out. But then if it works as a coolant in the running engine of his matrimony then there shouldn't be any issue. His wife is hospitable like most of the *pahari* people are. She will give you the best of bedding and the best of food cooked soulfully. But she will turn disdainful and impetuous if you commit the mistake of picking a raw corn not yet ready for consumption. She will show you supreme scorn if you steal her raw corn. She loves her trees, plants and little rows of vegetables.

I got the opportunity to witness the rainbow colors of a nice hostess at their old, traditional wooden hill house high on the mountain. The logs were ancient but the house carried a dignity of the purity and solitude of past years. A hill house that stands against snows, rains and winds for one and a half centuries becomes almost a temple on account of its survival, for its having seen many generations under its log roofs. The ground floor is for the cattle. The wooden steps lead one to a wooden balcony. The trapdoor on the landing in the balcony is shut at night. The men-folk in the hills drink with relish. So the gathering of drinkers in the floor-bedded hall would go to the side in the balcony and urinate over the wooden railing into the bushes below. I wasn't part of the drinking gang who did it profusely but still you need toilet at least once after the sundown. So I also did it with a guilty feeling. A dog barked from below, probably grumbling over such uncouth manners.

While the drinkers are snoring heavily, leaving the house almost thunderstruck, I have a dream. A rat snake is sneaking into the house. I spot it but feel ok because my knowledge about its non-poisonous nature avoids me from feeling the typical snake-born shock. Then another snake crawls in. This time it's a pinkish brown cobra. A man catches its hood from behind and squeezes it to let out many big squirts of poison. Another person is holding a syringe full of water to inject plain water in place of the poison in the empty poison sacks. How I wish I could inject love in some hateful people! I was just a silent, inactive witness to all this happening in the dream.

Down by the river, while staying at their empty new house, I have a lazy time observing and learning about the place. A tea-maker told me about a scandal. Kasab was trying to fleece away two sisters of Nepalese origin on the pretext of getting them *filmi* jobs in Mumbai. But they were caught at the Tiuni bus stand by the Rudra Sena activists. So the hills have their own little share of upheavals among these small hamlets.

This small hilly pocket on the remote Himachal-Uttarakhand border has its little page in regional history as well. Askot Arakot Abhiyan is almost a local historical milestone. On May 25, 1974 four students of Garhwal university, on encouragement by social activist Hemwati Bahuguna, started on a 1110 km journey, from the village of Askot on Nepal border to Arakot. Shekhar Pathak, Shamsher Singh Bisht, Kunwar Prasun, Pratap Shikhar undertook this 45-day journey to study the conditions of people in the hills. They stayed with the locals on the way to know more about their life. Since then Shekhar Pathak begins this foot journey once every decade on May 25. The participants can join and leave any time. You cannot keep any money on your person so that you have the only option to stay with the villagers on the way. The tea-maker, my local history guide, was part of the fifth *abhiyan* in 2014 from Pangu to Arakot, passing through villages, alpine pastures, *kharaks* (high altitude grazing fields), earthquake and landslide prone zones, *chattees* (ancient pilgrimage camping sites).

He tells me about *keeda jadi* (*Yarsa gumba*) smuggling in the region of Kosha glacier in Joshimath area where Dhauli Ganga river originates. It's used as a steroid. Forest fires are illegally started to melt the glaciers and catch the caterpillar fungus from the stones which emerge after the snow melts. The smugglers use even uric acid to start exothermic reaction to melt the glaciers. It's a very costly steroid, he informs me. The smugglers entice the local villagers to collect *keeda jadi*. People have set up entire camps with porters and ponies to extract it. They unleash forest fires in the lower reaches so that the rising smoke melts the snow.

If you love wandering in the surrounding forests, you may come across a little group of *Van Gujjars*, the buffalo-rearing Muslim pastoral migrants, the hill nomads. But tough forest laws make it difficult for them to migrate across the hills these days. They don't hold official papers for Indian citizenship and the police mistreats them very often. There have been some attempts to settle them at a place but they couldn't manage their livestock within closed limits. Many get jailed for transgressing forests laws. Some have turned laborers, but most of them just somehow roam the restricted areas, evading law, trying to protect their traditional way of life and living. It's the same old story like all the nomadic communities facing jeopardy in the plains.

'My first love and first *time* had been with a *Gujjar* girl, right there in those forests,' he raises his head towards the bare hillside high on the slope. I can't see any forests. 'The forests vanished. Like they vanished the very next day after our first kiss,' he says with a memory-laden sweet sigh. 'Maybe someone saw you,' I give a reason. 'Maybe someone saw, maybe it was just coincidence, but I got married and I'm a grandfather now. She too must be a grandmother by this time,' he again looked into the forest that was no longer there. One would always remember the first bud that opened into love even if one stays among an orchard of love for a century. 'Do you still miss her?' I ask. 'I just remember. Some things you never forget,' he says wistfully.

Sitka spruce on Campbell Island in Southern Ocean holds the Guinness World Record for being the 'remotest tree' on the planet. The loneliest tree is 250 km away from its nearest companion. It's named Ranfurly tree after Lord Ro, then New Zealand governor, who planted it in the early 1900s.

Tenere tree is, rather was, also one of the most lonely trees on the earth. It was a landmark on the caravan route in Sahara desert in northeast Niger. This and the Arbre Pendu (Lost Tree) to its north were the only trees shown on a map of 1:4,000,000. Tenere tree stood for 300 years before being knocked by a drunk Libyan truck driver in 1973. Even earlier it had been badly mauled due to vehicle hits even though there was all the space all around for a vehicle to pass. Its roots reached 108 feet to draw moisture of life. The camels didn't eat its leaves. The *Azalai* caravans didn't cut its branches to make tea. It was a kind of tribal custom mixing superstition and reverence for something so rare in the cruel desert. The caravaniers gathered around it before crossing it, so it served as a type of lighthouse in the sea of sand. A traveler said about it: 'An acacia with sickly trunk but nice green leaves and yellow flowers.' Then the vehicles started and it was badly mauled. There is a metal sculpture and pavilion housing its remains as a commemorative shrine.

Asia's lone redwood tree stands at CSIR Yarikha Tangmarg, Baramulla. It's primarily found in North America. The tree is 150 years old. It's in the shape of a huge mushroom, evergreen but the birds avoid it. In fact, no bird is seen sitting or nesting on this exotic tree. The CSIR has declared it a heritage tree. All efforts to create its progeny through cuttings in open fields, polyhouses, greenhouses and laboratories have failed. Even the seeds injected with growth hormones have failed to germinate.

As August hands over the baton to September, you have a fluidic canvas of blue, grey, white and black—loafs of clouds floating to give sunshine and shade almost alternately. Some naughty little cloud wets the cloth-lines even though there is sunshine.

One can even beat one's loneliness by looking at the shifting shapes and turn it into solitude.

After a brief spell of rain if you care to look among the fallen leaves under a tree, you may come across a dead butterfly. She too was a colorful flying leaf on the tree of mother existence.

The beauty of September rain is that it doesn't upbraid you directly like the previous months when the monsoon was at its prime. The clouds cantering towards conclusion, the sunshine capering about them forming a frivolous game. Then suddenly a brief drizzle comes to wet everything. And before you realize you see the clouds drifting away; they have many interesting shapes and silver edges; leaving behind a green world full of freshly bathed leaves gleaming under the bright sun. The butterflies come out again. Sometimes you get rain and sunshine side by side. You cannot help gasping with ravishing delight because the rain wasn't expected. But someone gets disconcerted because the clothes on the line are wet again. The September rain is in trilling accompaniment with mischief—old season's young spirit.

One such naughty spell of rain catches a blacksmith gypsy woman off guard. She is selling plastic ware. Iron-forging days are over. It's a world of plastic and fiber. The mass-produced items hardly leave any space for them to forge small iron implements and utensils in their little furnaces. So they trade plastic now. She still wears their traditional dress. But they are clearly struggling. It's impossible to survive as a wandering nomad these days. You need to dig your survival well at a congested place. They are trying to move faster by changing their bullock carts into bike-rickshaws, their sides having a cheap imitation of the nail artistry that those sturdy carts used to have. The big caravans changed to lonesome nomads driving the tattered bike-rickshaw piled with meager possessions and the family. But this swifter movement isn't enough. So they now turn squatters in urban areas at narrow strips of public land along the roads. They now expect the government to accept them as the citizens of India with identity cards, documents and some entitlements.

On a September evening, we have a brief but heavy downpour. Then the clouds part. The sun plays with clouds in the west. One ought to keep one's eyes ready for a rainbow in the east on such occasions. If you are lucky you will have your multihued arc in the sky. And coming across a rainbow cheers you up; just like finding a peacock feather on the ground towards which both a king and a pauper will run with equal enthusiasm. The fact is we are seeking colors. So if you don't get a rainbow on such a rainy evening, the clouds will make up for it. White, orange, red, yellow, grey blue, black—you have the entire range as the setting sun peeks through the rain-soaked veil.

The peacocks are into love games in September. Lots of dancing and you should keep an eye for their love-drops—master-colored feathers. If you find one, rush to grab it before anyone else, and hold it; it's an asset in many ways.

A bulbul and a sparrow are having a tiff on a wire. The swallows are angry that the little hawk, *shikra*, is here. They want him out. A squirrel hurries in dragging a strip of rag. It goes up a few feet on the tree and then takes a pause to roll the strip into a ball to crawl up easily and then adorn her house with the new decoration. But while she rushed in, she scared an adolescent gecko. The latter simply panicked at the sight. The leaves drip due to the shower they recently received. Thus passes a rainy September evening. All this is so familiar, yet so-so different.

Gajraj turned uproariously musth and became disgruntled and disapproving of the human bondage. He broke chains and ropes with immaculate show of hormone-boosted power, and tipsy on love-booze escaped into the forest with his six women—Chameli, Kaveri, Suheli, Pawankali, Kiran and Sulochna. They escaped into the solicitous greenery of the rhino reserved area.

Gajraj is a trained elephant in Dudhwa National Park. Basically he is a nice guy, cordially tagging around the forest officials in fulfillment of his duties, using his power with a well-checked iciness. But on entering the turbulent musth phase, he turned growling and fidgety; became forbiddingly aggressive and broke the shackles for love in free woods.

There are about 25 camp elephants in the national park for tourism, patrolling and conflict management in the zone of human-animal shared boundaries. Ingeniously timing the event he set out on the eve of the Indian Independence Day, making a big statement in favor of unchecked love in free woods.

The pachyderms are stationed at rhino rehabilitation area in Sonaripur range, a pristine 27 sq km expanse of *sal* and *damar* trees, nine lakes and mouthwatering grasslands. The area has 46 one-horned rhinos. I think he must have pushed them out of his playground in his state of heightened aggression born of increased hormonal activity in his system.

Gajraj was brought here in 2008 from Jaldapara wildlife sanctuary to keep a watch on the rhinos and patrol the area. He was ten then. He must have been on quarrelsome terms with Kamalkali because she didn't go with him on this escapade. Sulochna and Chameli were his childhood friends because they had arrived with him at the park.

Dudhwa tiger reserve officials panicked with the elephants' disappearance. Free love always meets a hoarsy retort. Love will always have its opponents, so the teams of forest workers, drone cameras and mahouts set out to capture the fugitives. A WWF team also arrived to assist the search operations. The tiger reserve spans an area of 2201 sq km richly imbued with greened freedom. A good space for the tremulous blizzard of elephant love. A zone of solitudinal sweet sighs as opposed to the stinking muck of captivity.

The park shares border with Nepal and if the lovebirds enter the neighboring country, it would be very difficult to get them back because elephants don't carry passports and Nepal might say they are their elephants. They are spotted after a couple of days. But just two days of love in the woods with his harem aren't sufficient for Gajraj, so he chases away the rescue teams. The teams kept pursuing them for the next two weeks. He turned his usual well-behaved self after a fortnight of triumphant and unhindered love in the woods. The love-satiated pachyderm was calm now when the rescuers reached him and escorted the runaway king and his six queens back to the camp.

Life invincible. A crack in the concrete wall. Some chance seed of a flower lands on the barely visible space in the crack. The rains follow. The dew forms pearls on the petals. The chance seed makes the most of what has been given to it and germinates. There you have a little plant high on the wall waving in the breeze like a banner of life in a zone where life has no business to thrive. The plant then proclaims victory and you have a little flower on the top of this tiny plant.

The triumph of life, the urge to manifest from the unknown to the known. Is the flower separate from the stone? No. It's mere extension of the stone from its cracked lip, its mouth open to the possibilities. I would say it's a smile on the stone's lips.

Even in its barren womb, the stone has the probability and potential for life. All it needs is a little crack, some drops of rain and a chance seed to transform that potential into reality. The stone smiles. The flower isn't something separate from it. It's merely an extension of it.

Manifestation is just a set of probabilities coming together from the infinite, ever evolving fabric of potential and probabilities. And of course it needs a set of appreciating eyes to witness this *leela*. It just needs some chance factors to acquire a structured pattern from the random factors sprinkled around like stars in the sky to complete one more little circle within the greatest circle ever; things going round and round; little cycles within the bigger cycles and still bigger ones to follow; going so big to again fall back into a point; nothingness and everythingness just the same.

Colors of beauty emerge from the stony ramparts of struggle, just like our very own journey through various challenges. There is an inherent inspiration in the cosmic fabric for this transformation. What drives this change, one may ask. Well, to the seeker of change, be it in terms of technical success or simple artistic evolution, inspiration comes from all corners. It's basically *hope*. An assurance that life settles back to normal after the chaos; that a new day comes after the night; that lovely spring blooms after horrid winters; that the same people who mourn over the dead will be smiling on new births; that tears of loss lose value in the face of a smile after success; that even dead trunks give live shoots.

I know it sounds poetic but there is an essential core of inspiration; a creative urge to renew and extend the present status. I think it's in sync with this cosmic expansion. All of us are drawn to expand the horizon in our unique ways in the fields of science, technology, medicine, arts, philosophy and much more.

Sometimes fame would knock at your door beseechingly even if you aren't seeking it and happen to be a whale. Fuddled with babbling public fancy, the strains of fame tugged at a particular whale's fins. The animated aquatic fans celebrated the whale as 'Russian Spy Whale'. The year before, it created a crisply sparkled ruckus in Norway as the government cautioned the people against any contact with the whale seen in a fjord near Oslo. It jangled the ears of common people like those of sleuths and spies. It was christened and given a name, Hvaldimir (Hval—Norwegian word for whale, combined with Russian name Vladimir).

As the people plentifully regaled at the sight, the whale also—quite surprisingly—looked at ease in human company. The beluga whale, initially spotted in 2019, stood at 14 feet in length and weighed 2700 pound. She had a harness apparently meant to carry a spy camera. The harness carried a marketing 'equipment' from a St. Petersburg company. So the people conspiratorially speculated that it was a Russian spy whale on a mission. Although Russia didn't make any ownership claim.

Belugas generally inhabit far off frozen Arctic waters. But this one seemed to like human company. The people got fascinated by its sight. The white whale was known to stay in the inner Oslo fjord near a densely populated area.

Then one day recently they found her dead. The news is heartbreaking for some people who had become its fans.

Life is happy and good because I receive a big carton of pears as gift. Juicy pears enter even the most desolate parts and fill life with joy. But during the transport many big juicy ones have turned pulpy. Joy is never complete; it comes with conditions attached. Here the condition is that I have to ignore the loss. But there is an option to use these partially spoilt ones—instead of throwing them, I use them as ceasefire table items.

It's Tuesday and the head monkey is visiting the locality with his family. His clan is bigger than the last time I remember. There is new addition to his harem. He is watchful as his clan eats pulpy pears. One little one is trying to catch butterflies around the *peregrina* flowers.

Fed with pears and the ceasefire still more reinvigorated I am going on my bike. I advise against being too bothered about the side happenings on the road. One has to be very focused on the job. One has to save one's bones amidst the thundering prancing of the travelling bravehearts. But some things will always fall in your zone of vision. You can't avoid them even with your brain all occupied in reaching safe amidst all the roaring runnels and gurgling gullies of driving passion on the road.

A massively fat policeman taking a lift on a slender splendor bike. The slim bike grumbles, the thin boy mumbles. I can't see the boy at all as I catch up with them from behind.

Shri Bansidham Gaushala Society (Reg.) written on a *gau seva* banner at the back of an e-rickshaw. The narrow and longish vehicle purring to the destination with chapattis, grass and donated food.

A lone quail trying to run and cross the road, making several failed attempts as the vehicles keep rushing past. Mr. Quail, why don't you fly a little and use your wings for a short flight? You will get trampled or get a two-wheeler guy tumbling on the road.

The infant lying on a cloth on the grass by the road under a forlorn acacia tree, and his/her three years old brother tending, keeping a watch over the baby. Already into the household duties! Their parents, the migrant *Bihari* couple, working on a construction site nearby.

A lapwing crushed on the road. The feathery carcass. I stop and as I pick it up to give it some dignity of a humble burial nearby, I hear the pittering, warning notes, maybe from its partner. A bird has little blood; it's more of flying spirit, airiness.

I reach my destination, the place of enlightenment of a local saint. I disturb the watery meditation of a fish as I step into the pond to take a bath. It springs up in surprise and panic, missing my nose by a whisker, going several feet high in the air and lands at a safe place. I nearly fall down.

The saint's soul reimburses me for the little shock as I, by chance, happen to enter his another ashram on my way back. The cook-cum-caretaker is a kindly man. He shows me the place—the guru's resting place, meditation rooms, and serves hot milk and sweet *petha*. He seems a lovely human being doing *tapasya* through *seva*. *Seva* is a very noble form of *tapasya*. We hold a very nice discussion about the life and times of the saint who shed his body about two and half decades back. His fragrance still lingers and many take solace from it.

He is sitting with a smug expression; in full acceptance of one's situation, which brings restfulness to life quite naturally. He is sitting on the roof of the tall new house of my neighbor overlooking my low but resolutely sprawled out old country house. Looking down upon me, eh! The world below is busy with routine exhaustless rambling. Despite the unrestrainable threads of mischief in his species' DNA, he hasn't yet broken the terms of ceasefire. No slimy gamut of mischief in my garden from his side; no detestable shouts at his mere sight from my side. Both sides contributing their respective share to peace. The best part about investing in peace is that it gets you the handsome most returns.

He is all focus at some point on the distant roofs. Men will be men—he is either eying a lady or some rival. I offer him a fresh ghee-smitten chapatti on the window slab of my terrace room. He looks at it just once and continues with his stare at the more coveted objects. My ego feels bruised and lacerated. Peace is very fragile and ego a hard stone. But I would advise one to keep its glass façade because it allows lovely sunshine into the room of your existence. So one ought to pay even extra to maintain peace. It will still be better than breaking the glass and again revamp, replenish and reconstitute the entire façade. So I quash the germs of malignity, gulp down insult and move from the place, feeling bad that he doesn't even look at my gift. 'Maybe he isn't hungry,' I think.

I return a few minutes later to take away the chapatti so that the visiting feral cat could have it. There he comes hurriedly but with confident ease. I stand at a little distance. He still keeps the ceasefire and doesn't snarl or growl. I stand hospitably and he takes away the chapatti as if it was his right and my duty. I think he is just putting up attitude, thinking that if he instantly jumped to my offer, he will appear like a beggar. So he takes it in a very casual way; as if it doesn't matter to him at all. This is what I term as *attitude*.

Given a choice I would just lie down all days, months and years, simply reading, studying, writing, learning. But this much of enormity of nothingness at the physical level will see the body rusting like an unused car in a yard turning to junk. So it's better to move, shake, stretch, bend—*chalti ka nam gadi hai*, as they say. There are people to whom physical exertion doesn't come naturally. They can take a detour to physical activity by setting up a target. For example, going for hiking and trekking in the mountains. So obviously you have to prepare. I mix another ingredient, faith. Since there are many high-altitude pilgrimage places in the Himalayas, I routinely plan to go on pilgrimages. So it serves multiple purposes.

I'm a Ganga Ma devotee, so going to Gaumukh nurtures my faith and the preparations to trek at an altitude of 14500 feet serve the body. It forces me to abandon books for some time and do some exercises. I won't enter a gym unless an assault rifle is held against my head. Too much muscular intimidation for a poetic man there. I get scared. So I have my own exercise alternative—walking up and down the open stairway (22 steps) leading from the courtyard to the terrace. A nice cardio exercise, good for heart, lungs and leg muscles, all key players in mountain trekking, be it for pilgrimage or plain adventure. So here I go and move up and down the stairs. Slowly lumbering up, gently clambering down, the breathing getting more labored with the passage of minutes, the heart beating faster, the leg muscles tightening and exercise-born sweat emerging on the skin of a poetic man! It's the eighth wonder brothers and sisters! I straggle up and down for almost half an hour. The drops of sweat fall on the steps. One, two, three... I count them. They look like big milestones of my effort. The little drizzle of my exertion.

Overall, the sum of pain, suffering, unhappiness, agony, tragedies in life—both individual and collective as a species—is far greater than the sum of happiness and joy. Happiness is almost like a few diamonds in a deep coal mine; the shying crystals hidden deep in the womb of tons of mud, rock, earth, stones and coal. But that's why we dig a mine. And exactly for the same reason we live; we dig the deep mine of life unearthing pain and miseries to finally reach the few crystals of joy. We walk through the darkest pits because we expect that life will someday get filled with color and joy.

A woman has lots of issues and grudges with life. Her life isn't too bad; it's defined by the routine Indian lower middle class challenges. But she puts herself under lots of stress while recounting all the lamenting stuff. I hear her discussing the tale of woes with her female neighbors so many times. I feel like gently reminding her, 'It could have been easily worse than this. You could have been an Afghani woman, deprived of colors from your clothing, robbed of the sight of your own hair, deprived of the freedom to walk, talk, exclaim, look the way you like.' But I don't think she would get this, so no point in telling her all this.

We have created so much electricity that the stars have lost their right to light the earth with their soft, gentle, twinkling smiles. The night sky seems lost. Maybe the sky now looks at the earth for inspiration—to come down, not rise.

I'm early in the town on some errand and have some time to kill—as they say—before the shops and offices open. The air still has some languorous contentment after the night rest before the awkward exuberance of the day shoves it alertness into the fray; thus notifying everyone to be ready for the engaging statistics of a busy, crowded day.

An inspiration to *make* time instead of killing it sprawls its arms quite expressively. I decide to use the opportunity offered by a fine little park by a road. It's a long rectangular park with a newly laid chocolate-colored walking track. One complete round roughly measuring one kilometer. A senior citizen is walking quite briskly. The ruddy flush on his chubby face show hard determination. The shambling strides with bandy legs carry unabated zeal for an active life. The sight pumps enough inspiration in my legs to start walking and *make* time rather than *kill* it.

This is Monday late morning, the monsoons resting after many rainy days. Someone passes with knitting brows and gritting teeth for a bashful stroll. Good way to spend energy instead of pouring it upon someone as scorn. A woman is walking with impatient unmeasured strides. A girl looks tipsy but curt and agile—drunk with youth. A young boy with jaunty strides. An old man going sedately mindful of the lack of axle grease in the wheels of life at this stage. A middle-aged man looks amiably, another stares distrustfully and guardedly. Well, enough of spying on others. Let me mind my business and start walking instead of just standing and staring at people.

The leafy trees on the sides of the track and over the narrow length of the park full with green luxuriance, almost shading the stylish cast iron lampposts. There is a busy road on the one side; a housing block the other way with its caged-in backyards to undo encroachments by the man- and monkey-kind. The long narrow rectangular strip has overgrown grass. Assured of not being flummoxed by a predator, a rat is out on a stroll too. Seeing me coming it scampers off with a snooty frown and hides in its hole by the base of a long mercury light pole. A monkey sitting on a branch stares out of the corner of its eyes to ensure if I carry some eatables, and if yes how to waylay me at some isolated spot. A few squirrels playing on the track, flicking their tails and fidgeting coquettishly. One flounces this and that way, wrangling with uncertainty, a chance juggler or acrobat. I have to stop in order to avoid treading over it. One angry type runs with me in a retorting and obstinate manner as if accusing me of accidently barging into his girlfriend.

An injured monkey, its mischief all crumpled, is thankfully well behaved as I pass just a couple of feet from it. But a mama monkey is gripped with tension and mocks a cunning attack to help her son lick mossy water from a puddle nearby. Another one surreptitiously stares into my pocket. I put my hand on it to save my phone from getting stolen. He seems a hard-boiled character and slyly follows me with a jagged, jerkily swaddled walk.

A friendly Labrador is walking leisurely, while its pet father is exercising with tongue in a political debate. State elections are just three weeks away and thus consume lots of tongue energy among the masses. This I would call the real slaughter of time. I would prefer anything but not this. It makes me very miserable after political talks. Why kill time while the politicians reach the glittering zenith of fame, money and power, while we remain the same despite all the promises bombarded upon us during the election times?

A young boy is running. I really appreciate this—a kind of real polished insignia of youth. It's better than moonlighting the nights with the phones and getting into internecine struggles over girls. Good going boy, first make yourself and then give yourself a break.

A young girl, student most probably, is sitting on a bench, surfing her mobile phone, caught in the thrilling myths of love, lust and growing up. Completely ignorant of the fresh air and the nice walking track, no wonder she gives a sickly feel. The heady smell of youth haloed in mist.

There are love-birds on a stone bench. Her dress, blue *kurta* and black *salwar*, clearly shows that she is a private security guard at some establishment. They have time till their office opens. She is sitting, he is lying; his head in her lap, surfing the phone; she rummaging her fingers through his hair. He must have used a nice shampoo this morning. I assume it to be an extramarital affair. Both of them look married but husband and wife would hardly have enough spirit and love left to allow it to spill over for a public display of affection on a Monday morning. Well, let them have their bleary ecstasy among all the clammy and artless folds of life.

A man is working in the open gym, adroitly ferreting out bundles of energy to pump into thick muscles. With edifying alacrity another man is walking backwards, looking this and that side to peer behind to avoid collision. He moves steadily and ardently. I hope he hasn't been punished by his wife for some mischief to go lapping backwards as atonement. Swings and slides are resting. The children must already be in their schools wearily waiting for the classes to end and then feel the seething chill of freedom on the closing time. The swings will be creaking in the evening probably.

There is an overweight pulpy group of men in their fifties and above. Their nerves wrung taut. Garrulous debate, flushed faces, ominously forcing their points. They arduously drag on, stamping nuggets of their political truth, which is in proportion to deceit and falsehood. Among them one dried up wheelchair-bound old man looks flummoxed and puzzled. He is resignedly listening to the excited talk. Thank god there is national flag on the top of the round open pavilion nearby to remind them that they are all Indians and need not break their heads over different political flags.

The traffic is light on the road so I can hear the pleasant twittering of birds. A merry mynah. A vexed tailorbird. Beseeching, imploring notes of a *koel*. Impish guttural cooing of a pigeon. Rockchats with their morning-time pleasantries. Enchanted blubbering of a babbler. A crow cawing with uncertain pride.

A short old man takes a pinch of snuff to boost his moral. He is the cleaner with his rickshaw, doing his work gently with nice focus, piling his rickshaw cart with fallen leaves and other littler that uncaring people would always fail to put in the waste bins so prominently placed in the park. He walks amiably, almost with evocative courtesy, placing his steps with a age-born limp, dragging his cart around the park. He need not talk. His work itself is a big statement—the best use of time anyone in the park is having at the moment.

A plump woman in peacock blue *salwar-kurta* topped with a white lab-coat. Her broom is tied to the end of a long stick. She is seriously working, cleaning the dirt, fallen leaves and litter. I wish she had the rights to hit the political debaters with her long broom and remind them the purpose of the park—an avenue to shed some fat from their bulging paunches.

I walk for about 45 minutes and thus *make* time instead of *killing* it.

A tree sings through the birds sitting on it. Smiles through its flowers. Doles out charity through its fruits. Becomes a loving host with the shade under its canopy and the nesting space among its branches. When the wind blows, the murmurs and rustle of its leaves are the words filling the silence. And silence drips from its rustling words. The cut marks on its trunk are the eyes; deep seas full of unshed tears; vast stretches of water. The waters sometimes storm-driven by adverse winds; sometimes calm little ripples gently pushed by the breeze of sympathetic touch on its wound by a poetic heart.

In losing forests, lakes, pastures and rivers, we are losing a big part of our own self. We are turning strangers to our own self; weird shapes building within us. No wonder we seem like ghosts to each other. And the ghosts hardly listen to the message of love and peace.

The mankind seems mired in the bog of liquid melancholy. The species of living ghosts. Shame loaded over their skin in thick layers, giving them a sturdy armor, a shield against light, truth and openness. Lies and falsehood pile up in the body imprisoned in the armor. A junkyard.

Dear reader, walking among them, slowly losing to melancholy, losing light and hope, your greatest fears will scare you. The slurs shouted at the top of their voice don't hit that hard as do the silent hate, accusations and judgments pouring out of their eyes. Don't just back off and run away. If you enter the ghostly cave and manage to keep walking, it will take you to an opening leading to unimaginable freedom.

At the basic level of survival we walk inwards, to shrink, to give more concrete shape to our interests. And the protective walls around us—that we inherit collectively and also that we make individually—look like our defense ramparts. Yes, to begin with we need defensive walls. These are necessary because we are born so weak and vulnerable. The initial yolk of our existence needs the protective eggshells. From that we acquire more specific chick shape. But doesn't the shell has to be broken by the chick to grow further, acquire wings and fly to live life fully? If not, that same protective wall becomes a barrier, a trap for death.

Usually our protective walls, which we naturally needed to begin with, stay with us. And we continue—out of habit—erecting more individual walls even when we no longer need them around us. So instead of dismantling the walls we keep strengthening them. The foolish prisoner who works to consolidate the prison walls. Then these walls become a barrier, a trap for stunted growth; shackles in our legs; rings in our wings—to stop us from flying and maximizing the full potential of our seed of existence.

To become a maker, one then needs to be a breaker of these barriers. The eggshell that incubated us, but now needs to be broken and discarded. Be a grand laborer holding the hammer. Strike forcefully. *Break* the redundant shell. Come out and *make* life like an artist.

Thus speaks a tree that has been killed:

They uprooted me. There was a murderous glint in their eyes. Pulled me out with wild enthusiasm. My spine, my main trunk snapped. My lungs shattered and dusted. My leafy head grounded. My fingers, my branches, chopped off. But my legs, my roots, had the sky to look forward to. So I pushed my roots into the sky. That would be my earth now. And they can't rob me of it. Because my roots will grow into the invisible airy fibers. A reverse tree in this steely straight world. Or a straight tree in an upside world. Choose what you prefer to say it. But I'm a floating one definitely. I can just go like a cloud from place to place; laughing at human follies. Sad for them; joyful for myself.

6

BROTHER, whenever you fulminate with pride, remember that we are mere chance seeds thrown around. If we land up in a corner where sunshine, soil, wind and rain help us germinate better, it's sheer luck. Accept it with gratitude. Some other seed landed on a stony barren terrain, some in a bog, some in a drain, some on a waste dump in a slum. These seeds carried the same potential as you. They just landed in saddening, squabbling, feverish conditions. The potential withered in the womb of germination. They got stunted, fragile, poor, disadvantaged and enchained by crippling circumstances.

We are the products of nature's unpremeditated plans—the open-ended process; the unplanned plan that progresses with fixed laws of nature. I know the flippant rhetorician in you will scoff at the proposition that we are the off-shoots of chance seeds. I know you have been customized to believe that the mankind has to forge his destiny; that we create our circumstances. But mind you, this boasting loquacity is simply a chance given to you by favorable winds.

One seed falls in squalor; the other in fertile soil—isn't it already a favor to the latter? When you start acknowledging the role of so many circumstantial factors in shaping your better destiny—your birth in a better family, meeting supportive people, being present at an opportune time, favorable winds blowing, being healthy in your natural constitution—you will feel gratitude for what you have received. Once you feel gratitude, you will see the positives hidden behind the apparently tough situations you have faced in life. If the skin has a boil, you will be thankful that at least the bone inside isn't broken. And despite all the routine struggles of life, you will accept that at least you are alive today, while so many died on this very day.

It's a gift to have a blue tiger butterfly among your peregrina blossoms. The status of the bearer of these crimson clusters of little flowers lies between a plant and a tree—a shrub. But give physical care and emotional support and it turns out to be your tree. A small tree but always smiling with its bright flowers. It's perennially in bloom.

Throughout the monsoons and even later lemon-green butterflies have been feasting among the blooms. But today we have a visitor—a blue tiger butterfly. It has lovely black patterned with bluish spots on the wings. Butterflies can directly absorb sunlight on their wings to get autonomous flight. And we still boast of the solar panels in our satellites! The dark areas on its wings enable greater absorption of heat and fly with ease.

The blue tiger butterfly is bigger than the lemon-green butterflies who I think consider the peregrina tree as their residential tree. It bullies them across the clusters of flowers. It wants to have the entire little tree to itself. It just jumps into the flower where a lime-green butterfly is having tea-time snack. In this airy scuffle many ripe flowers drizzle—little drops born of a fight among the butterflies. Surprisingly it's successful in driving them away. There it has the entire set of flowers all to herself and enjoys its time, flying from cluster to cluster. A bullying butterfly. But looks beautiful.

As the day moves towards twilight on musty September evenings, and most of the birds already settled home with the setting sun, the wire-tail swallows go swiftly scouring the sky for midges, fleas, mosquitoes, dragonflies and other flying insects. The insects come carousing in the air in late evening. The swallow couple has successfully raised their chick. I see the three of them flying around. It has been a few weeks since it came out of the mud nest. In a bigger flock it might have started its independent life by this time. But the days of big flocks are gone. So in the grease and grime of survival, it sticks to its parents forming a perfect modern day nuclear family.

They have the word 'wire' in their name, so they have every right to consider the electricity wires and cables in front of the house as theirs. I usually see them perched on these cables. In late evenings a *shikra* also comes and takes a sniper-type patient stance on the wires as the tired day is slowly moving towards the twilight. It mostly looks for any casual gecko on the walls. But its presence is objectionable to the zealously roving swallows. 'It's our wire!' they chip-chip angrily.

They can maneuver their flight like fighter jets, or rather fighter jets imitate them. They pester the small hawk, taking advantage of this aerial skill. They come chip-chipping in consternation, almost bang into him, take sharp turns, follow puzzling curves and fly away only to come suddenly with a big surprise and shock element—necessary for a dogfight midair—from another direction. They dash in from different angles, sometimes attack together in perfect dogfight formation.

Even their kid's courage gets buoyed up as it sees the hawk perplexed and dodging to avoid collision with its parents. It also takes an attacking sortie and passes near the hunter's head with reasonable accuracy for a beginner. The parents must be happy that their child is learning the art of life, which is basically survival at this level of existence.

They have botched the hunter's crouching stance and hunting prospects. It leaves their wire petulantly letting off a shrill hawking sound and flies off to a place where it can hunt in peace.

As a sultry day hands over the ashy grey baton to the twilight, the swallow family is chipping away mosquitoes and fleas in swishy merriment. When they dive so effortlessly, dip easily, turn around and change directions it makes me feel as if they are in very jolly mood. A kind of merry and genial version of air itself. But of course the hawk would think them to be a nuisance.

Why should one's soul be in love just with the spring? All seasons have their unique offerings. Look at the lovely autumnal surrender. The trees shedding the extras for a walk through the cold winters. The fallen leaves must be murmuring a lot. Listen to their story.

These are old leaves rich with age, gladly abandoning their hold on the branches and falling down with the cool breeze. This is a beautiful version of what we call death, but which is just a transformation in the eternal cycle.

Autumn is basically a collective phenomenon of detachment. Stand in the mist of such mass-scale leafy drops; detachment almost raining with the leaves. Make the most of it; listen to their murmuring rustle of joyfully quitting the stage of life.

And when they quit life with such a soothing rustling song, it shows how fully they have lived.

The fuller the life, the less scary is death. Death then doesn't appear like an abstract entity, something cut off from life. It then appears like life is shifting to a new level, a new dimension. It then gives a glimpse of a continuity, not something like a dead end.

Videos and thoughts can't catch such a phenomenal experience. It's like we try to catch air in our fist by clenching our fingers and it slips out. But open the hand and it's embraced by the all-encompassing presence of air around. These are the moments when we are totally open with our vulnerability and innocence—like the open hand—and are embraced by a larger presence, undefined and unbound, which hands over a portion of its freedom to us and we feel joyful.

My slice of autumn has a flowery color to it in my yard. There is a flowery drizzle in place of falling leaves. I have collected a huge pile on my table. This is just a portion of the flowers that drizzle in a flowery, scented rain from the two *parijat* trees in the yard. Scented, dewy, flowery nights; and the rain of flowers in the cool mornings. With so many flowers around, no wonder I find my spirit dancing, intoxicated with the beauty of the countless blooms and the scented breeze.

A tall building has a deep foundation. You cannot be incautious about the foundation if you want to bring about an element of indestructibility, be it buildings or personages. A building with deep foundation can withstand malevolent storms and inveterate earthquakes. So don't be willful, sprightly, gliding and hastening in erecting the façade; don't be just expansively bothered about the above-ground decorously gleaming ramparts. The creation should be firmly welded to the basics—the ground level and the sub-surface set of realities.

The energetic system of our physiognomy too is a vertical stack, a building of seven storeys—from *muladhar* to *sahasrar*. *Muladhar* is negatively judged for its basic tendencies and worldliness. I would call it a jaundiced view, something ungracious. Most of the spiritual traditions feel vexed about the root chakra and quizzically look down upon it. And glorify the higher chakras as the plausible pathways to divinity. The lowest chakra is taken as something incorrigible that will instinctively draw us back to the base-level survival. It seems to be dealt with too abstractedly. In divine facetiousness, the spiritualists have devised tools and techniques that work on the higher chakras for raising consciousness to a higher dimension of experiences, thoughts, emotions and perspectives.

Kundalini yoga is one of the most straightforward means to leapfrog onto a higher platform and align one's journey in symmetry with the vibration of higher chakras. In this hurry the poor, boorish lowest chakra gets almost jeered at. In their rush they simply bypass the *muladhar* chakra lying in its obscure lodging at the perineum, taking it to be the carrier of covertly topical tendencies to pursue desires and hence getting trapped in the cycle of pain and suffering. They dart about in full enthusiasm to pursue the higher chakras leaving the *muladhar* chakra dismally neglected. They hurry past it, leaving it weak and go spiritedly building the upper storeys. There you have a tall building with garishly upholstered rooms on the higher floors with a weak, almost decrepit foundation. A tall building with shallow foundations seesawing to the ordinary ambiguities of life.

If you want to know the proof of a tall building collapsing due to shallow foundations, kindly consider the cases of accidental *kundalini* awakening. The structure isn't prepared, no plan, just a chance whimsical thunderbolt of energy surging upwards. There is a thin line between the devilish and the divine. It's the same energy—misdirected in the former and well-directed in the latter. A tall vertical shaft of huge energy with no physiological foundations— which the *muladhar* provides—to keep it channeled and rooted. The body precariously argues with the new, unfamiliar energetic waves cascading through the nervous system. It falls apart in utter bafflement; overheated by the hyperactivity of the hyper-charged nervous system, the physiological structure collapses and various diseases strike. Madness of mind and decimation of body are frequent outcomes.

It happens simply because the body's structure isn't in alignment with this level of sudden nervous activation in the brain. There is a pungent discord in the nervous system. It's too much for the system; just like a simple indoor 240 V cable suddenly gets a current of 10,000 V. Of course it cascades thorough the system wolfishly. It will burn, let off sparks. It capriciously grizzles the nervous system that is simply sufficient for the monotonous and expectedly tedious load of mundane life. It becomes a sneering hussy trying to even break the impenetrable silence deep in your being.

We crawl on the ground. We come from earth. We carry her in us as the most predominant element. But we look to *akash* for salvation; the *akash* whose just a minute portion is present in our energetic anatomy. We try to build a top-heavy tower with a narrow base. It falls. No wonder, the majority of the people on the spiritual path are more depressed than the simple folks grounded on earth.

So, o thou spirituality aspirants, work on your *muladhar*, strengthen and solidify your base, your foundation, so that your energetic tower withstands the thunderbolt of elevated consciousness. Bow down to mother earth; walk on naked feet; eat a well-balanced diet of *satva-rajas-tamas* food to nourish yourself with groundedness; do yoga, *pranayam* and plain physical exercises in balance; read scriptures but also go to watch movies for light-hearted, feel-good entertainment; read holy books but also romantic fiction; get into relationships; laugh when you feel like smiling only; be a creator. Let all this be on the ground and not in the heaven. Plug into the socket of divine possibilities for drawing your share of energy and harness it. Just keep working on your foundation, your base. Mother existence will Herself take care of your tower above.

Mid October—a season of mild acclamations by both summer and winter. An inexpressible, unspeakable dewy delight when nature seems so restful and poised, almost balanced. A beautiful cocktail of cool and warm. The highlight of the season—the *parijat* flowers in full bloom. Do they bloom for the fairies at night and drop so peacefully in the morning? It's mother nature's quintessential sweet conspiracy. I let it stay as a piece of wonder only. It's a kind of flower shower if you are happy enough to feel it.

He also seems very happy this morning, an astounding whirlwind of energy hurtling ahead with its inexhaustible sense of mischief and playfulness. In complicity and connivance with mischief, from the terrace he jumps to the top end of the electricity pole and gives it a vigorous shake. Then he sits comfortably on the parapet wall maybe feeling giddy due to the burst and explosion of energy. The ceasefire is still practicable, the skirmishes on hold. The ceasefire is always quivering and fluttering and one party has to contribute extra to counterbalance its tremulousness and give it some stability. I understand its grave significance and accept the role of this extra contributor.

In league with typical simian gaieties and pleasantries, he has broken into the house a couple of times during the peace times as well. But it has been more like an uninvited guest instead of his earlier robber avatar. I have to understand that he has to cope with titanic heaves of mischief to give the smaller bit from his end to maintain peace. I digested the fact of his taking away the bananas

130

and coupled it with faith for Lord Hanuman. Overall, I think he is trying his best to hold ceasefire.

I offer him a stale chapatti from below as he peers from the terrace railings above. It takes a few cajoling words for him to come down onto the compound wall and take it. We have to give our best to maintain peace and not leave it to be decided by the fate's swinging scale. There is tension at both ends. He hasn't yet taken anything directly from my hands. So it's almost a snatching as he hurriedly takes it away. His lack of enthusiasm in straightaway gobbling it down bears testimony to the fact that he isn't too happy about the stale gift. He likes them fresh. But since he hasn't thrown it outright proves he has improved a lot in manners. He pulls apart the softer upper layer to eat it with casual munching, as if doing it to keep the friendly terms intact. The rest lies in pieces around him.

Seeing him better behaved today, I offer him a carrot. This time he takes it—not snatching—gently; there is no rush or overcautious pull. He thinks he should peel the outer unimpressive layer to eat the inner substance, but ends up peeling to the core. He takes a few unwilling bites and chews with cutely drooping eyes. Then he finds chapatti better in comparison and picks up the discarded pieces and chews with better facial expression. For a change of taste, he stretches his muscular arm and plucks a small, raw guava and takes a few bites. It has no taste either. He throws it away. Then a small tailorbird nest finds his attention. It's smartly snatched away from among the leafy camouflage. Thankfully it's an abandoned nest. He tears it apart. No broken eggs this time.

He is sitting with his back to me, his way of telling me that we aren't at least foes now, if not good friends. No typical apish snarls from him; no angry cuss words from my side. As humans, we have to invest more in buying peace because it's we who have made it a rarity. I do it from my side in this little human-simian equation of peace.

Do you believe in guardian angels? A man of faith will say yes; a man of science and logic might say no; and many others may just shrug with indecisiveness. A man of faith has belief in a beneficent external force, existing around to protect him, his interests and facilitate his journey. His belief would keep the thread intact despite many contrary, adverse experiences. So that is basically his inner force which keeps the little lamp of faith from being blown off by the winds of fate. This is a very sublime form of karma, a kind of invisible foundation on which, as a natural consequence, his physical world will manifest.

An atheist—but a practical, logical and confident man—carries the same light and dream. The only difference is that he needs more tangible proofs of being in control of things as a doer, as a manager of his affairs. He needs to pacify his reasoning mind to be assured of his safety and goals. Nothing wrong with that. The man of faith has lamp in his soul; the man of logic has a physical torch in his hand. But both of them have a source of light with them to move ahead.

One might sometimes consider gratitude to the guardian angels for putting us in a situation where we have more chances to life than the millions of deprived people. There are people caught in slums, genocides, civil wars, climatic catastrophes. Gratitude allows us to be more in love with our self as we are.

Just consider this point. Most of the seeds have almost the same potential to grow and expand to luxuriance. And if there is some variance in fertility within, doesn't it prove that again it is a chance factor because tell me of a seed that had a choice to determine its fertility or some patronizing force that bestowed more fertility to some seeds at the cost of others.

The seeds are thrown randomly. One falls in a sewage drain and is gone as sludge; another falls on a barren patch and is eaten by dust; one lands in a swamp and rots; one gets trampled under the feet; one is eaten by a bird; one germinates but wilts under the harsh sun; one grows luxuriantly but is eaten by a goat; one grows well but suffers an infestation; and one grows to be a beautiful tree. The last one is almost a miracle of random favorable circumstances, which allowed the seed's potential to bloom fully.

The chances of disorder and chaos, of things going wrong are open-ended and countless. Every individual has millions of his very own sets of probable things going wrong. The mere fact of survival is a miracle in the face of so many undoing probabilities. And if we happen to be lucky enough to creep out because of favorable chance factors accept it with grace and gratitude. This I consider to be our set of guardian angels—the set of protective probabilities that allow us this journey in body, thoughts and emotions even though so many things can go wrong every moment. Bow down to it because you just can't imagine how lucky you are in this form while massive stars are getting sucked by black holes and galaxies are breaking apart across the cosmos.

Anything can be written, thought, felt, analyzed and interpreted about an empty page. Its emptiness is the limitless, infinite womb of creation. Its nonbeing is the soul of the entire substance of being. The word is an echo of the wordless. The noise is a mere chiming announcement on the timeless clock of silence, intimating the eternal presence of silence. A buzzing, stirring, musical rhapsody—the sound of the soundless.

The manifestation is a mere indicator of the presence of the eternal, unknowable void. All that is perceptible to our senses is merely a motley bunch of thoughts, forms and shapes from the pool of a tangible wider wit, which itself is a known ripple on the outer margin of the unknown, the latter itself just a corner of the unknowable.

I'm smaller than what I create—writing, art, good deeds, smile, positivity, architecture, innovation, discovery. Because I'm just a facilitator, a conduit, a mere humble means to a little end. I represent something indirectly; a mere reflector of it—light. But I'm bigger than my wrongs, moral lapses, negativity, hate, greed and harm. Because now I directly represent something—darkness. I'm liable to be judged by others (and by myself) as the bearer (not just representative) of that darkness.

One can indeed make a perfume of one's pain and take copious sniffs of freedom in it. There is no point in being a truculent, blackened, smoke-blenching fire engine—a self-sacrificing, infuriating, haphazard sprawl of energies; a gloomy and haggard version of oneself. Princess Mahra Bint Mohammed Bin Rahid Al Maktoum of Dubai did it. She got fed up with her husband's philandering ways. Divorcing on Instagram makes a big, modern statement— a defiant declaration of women rights by an Arab woman. Giving an absorbing example of wisdom and maturity, she then puffs her anger into a perfume brand, named Divorce, launched by her. Her perfume is costly though at $272 a bottle.

Insulate yourself with fears, insecurities, phobias—and your guardhouses against them in the form of customized remedies, the collective, majoritarian safeties, the safe options—and you lose your freedom.

Grapple with instinctive short-cuts (which appear as safe options) and remove the insulation—they would warn you that it's only risk-taking and dangerous—and you hit the real treasure of life.

A lot many conventions may insulate you from the routine set of the so-called harmful elements, the expected ubiquitous hardships, but they keep you cut off from extraordinary freedoms as well.

It's a world of far less open spaces now. Even the birds are settling down. Earlier they would make nest at a place, raise their hatchlings, fly away and start life at some other place. They had many options. And wings mean freedom, so they won't fall into the trap of getting bound to one particular place. Not anymore.

The wire-tail swallow couple is a resident bird now. They have lost their colonies. It's a lonely pair. They know survival has better chance if they cut down on the freedom of their wings. They sleep in the mud nest in the verandah and spend the day darting around in the locality, taking rest on the same wires.

The gypsies are also getting cornered. Earlier their nomadic boats went bobbing over the geographic sea. No more open spaces to allow them temporary settlements. Every square inch is precious now—the land. They don't have any landed property. Earlier they owned all the land due to their free movement. Now they are landless in the real sense.

To avail any survival chance they are now finally putting down the yokes of their bullock carts and settle down. But they don't hold any rights. So they turn squatters in towns and cities. They will have to sacrifice at least one generation before they get a footing and some rights.

In sublimity with natural force, grass would try to reach beyond permissible possibilities to become plant; a plant would try to grow to be a shrub; a shrub would strive to be a tree; a tree something beyond, aspiring to kiss the sky.

The *champa* in the yard has little space to grow among the small cluster of trees. That's its set of close-clipped circumstances, its pathway to possibilities and originalities. The monkeys have rambled through its branches with mobbish fun and broken many branches. But the plant exactly knows what to focus on despite the limited space and the monkeys playing truant. It has its tiny portion of sky that beckons it. And the shrub gears up to inch towards being a little tree, adding to its trunk strength and woody girth, little by little, with patience, precision and prudence.

It has a beautiful five-petaled flower with yellow starting from the centre from inside and fading into milky white around the middle of the petals. The flower has a lovely subliminal smell, which it holds close to its centre, as if it's an introvert; not an extrovert like rose that freely spreads its fragrance to the air around. You have to strum the strings of its smell to get into the fluid blend of olfactory notes. It's a strong fragrance but for that you have to bring your nose very close to the petals; just like to get water you have to go to the well. But once you do that it opens its lovely opulence. You can then inhale with a long, slowly drawn breath and enjoy the classical verses and delicate *ghazals* of the scented world.

Don't pluck a flower, try to pick one from the ground—if your necessities recommend this. This is my subdued protocol. Usually the plant is happy to offer me a couple of flowers, sometimes even more, while I walk around the yard. I pick up the scented gift with gratitude.

I walk slowly, holding the flower to my nose, inhaling deeply like I'm doing *pranayam*, enjoying the fragrant elegance and luxury the flower has to offer. Do it with alertness, patience and it becomes a walking meditation—*pranayam* saturated with lovely smell. It goes deep in you and resurrects the innermost stale corners with freshness. It's enriching. It's better to be full of lovely smell in this world brimming with bizarrely contemptuous distortions and misconceptions. If you do it for 15 minutes, you get a high; drunk with the natural cocktail of smell. Its trove of smell is exhaustless; keep inhaling. You will be tired; not the flower. Later I put it in my room on a table. It's better to have a source of beautiful smell around you. It harmonizes the energy field around you.

It's a sturdy flower and doesn't wither easily; just its edges turn dark brown—the signs of its saying bye to the world. But the yellow pool of smell in the centre still welcomes you with a gentle waft of fragrance even in this heat for two-three days. Then it goes for eternal rest in the flowerbed.

Whenever you feel beaten, try to think that it could have been easily worse, for there is no limit to the things going wrong, disorderly, messed-up and chaotic. The things going right are just minute traces of orderliness amid all this meaningless cosmic chaos. And that's where the purpose of life lies: to give it a meaningful push, to provide it a definite shape out of all the fuddle-duddle and random flux of events. The unknown and the infinite is looking at your hands to give it some more meaning. You are its potter, its arm, its tool, its heart, its soul; one more shoot on the tree of existence to sprout and add to its luxuriant quotient of infinity. Knead, mesh and shape your clay well. That's life—an operational unit, living; a verb, not just a noun.

A huskily building twilight losing itself to the imponderable quest of the artificial lights in the town market. The whinnying tenor of shoppers conveying some oppressive clanging even among the festival chimes. This is Diwali eve. A dissolute sense surreptitiously serenading somewhere in the crowd's eyes.

Shop fronts are glittering with lighted strings. Almost a hemorrhage of consumerism. Allurement lurking precipitately from tables, shelves, display cases and shopkeepers' faces. A plethora of presentiment. Colossal and gigantic stream to buy and sell. The worshippers of gold gathered in swanky jewelry temples. Most of the hypnotized people bow with prodigious prostration to gold.

The sellers seem invincible today. And the consumers sleepwalking with some unknown enfeeblement of senses. Sweet-makers with mounds of sweets; offering sugar lumps against life's embittering experiences. The collective enthusiasm going with colossus undulations among the crowd. Almost sepulchral sovereignty of profiteering leer. The crowd in intangible trepidation. It's the occasion to look up and move forward. Guttural, hoarse hiccups of the consumerist, capitalist desire.

Lots of firecrackers selling openly despite the ban. Spicy street food stalls catching tongues with the adroit endeavor of a chameleon catching a fly.

There are insects on the dirty ground below, under new boots, sneakers and fancy heeled footwear. And there is a bigger pair of insects, let's say bigger beetles or cockroaches. A father cockroach and a child cockroach. Victims of destiny's selectivity in turning some fates to cockroaches and others to earthly gods. As the bigger world of festival eve humans goes with a burgeoning whoosh, the father cockroach broods over the baby cockroach that is lying like a little bundle of garbage.

The father cockroach's clothes are so dirty and hair so wild, shabby and unkempt as to make him some humanoid form of mud in the drain. The child cockroach is lying on a dirty cloth. His head bandaged, yellow antiseptic visible at places. The feet are also bound in dirty dressing. In all probability he is a made-up patient, opiated and dumped by the father to gather some survival grains of human sympathy in the dust. A tragic little brigandage. They have made themselves so dirty and stinking that nobody dressed festively would dare and touch the child to verify the truth and would just throw a coin to move away from the ill-fated dirty cockroaches.

Jump from the pinnacle of your loneliness. It's a nice height to go for a dive. Sometimes standing there, mulling over your bruises gets you in a sadistic attachment to them. They give you a sweet-sour itch. It's on the surface—a big, spacious expansion on the outer layer. It doesn't even teach you much. It's shallow and shallow teachers aren't good guides. Even if the little niggling thing—that grasps the outer layer of your attention and fuels your loneliness—turns to a scar because of a fall after the dive.

You at least break the stalemate; you leave that point. You might get a bleeding scar instead of a mere bruise. It's but an avenue for the pent-up darkness to come out. A door opens to the soul. Earlier it was a mere grilled, meshed window to the body. Yes, it will be a bit more painful, the opening of this door. But then light comes in. This is your little penance. This isn't self-inflicted injury. This is healing. This teacher is deeper; will give you profounder lessons. The scar will be healed; its imprint on your body a kind of trophy earned during the journey.

When the plant is happy, it gives you a flower. When the tree is happy, it gives you good fruits and shade. When the sky is happy, it gives you rain, sunshine, shade and prismatic play of clouds. When the birds are happy, they give you a song.

What do you do when you are happy? Think it over brother. You too are no less than any of these. You too give your smile, sympathy, healing touch on a shoulder, a bit of clarity, some kindness, a tear of loving kindness, a little bit of helping hand to someone fallen. You open your treasure when you are happy. I know we can't be happy all the time. We have our off times when we fret, fume, snort and get sullen. Then we automatically close the vaults of our treasure. Happiness can't be maintained forever, but we can keep it in mind. That's an option. We can lure it back from the secret hiding place it retreats into after briefly spraying sunshine in our life.

There are times when you even hate yourself so much that you don't even want to look at yourself and turn the mirror to the wall. No problem. Don't worry too much. There will be more happy stories on another day. Just remember this.

It's Diwali, the festival of lights. The two *parijat* trees in the yard have carpeted the earth below their canopies with so many flowery drops as to make it a flowered floor. What celebration! The rains have been good and the plants, especially *tulsi*, have acquired a bushy jungle shape. The tailorbird parents have their hatchling out, a greenish tailless funny guy almost as big as its parents. It hops around the leafy tangle during its post-nest training phase. It's a mischievous guy. I saw it running after a good-behaved elderly Indian robin.

Everything is perception-based at this level of existence. So this particular section of the yard is the tailorbirds' house, just like I have the same perception due to being born in the house. They deny my entry to their section. They raise a brain-hole-drilling din the moment I reach the spot. The wire-tail swallow couple does the same. They are agile fighter-plane type fliers. They dart with chipping sounds, coming dangerously close to my head whenever I happen to be near their mud nest on the ceiling in the barn verandah. I understand their position. We humans are also darting around with angry chipping sounds, insecure and afraid of losing our position, interests and stakes.

The white-browed fantail flycatcher is a distinguished bird having a white forehead with a black strip running from top to the nape, blackish top and milky white underside. It's very lively and flicks and spreads its white-edged tail quite frequently. With its long broad white eyebrows, it flits around almost tirelessly. Flaunting white spots on its throat, it fans its tail, flicks its wings, giving quick hunting dashes midair. Fleas beware! It's wonderful to have a pair of flycatchers in your yard. I love them for their midair antics and lively attitude. They look playing all through the day. These playfully restless birds consume so much energy due to this tireless physical activity that the entire day is spent in catching fleas midair. Can I ask for more? Make your hobby your profession. Like they do their midair antics while going with the profession of survival—playing and gathering food going side by side.

There is an icing on the cake as well—they aren't too scared of my presence. Their confiding nature allows me to stand a few feet away and enjoy their fun as a spectator. Then there is cherry on top of icing—their song. It's a melodious song comprising six to eight notes, ascending, sometimes descending. Sometimes they stop it midway, leaving you craving for the entire performance.

Both of them look the same but with the spirit of an ornithologist one can spot the difference—the female is slightly paler with browner head, while the male is black with greenish gloss. I had to do a bit of research to find out which of them is doing this tireless exercise in front of the little old car parked in retirement mode in the yard. No wonder it happens to be the girl in the pair! Who else loves a mirror so much?

The car is 21 years old and deserves graceful retirement as a vintage souvenir in the yard of a small-time rural poet. After all, it was with me during the challenging and complex cluster of life and events during my urban innings in editorial jobs. With our limited capabilities, both of us suited each other really well. Now it becomes the dressing table for the female flycatcher. She is such a narcissist. She spends her days ogling at her reflection in the rearview and window glasses.

It's a rural set-up, so there is no problem of food, I mean fleas. The humans to fleas ration is infinitely in favor of the latter. She can continue ogling coquettishly at her reflection and take little bites of food as the fleas naturally happen to be within the range of her dressing table, dressing car rather. Such tireless flapping of wings requires lots of food. It means less fleas in the yard of a poet. I note that she drops her extras quite frequently. So cleaning the bird drops on my little souvenir at the day end is the service charge I have to pay.

She thus is a homely girl. Her husband, as can be expected, goes outside to loaf around. But he returns quite frequently to check on her. When he disturbs her dressing-car time she gives an angry, agitated, grating *chuck...chuck...chuck...chuckrr* reprimand. The moment he starts disturbing her self-loving ogling at her reflection, she throws these irritated notes and shifts to the other vehicle, a bit new and a tiny bit bigger than the older one, which seems to be her favorite. I hope she isn't fed up with this guy—or suspects him of double dating during his sorties outside the yard—and has fallen under the illusion that a handsome prince is imprisoned inside the car and thus goes calling from all sides, asking it to come out.

The zero. The imperfect. The perfect. Three basic concepts which the mind can hypothesize in trying to understand the cosmic equation. The imperfect is forever striving to become the perfect. That's the basic functional element in the play of existence, the *leela*. The imperfect running timelessly and endlessly after the perfect becomes the infinity. The infinity is just the ever-persistent, eternal impulse of the finite to become perfect. And perfection is impossible because one point of apparent perfection is just a transient state, a mere beginning of a new stage of the imperfect looking to further its path to perfection. The flow. And infinity collapses to zero, the empty.

I was expecting a pollution peak on Diwali night. Everything has been politicized and everything within politics has been communalized. I saw lots of social media content giving a clarion call to the Hindus to celebrate Diwali with clanging, banging gusto, especially when others can kill animals on their festival, so why shouldn't we slaughter the clean air on ours. It had its effect. Despite a ban on the firecrackers in the Delhi NCR, these were sold in open, purchased with a right to unrestricted religious celebration and banged and burst with yelling enthusiasm. I also love to celebrate Diwali as a Hindu, but I care for our lungs as well, especially the elders.

The night was breezy which dispersed the pollutants. In the morning there was no eye-burning smog. A cool breezy morning with tolerable level of pollution. Elated over this I carry my Diwali celebration into the countryside with a walk in solitude. Many parts of India are celebrating Diwali today because the lunar calendar overlaps two days of the sun calendar. It gives us the option to celebrate our festival on two days. Good for business; good for the people as well, enabling them to carry extra festive spirit.

It's a bright day, the horizon slightly smoggy in the distance. Mother nature spreads a breezy cool hand like a windscreen wiper to take away the pollutants. A perfect time to appreciate *Celosia argentea* or Plumed cockscomb blooms in a corner. All it needs is a bit of sunshine, dewy moisture, cool breeze and no human foot intruding, and mother nature offers a lovely bouquet of smiles to a solitary walker with poetic sensitivities. We humans might consider them as weeds but they are a perfect breakfast table for a flock of moths who are high on nectar. These are lovely finger-shaped creamy blooms with pink spires on the top. Plumed cockscomb indeed—fluffy with a slightly curved creamy erection, milky white head topped with a pink spire.

There is a lonely date palm standing in the empty harvested fields. Dry paddy crofts too low and lifeless to give it any sense of clothing and company. It must be missing the company of its brothers. Sadly, there will soon be a world when the trees will be barcoded and numbered. No worries. Let's make the most of what is left. Thankfully we are the generation that is lucky to see unnumbered and uncoded trees.

In a corner there are golden shades of ripe paddy waiting to be harvested—a prelude to nice, luscious aroma on your table.

I stand under a blackberry tree and stare into the bluish haze in the east. A trickle of sunrays plays on my face giving me an insight:

There is light everywhere and darkness alongside. You have to position yourself in life to have your portion of light rays and your little puddle of shadow.

When chaos is unleashed in the name of pseudo-security, pride and supremacy, the rulers take falsehoods, lies and dirty tricks to unprecedented levels. The ideal citizens then are the ignorant fools who can be customized to make them blind followers through fake news, passionate narratives and twisted history. The raised and ruffled passions divide the society. Falsehoods rule and become the new-age dharma. Under such conditions, the one who has a mind of his own, a simple man who isn't blinded by the sandy blizzards and can see the reality, becomes an enemy.

Truth is taken as a sin as per this new dharma. Those who know the truth are viewed with suspicion by the rulers. And out of these, those who speak the truth are the outright enemies of the *set-up*.

The rulers aren't afraid of the plain thugs and criminals because they are the foolest among the fools. It's a simple law and order problem. In fact these bigger fools become great tools to be used by the rulers. So those who speak truth are the real terrorists for the rulers. They are systematically penalized. That was how it was in the past. That's how it's now.

This existence is like a fiery dragon whizzing in a circle. It eats the same excreted stuff that comes out of its tail after the previous food is consumed in the guts for fuelling its fiery dash. The excreta then becomes the same stuff that was previously eaten by the time the head comes circling again at that point. At each point on the circle, what it now eats was formerly left out of the tail after consuming as fuel for its journey. Nothing added, nothing subtracted. But still such a rollercoaster ride! The question arises, 'Who set the ball rolling initially?'

Where does such a weird dream come from? I'm clueless. President Trump is working as an electrician in my depilated room. It's the old style, laborious electric wire fitting he is working on. A lurching bamboo ladder laid against the wall, he has a hammer and a chisel in his heavy hands, making a little hole in the plastered upper wall just under the ceiling to fix little wooden bits in the grooves to nail narrow wooden strips on them. These were used to bind wires on them during the good old times.

The room has dusty green, peeling limewash coating on the walls. A green dust has settled on his lovely orange hair. Me and my father—who departed 15 years back—are watching him with intimidating curiosity. He takes a break and climbs down the ladder. We are embarrassed. Surprisingly, President Trump doesn't seem offended or angry. I mumble apologetically, 'You are the most powerful man on earth. I don't know how do we land in your life. But I see the tough phase of the task is over.' Frankly speaking I don't have any clue as to how such a thing lands in my subconscious to surface as a weird dream.

Full riot of life and colors embraced by spring flowers. Then in boiling summers, the flowers wilt, as if fighting to keep the memories of spring away. The dying petals seem struggling to get a whiff of long-forgotten smells. The force of disintegration meanwhile eroding big chunks of whatever is still present, the faded smile and feeble scent.

The dying flowers struggling, still hoping to build a bridge that would allow them to come to terms with this seemingly tragic transformation—spring's luxuriant kiss to summer's sun-burnt lips.

It looks the flowers died; but they changed to seeds. The dry, crumbling specks, wispy and hairy, will be scattered by the wind. And a tiny hairy speck of seed, carrying the entire code of flowery luxuriance, flows and flies and lands at some place to again blossom one fine day in another lovely spring.

'Where is death in this?' I wonder. Brothers, life is crammed with symbolism of the eternal truth. It's a book of very easy codes. To read them we don't need sophistication of mind; we simply need simplicity of heart. It's a very lovely exercise to try to learn and read nature's book of symbolism.

It's a beautiful sight in the morning. A loving precursor to the poem that would follow soon after it. The love dance of a peacock on my terrace. I'm the excited peeping tom looking from the terrace room.

The surrendering spectacle unfolds. The love-lynched bird spreading the wings of desire; swaying the fantail of passion to catch her, the peahen, in his airy love-loops. She stands still, full of wonder about this colorful show, the buzzing-humming shake of his spread out fantail. Her time stops as if snared by the net of love.

His colorful invitation. Her curiosity, silence, acceptance; a space for the manifestation of the nonbeing to acquire the shape of a little colorful being. And of course the unnecessary worldly noise that is always seeking to spoil the love game, the futile barking of the puppies in the street who find it a nice case study to learn to bark.

7

SOMETIMES in our impatience to create the *new*—too hurriedly—grafting it over the *old*, we bring down even the settled *old* along with the unsettled *new*. Certain fundamental laws are broken in this storm. The naked passion, blind impulse and uncontrolled force are hardly the reasonable tools to forge something new.

So build slowly. The past is a platform, a foundation, a book of lessons about what to do and what to avoid. It's a set of good and bad, but a box of lessons nonetheless. So handle the old with care while you go for making the new. Impatience with the past is a blasting revolution. Yes, it destroys the past quickly, but it's very chaotic. It doesn't lay a foundation. In the name of foundation it goes for repression, killings, deweeding. It crosses all limits, uproots everything in the name of change.

Most of us are imprisoned. We are the prisoners behind the walls of fears and the wires, bars and grills of the supposed and assumed securities to ward off those fears. The wall of fear is the mammoth panic of death and the unknown; anything we can't see beyond the normal perception field. The wires, bars, barbed mesh and grilled fence comprise the rules and conventions; the tools of collective securities; the expected; the commonality.

We are heavily laden. We carry loads of guilt, shame, fears, secrets, judgments, hate, jealousies, malice. Sometimes it feels like we would collapse if not for the minor trace elements, the uplifting brief feelings of joy and happiness. They are almost weightless, feathery, floating; something like anti-gravity. They mysteriously manage to counterbalance the tremendous load we carry.

A broken doorway. But the interior of the house still safe, welcoming and cozy. In contrast, an illustrious, ornate, imposing gateway, aglitter with form, design, authority, shiny paint and much-much more. But the interior broken, stale, unwelcoming, hitting you in the face with its unfriendliness. That's how most of the people are, the latter category I mean. Brand new clothes, stylish haircuts, designer glasses, costly perfumes, fat attitudes, sophisticated looks, illustrious footwear, daunting language—massively adorned gateways to their personality. All focus on the superficial, introductory gateway to the their self; entire energy and resources spent on the surface varnish. But the interior—the real self—poor and neglected. The door of a palace enclosing a slum within. They would hit you with selfish venom at the littlest provocation. The first category are rare individuals—a poor-looking door protecting a palace inside. An oasis in the desert. Soulful. With a loving, healing presence. It needs mother nature to have thousands of the other type of people to bloom, nurture, protect one such person.

Probably we saw the lasts of big swarms of the soft-bodied beetle that flies with a glow—fireflies. Their habitats declined and the fireflies that spun the dreamy webs of imagination, poems, stories and parables vanished from the nights. What do they need? They just need that which used to come naturally with nights—darkness in the moist, shady bushes during the monsoon days. The days would be bright, musty and green and the dark nights had fireflies. Now when the lights remain on all night even in the villages, spotting a firefly has become a rarity. Too much light pollution. I think contrary to our negative impressions about darkness, it must be washing lots of lighted pollution that we unleash on a daily basis.

The fireflies dance using their bioluminescence, the males and females looping with their own types of bio-sparks. Aren't they such beautiful dancing lights! When there is too much of bright artificial light, their bioluminescence becomes ineffective in the males and the females spotting each other.

The vegetation is vanishing, the nights are losing darkness and so the firefly love-festivals are gone too—almost. The agricultural fields use insecticides on a large scale. Where does it leave any place for this soft beetle? For those who might care to listen, let me inform you that when a firefly boy and girl go on a love-dancing date, they enjoy feasting upon mosquitoes on the dining table. So those who have had dengue and malaria should have empathy for them.

As the 22-month-long pregnancy nears its end, the female African elephant starts eating *Boraginaceae* plant leaves to induce labor. Has anyone taught the elephants about it? No. There is natural intelligence. It pervades around in sync with natural laws. It guides natural processes across the species.

So many destinies are poorly scrawled, almost illegibly, by adverse circumstances. Millions of meaningless destinies—except being meaningful in pain and suffering—shaped by wars, natural hazards, poverty, social strife. Destinies decided by the random casting of the cosmic dice—just being at the wrong place at the wrong time. And amid all the sad scrawling, a few nice lines, legible, the chosen few with an apparent meaning. A few people at the right place, at the right time as well. They serve as beacons of hope even though there are daggers of jealousy thrown at them by the poor and the destitute. They are the lighthouse in the dark, choppy sea, beckoning the struggling, gasping swimmers to join their league.

The winds are drifting. That's their nature. The fragrance of rose from this side. The scent of jasmine from that. And other lovely smells from other directions. So if you happen to be someone's rose at the moment, don't be haughty and vain about it. The wind is merely blowing from your side at the moment. Just that, nothing more. And if we simply, naturally raise our nostrils to the wind to inhale, it's plain normalcy at work. That's our nature. We are needy. We need fresh fragrance to beat the routine boredom-born odor of life. But then the winds shift as well. That's their nature. Now that special person, the apple of your eyes, inhales the scented breeze coming from a different flower.

Sometimes you have to walk to the edge of the roof of your being, your existence—to stare at the depths below, to gauze where do you stand in life, to evaluate your position. For security you might decide to step back and be in the little safe square around you. But sometimes you ought to just give a long, hard look into the depths below. You evaluate by focusing at your lowest point. The low point lying there among the dusted ground realities far away from the lofty heights. And if the call of the journey assures you of the sweet-sour pain of a fall, but with a reasonable chance of survival, you then just jump and make your path beyond all confines and fears. You untangle the messed-up spools of the past lying in the shadows of those low points. That's when your real journey begins.

And who would triumph these days? Faker than the fake most. Not probably. Definitely. And who would rule? The fakest among the top fakes. A darkness that eats the little silver lines of light. That's its diet. Darkness rushes in from all sides to eat the tiny slivers of light, just like a flock of goats and sheep running to nibble a few dry wisps of grass in the desert.

It requires character not to be defined by one's losses. Because if not, then you turn out a very sour, bitter fruit. Don't allow the loss, the rape, the plunder to define you. Growing with a feeling of victimhood is gross self-injury. A degradation. It's better to be defined by life and hope beyond that wound.

There are pirates crouched down in the crowded sea. They emerge suddenly and quickly rap your bottom. And here you are left with a Beslery or a Kenley. The bottles look exactly like the original: same shape, wrapper, color and marking. Just for the one letter difference. Nothing frightful apart from the fact that you drink simple tap water for twenty rupees. You get a livid look on your face once you have consumed it and then realize the difference. You have been tricked and feel like an utterly callow person.

Me and my friend have our respective Beslery and Kenley and reach the Sunday Book Bazaar at Mahila Haat, Delhi. The boy fraudster melted in the crowd.

There is a mute hawker of small items like socks, belts, hankies, purses, pen and key rings by the entrance gate to the book bazaar. It's a smart geographical location because the clients are less thuggish if they are going to buy books. And who would bargain with a seller who cannot speak? At least bookworms won't. But he is not deaf. He can listen and that's more important. I have a doubt that he has a very nice tongue to speak. In that case it's a nice strategy. He easily sells four sets of cheap socks to me without the slightest opportunity of bargaining from my side.

There is a lot of springiness in the air because many girls are buying books. It's a lovely sight at the open-air book bazaar in late October. There is a great book lover moving diligently with a haversack half full of books.

A scratched placard fittingly displaying old classics stacked in compact horizontal rows on the ground, their spines up to catch the bookworm in you. Bookworms get a tremulous kiss by the fair-lipped maiden—the urge to buy books. There is a problem of plenty actually. As a book lover you have to squabble with your urge, an onerous task—to not buy everything on account of how much weight your wallet and back can carry.

There is another real book lover—a lovely wayfarer amiably walking pulling a trolley bag to fill it with books, the lightest and the loveliest weight one can carry.

A girl in aromatic rumples of sleep carried by her purple maxi. She looks just out of bed after the soundest sleep. A very short guy with her walking with the longing of a lightening bloodhound. He gives the feeling of pork; she stewed vegetables. I'm lost in books, my friend in her loose hair. She flicks her hair so suddenly that I'm startled out of my book-spell. She looks back at us with an unreconciled haughtiness of the young for the uncles nearing middle age—as if reminding us that we were born too early; that the dreams of our youth are a common stale reality now. Aah, unsubmissive youth! My friend feels the pangs of inter-generational enmity. His spirits plummet, the steps lose energy and he walks as if clad in grave-cloths, his mood swaddled in burial attire.

A friend has a sententiously honeyed heart. He is as observant of the present carriers of youth—the opposite gender, of course—as I'm of book titles massed around. Recently his father received a WhatsApp call, 'Your son is in custody on rape charges.' The fake police officer spoke with gruesome, jarring authenticity. With exulting clamminess they continued, 'If you want him out, pay money without delay. There is no time to lose because there is pressure to register FIR. If it's done, nobody can save him from prison.'

The malevolent bluff is then surreptitiously changed into reality by the menacingly maneuverable algorithms of artificial intelligence, which gleans facts about a person's voice, image, manner and produces a virtual reality—the life-like audio and video of that person. 'Father please save me!' his son is heard pleading in the background. The artificially generated voice of his son beckons paternal fears. His father finds it plausible just like my father would believe if the fraudsters had called him saying his son has robbed a bookstore. It was sheer luck that the old man's account wasn't plundered by the ultra-modern heathens. His grandson arrived as a grand good-luck gift. He called his father immediately who informed him that he was on the way from office.

Osho tells a beautiful story of a *sanyasi* named Bhavani Dayal. He was on a pilgrimage in the Himalayas. It was a very hot noon and he was moving up the hill with his bedroll on his shoulder. The *sanyasi* was sweating and breathless because of the weight and the steep climb. In front of him, a small hill girl was carrying her brother on her shoulders. She herself was very young and that is why she was also struggling, panting and sweating. All breathless, the *sanyasi* said to her, 'Daughter you must be feeling a lot of burden and weight on you.' The girl said, '*Swami ji* the weight and burden is on you. Your bundle. I carry no weight. He is not a burden, he is my brother.' The *sanyasi* was shocked. A small hill girl taught him a big lesson of life. Where there is love, there is no burden in life. It was joyful for her to carry the physical weight of a little brother, while he joylessly struggled under the physical weight of his belongings.

I don't believe in a fixed life term because we are a process; continuous shedding of the old and becoming new. So of course body chemistry can be managed to alter the lifespan. It's also a fact that outer threats such as accidents are always present to undo all such efforts. There are also internal threats like something unreasonably going wrong in the physiological system. But within these possibilities we have the choice to create a third dimension of possibility, the possibility to change and manage our life with conscious effort and that includes how much time we want to spend on earth.

There is an art and craft of health optimization through proper nutrition and holistic practices to take body functioning to its peak performance. People are fond of hacking these days. So bio-hacking means slowing down the biological aging rate. Some have managed it to be 34% slower than the normal aging rate. Targeting longevity through healthy lifestyle is a nice goal. All of us can have personalized health strategies. So chalk your own individual robust health regime. It includes dietary and lifestyle overhauling.

Jinping wins (Tibet atrocities and Xingiang concentration camps), Putin wins (Ukraine massacres), Trump wins (Convinced felon), Modi wins (…). Now is the time for us to be like three deaf, mute and blind monkeys or shift to some other planet, for which unfortunately there is no choice except Musk, Zuckerberg, Bezos and a few others. But Musk won't take that option. He is the bright-eyed, super-genius macho man of the mighty Trump. The rest of the billionaires beware. Take your rockets out.

In any case, the mighty four have the power to dispatch anyone to some extraterrestrial planet—I mean if not in body but soul at least. The super-strong guys are actually eligible to share the same table and have relaxed talk over wine. Modi of course will have milk. Then who will be their common enemy? Maybe small people like you and me who think they have their own mind and feel like speaking the truth.

Democracy will get diluted like never before. It has already thawed quite significantly in the world's biggest and the strongest democracies. I think Putin and Xi Jinping are the trend-setting big, bad boys, inspiring the rest to follow their steps.

Who will they hunt if not each other then? Because the most powerful can't help hunting. They have to go on their predatory prowls. It's almost natural. I think they will hunt the little voices of liberalism, freedom of speech, truth, human rights, equality, gender parity, etc.

Putin will be allowed to retain whatever he has captured in Ukraine. China will be allowed to take over Taiwan somehow (with the sham show of American opposition to that; and in return for substantial economic gains in bilateral trade with China). If India plays its cards well, it might have some more chunk from the PoK. And America? It will be allowed to have the symbolic chairmanship on the table of the four. The mighty tigers then will be free to play cat and mouse with the little mice, the liberal intelligentsia But who knows the aliens, who have been taking reconnaissance of our small planet for decades, will finally step in and present a common challenge to the four. Then it will be quite interesting.

As a non-American global citizen I respect the Americans' choice in electing Trump. I can't analyze on bigger issues but I think the major gain from being mere Trump to become President Trump is that he will be able to terminate the federal legal cases against him and suspend the state cases till he occupies office. And of course more trade for himself and America in general. As a layman I view it as the major take away: the ability to become above the law. That I think is the real *Power*. President Trump, wish you a powerful, bombastic, fantastic time in the seat of *Power*! Our leader is also a big fan of yours. So we see benefits for India unless you get irritated with us.

Now I believe, President Trump, that you were supposed to become the American President. Fate saved you from death just by a millimeter. It had plans. To reward you with power over millions of square kilometers on earth. Sometimes being one millimeter short of death means trillions of square yards of powerful life. The world will be at the mercy of your temperament. Please rule with mercy, benevolence and wisdom of an elder. Because you are the *Global Elder* now.

Teenage girls of the present generation are hyper-smart. They know exactly how to act as pickpockets on sweet-toothed, grey-haired, balding uncles who easily believe in fairy castles. Just to feel the breezy spring of youthful, naughty talks he has a few teenage girl-friends who keep stabbing his pockets for buying costly gifts for their real, young boyfriends. One of his little friends cajoled the liberal-hearted uncle with honeyed words to an extent that it found him joyful enough to open his wallet, fully allowing himself to be stabbed deeply in pockets. It enabled the little girl to buy an Apple phone for her local history-sheeter, goonish boyfriend who had grown glum after a recent beating by the police. So in a way the gentleman helped them in darning the torn collar of their shirt. Of course he didn't know about the end point of his gift; wasn't aware that his gift has landed in thuggish claws instead of her soft, fair, pinkish hands. He came to know about it from another source. He was bawling and snarling for a few moments but then his aggrieved energies subsided as they are supposed to be for a man in his late forties. With grating but muffled anger he told me that she had lied to him. 'We have four cars and my father runs a business,' the smart teenager had lied about their financial standing. She turned out to be the daughter of a small corner-shop tailor in a narrow alley where a car couldn't even enter. Her father had a rusty moped only.

Another little one tried the same trick with me at a popular eating point, named Madras restaurant, in the town. I'm eating a *dosa* with unhindered zeal, having arrived from a trip to the Himalayas, and feeling ravenously hungry after the daylong journey. Maybe she got this sweetened assumption that a graying man in forties spiritedly gorging on spiced *dosa* is still caught in the unwearying aroma of youthful desires. This proclivity turns the purse strings of such men very loose.

These are very smart kids with their personalized set of endearments to fan the air of desire in the men in their forties. From their clothing and bearing they estimate the gentleman's financial worth and calculate that thousands can be easily drawn out, while a young man would give hundreds only in terms of dining and petty gifts and would demand much costlier returns in privacy.

She is sitting facing me; her young, boyish boyfriend facing the other way. She ogles at me with love-drenched eyes—at my purse rather. I'm eating very spiritedly, so she thinks I have enough youthful strings to be hummed by the fingers of desire and lose my grip on the wallet. The maiden finery spreading sensuous shine for a liaison. She spreads her arms on the table, puts her chin on the back of her palms and takes a sniper-precision aim for long moments, spraying translucent bullets of fake love. The air around me is profoundly speckled with feigned love-notes. Little does she realize that I lose myself to books only. I smile, get up, pay the bill and leave gently. I take a last look from outside. She is grimacing. 'Of no use anymore!' she must be judging me. Well, I'm happy to be of no use in the way they mean it.

A couple of uproariously adolescent monkeys, a lacework of mischief, with beet-red bums, jumping around for fun. They greet "how-d'you-do" to humanity in the morning; running to jump onto the electricity poles, shaking them with a sadistic pleasure; gratifyingly wheedling, spinning, twirling to leave a tornado of misbehavior. I watch bewilderedly. A gabbling spirit of youth an energy—fresh-morning youth with moistened tremulous lips.

The big dark-grey goonish feral tomcat, the hideous scourge for the birds among the trees and plants in the yard, is sprawled for sunbathing. Tailorbird bickering, bulbul gabbling, babbler ailing, squirrel *tik-tikking*. But they cannot come near because the foe has a crafty shiftiness in its eyes even while resting. Then the flycatcher takes the lead. It has a spurtling maneuverability in its wings; a rousing charge and dandyish twists and turns from a close range. So the beautiful agile flycatcher goes for a helicopter sortie over the cat; flicking, fluttering, flying at a point just a few inches above any world-record holder tomcat would jump to catch a prey midair. The cat looks vanquished and helpless. It gives a sinister, vicious scowl to which the birdie helicopter gives indignant, whinny clangor of notes in triumphant spirits from the side of all the birds.

Mating fleas taking a tumble on my newspaper. It has happened thrice in a week, so need to note this. Falling in a torrid unison of desire, like a little pebble on the soft newsprint, almost crashing through lesser news. A flabby and pulp love drop. Sweltering passion in cool October breeze. A spasmodic and riotous carousal humming in the wings and two sparks colliding into each other with lightening swiftness, giving good news for the flea kingdom on human newsprint.

I wring clothes before putting them on the clothesline to dry. Soapy water gets squeezed out forming a few little puddles on the brickyard floor. Three Indian robins make the most of this. Flicking tails, wetting wings and taking few sips in between. Rejoicing rills. It's a lovely sight to watch birds playing like this.

On my solitary walk a spectacle of motherly love. In a marshy overgrown patch among the ripening paddy fields the angry trumpeting notes of a mother *sarus* crane. A mother would jump head first into danger to save her little ones. She has eggs here and some dogs have arrived sniffing the grass. So she dexterously feigns to be an injured and sick bird, not able to fly, giving agonized cries to draw them after her away from the nest. They follow her despairing notes and sickly strides, sensing victory in catching her. When they seem like catching her, she takes a few seemingly labored wing-strokes to just fly out of their mouth and land a few feet ahead and then run again to keep them on the hunt. And the befooled and lousy devils being drawn into the fading light towards the pink ball melting in the twilight dark grey veil lurking over the horizon.

A revisit to the town park after a month; enough for father time to show you its freshly cooked plans. The female sweeper in peacock blue dress is working without her white lab coat today. But with more colors visible, although partly, she has a cute round girlish appearance. It's the day after *karva-chauth* night, the fasting day for the welfare and health of husbands even if they spoil yours. Her hardworking hands have henna for the occasion, an indication that she has a tolerable husband whose life can at least be celebrated once in a year. Like the last time she sweeps quite methodically and instructively.

Instead of the old man today it's a younger cleaner who comes paddling the rickshaw cart laden with dry leaves, the thin strands of not so prominent north Indian autumn. He gives a snuffling and moody appearance, in contrast to the peaceful and composed old man. Where is the old man, I get worried. Hope he hasn't been fired or fallen sick. Some genuine souls—even strangers—leave you with invaluable keepsakes in your memory just with a few glimpses of their kind, gentle presence.

There I find him! He is doing something important today—preparing seedbeds for winter flowers. It's a laborious task using a spade. But he seems to be a gardener first than a mere park cleaner. Any opportunity to create more blooms must come solicitously, quite naturally. Then sweating and hard labor don't matter. He has worked on a long, narrow row along the walking track, freshly dug soil giving a trajectory of his nice work since early morning. Imagine the winter flowers along the track after a few weeks! He is resting on a bench, probably giving some respite to his stiffened joints. He has a grandfatherly ticklish look into my eyes, as if to say, 'You can exercise with the shovel on the seedbed.' I toddle on with a little movement of head, acknowledging his great flowering job in this deflowering world.

The election fever has gone down with the formation of a new government by the same party. So the politicking group is talking about mundane things that matter. The park feels far more calm in the absence of political vainglory. They are off the entranced political cart, hence the bass voice has normal drawl, no tension in tenor. Today I don't feel the heat like I did the last time as I pass them. The old, gaunt, wheel-chair bound figure of last time, sitting languished and petering out of the stage of life, has improved. He is off the wheel-chair, and although still very fragile, looks taking a clasp at life in spotless whites, sitting on the ground doing *pranayam* while others talk about mundane issues of life. He has a very firm ostrich like face looking determinedly to improve his health.

A sixty plus grey-haired man with his unique set of exercises. He has a good athletic physique for his age; a focused man humming in accord with the fresh autumnal air. His shorts, sneakers and T-shirt muffling the bugs of age through a punctual exercise routine. He spins in circles with a vigorous shake of hands, as if redeeming energy from the not yet spent coupons of energy in muscles and nerves. He then jumps on one leg; then the other; followed by unique twists and turns; then copiously inhales morning air through *anuloma-viloma* breathing exercise.

Two gentlemen walking with firm steps, both of retired age, one carrying a jailor's cane. His friend seems a jolly guy, somewhat undoing the rigid authoritarian air carried by the cane-wielder. I keep distance from him. The cane seems an extension of his striking promptitude.

A fat woman with hennaed hands and lots of *sindoor* in her hair parting lazily sitting on the grass. She is busy on a video call on her phone. Her face is slightly blotchy but lustrous black hair cover up for that. She has a husky, jeering tone. Given her happy spirits, no gainsaying that the man on the call is fond of her.

Another fatter woman, very short in stature, in fluorescent green top and tight dark leggings and shiny pink shoes. She seems to pursue the rapturous prospect of thinning, slimming rather, and gives an ominous blaze of enthusiasm, bulldozes past me, almost toppling me off the track just by the stormy wind unleashed by her passage. I'm shell-shocked for a moment but then with a benign look wish her many-many rounds and the fat getting melted from her body. But my exemplary, honorable thoughts come to a naught. She barely makes one round, runs out of wind, or maybe finds it silly and boring to rush around like that while better things can be accomplished. She dumps herself on a bench and gets busy with her phone, the best buddy who isn't bothered about her weight. She gives me a brief look of vague hostility as I breeze past with my slim structure. Maybe she is wishing to pump some of her extra fat into my thin frame for betterment at both ends.

Two old women walking briskly. One thin, the other buxom. They waddle determinedly, chests thrust forward. Real mothers who fed milk to many kids. Their copious breasts bouncing on their stomachs.

A few old women sitting resignedly on corner benches. The last time they were singing devotional folksongs. But today the song is missing. In fact one of them is lying on a bench; one sitting with legs drawn up. It gives a sad, resigned look to the group. Their well-worn clothes evincing a hard-fought life in the villages, fighting the abominable reproaches of a patriarchal society, their fate wrung out as much by providence as by the back-breaking household and farming chores. Wriggling to forestall newer and newer tests. Then tiredly shambling after their sons who shifted to the town. Tagging up to bring up their grandchildren and forcing their way into new set of chores to keep them relevant.

Seven or eight high school boys in school dress; boys from poor families, thus going to the highly crippled state schools. Giving a free way to their unguided, precipitous, adolescent energies. They are setting up an infuriating new benchmark for the monkeys in the domain of silly pyrotechnics. Convulsively shouting, jumping, throwing cuss words, hanging from the upper bars of the swings, hurling big pavement tiles at each other with full intention of breaking bones.

An elderly man rushing in with the evident hurrying intention of finishing few quick laps. He has sprinted forward like a deck-based fighter jet on an aircraft carrier. But then screeches to a halt putting power breaks. His big car is parked by the park's gate. He gets unsure whether he unlocked the car or not. There he raises the key remote in its direction, presses the button with owner's pride. 'Qui, Aye, Yes, I'm locked,' the car beeps and blinks. He waddles forward and I exit through the gate, startled by the sudden activity in the car.

Those were almost decrepit establishments, almost filching with moralistic shame. Even the most liberal person would pass by them with a judgmental smirk. There seemed to be something incoherent about it, a kind of ashen-faced entity, almost embarrassed by its very existence. And its clients would seem to be trying to guzzle all their conscience and commiseratively—shoring up courage—approach the prison-like bars on a front defined by stale paint and peeling plaster.

The interior was laden with stifling privation in semi-darkness. Dispirited and caught in miry ruts of social chastisements. The racks inside—cold, plain, blackish shelf-racks—staring icily. A sort of implacable tragedy held up in the musty dim-lit interior. And the shop attendant behind the grills seemed a prisoner, sullen and brooding. But the bottles contained the magic potion of riotous revelry—alcohol.

That's how the wine outlets of the last decade looked in the towns. Almost facile and nauseated. Then the number of drinkers busted the ceiling. The spirit had a temporary puddle to douse the scum of life for a few hours. And with a plum glee (like rain pattering on lush green foliage), the wine merchants prospered. Alcohol and spirits acquired mainstream position to douse the scab and slut of life. The ill-boding, nit-wit image was gone. The cloth wallet changed to fashionable Gucci purse.

The ultra-posh, shiny wine outlets are now making up for all the undemonstrative, ragged past. They glitter like jewelry showrooms with fancy lights and plush interiors. The bottles gleam with naughty assiduity in fancy illustrious displays. No longer the squeamish and morose attendant. It's confident staff behind lovely counters. Of all the trades, alcohol industry has made the loudest mark in terms of change in the shape and look of their outlets. It just shows how much money is now pouring into its coffers.

This is for the history-minded common people who care to know about small things. We trees are highly underpaid and under-appreciated. What's something preposterous is that it's we who have sired the evolution of mankind and now we depend on him for our survival. We are numbered now—from that countless status when mother earth was lush green earlier—and there will be a time when the heritage lobby will be fighting to keep our ruins as a memorial for the past when mother earth was alive. There will be machines all around and the human brain itself will be replaced by artificial intelligence.

I'm a *seemal* (silk cotton) tree standing by the canal-side pathway. It used to be a beautiful thin ribbon of solitude between the canals overgrown with few trees and lots of grass, bushes and reeds. A poetic man would walk in somber profundity on the path. Then the developers hoeing the dirty grind of parasitic business arrived. The sand mafia would arrive at night and scoop away the sand from the canals and the path between them. The chauvinistic pigs would scrape out as much grains of sand as possible to build their big buildings. The earthmover's claws were lucid, pertinent and driven by soulless precision. I'm scared of an earthmover more than anything else. It works with a pure sense of abstraction. Its steely zealousness cuts the upper lateral roots of we trees to dig out more and more sand to fill the truck to the brim. The solitudinal luminosity for the lone poetic man was gone; the grass, reeds and bushes obliterated; the smaller trees fell and bigger ones like me survived the onslaught with bruised limbs and big gaping wounds. The cast and crew of development are too big actors now.

When the poetic man came and saw my big roots exposed and cut, he put a sad but healing hand on my trunk. The edifying notes of his love touched my innermost rings in the trunk. He made a very little effort, this is all he could manage being a poetic man, and sweated for a couple of hours to gather soil around my wounded roots. For me the spiritual symbolism of this love is beyond its physical limits. It feels good to be cared and one's pain acknowledged. But a small group of thugs took away even that little heap of earth this man's poetic hands had gathered around me. I think they did it specifically to make it seem self-mocking to the poet—that your kind of emotions are meaningless in the modern age; that this artistic outlet is nothing more than a speck of dust in the face of the horses of greed on full trot.

Since then I have tried to muster up courage to the extent of granitic endurance just for that poetic man who sometimes comes and puts a friendly hand on my bark. But I missed my flowers this season, the beautiful big red flowers, one of which I had intentionally dropped on his head as he walked under me. That's when we became friends. So there have been no flowers because I have been using all my energies in keeping myself up with the remaining roots. My foliage also has been the same for the last one year. It's pale without any new shoots. I'm still in mourning, you know.

They have cut a little square on my bark, a sort of numbered nameplate declaring my number, a kind of my leasehold to stand on this small portion of earth till they decide to terminate it any time. I sanctify their insinuations and grotesqueness by oozing my sap, my tears, through the square marking. This disquieting incision on my skin keeps reminding me that I'm their numbered property under some forest law that easily allows some thugs to lacerate me.

I have a message for the bloodhound. I let out a yellowish sap through this little square of licensing cut. It coagulates to a meaty sanguine blob. I have obliterated their despicable number that they had assigned me. It's my revolt. I don't agree to their lease contract under whatever forest laws they have. The law that doesn't provide me any protection and leaves me open to be vandalized by any thug whose spirit itches to play truant.

The poetic man sometimes comes and puts his gentle fingers on the protruding sanguine crust oozing from my guts. I see his mournful countenance. This human touch is astonishing. It snaps off the thread of pain for a few moments. How I wish more humans could touch we trees like this! How I wish more humans realize that we are half of their lungs!

Kaka *Maharaj*, the old *sadhak* who stays outside the village, fell out with worldly elements and left his hut—where he was staying for the last two decades—in anger. He had groomed the hut with so much love in solitude. It's a high energy place, one can feel its energy the moment one enters it. I have been trying to convince him to come back because I feel that he ought not to abandon his spiritual seat; it's a cocoon of love for his guru Kude Bhagat.

The other day I went to check the hut and sat for meditation near his fireplace. It was a sad sight to see the place abandoned in one stroke after decades of careful nurturing. The ramshackle thatch door closed. His old, worn out mismatched pair of footwear placed in front. The little grove of trees he has planted, which is a tiny forest now, sighed with sadness; the tiny rows of vegetables lying like orphans without any parental protection. The open fireplace and the heap of dry fuel wood lying like the ruins of a historic site just within a few days of the master gone. I gathered few cheap, dented, blackened aluminum utensils that I found outside and placed them inside the hut, hoping for better days for them.

Sitting by the fireplace inside the hut is like plugging into an electric circuit of high energy. Despite my clear intension to sit still and meditate, I couldn't sit still. Involuntary movements would start the moment I closed my eyes and stilled my body. I just allowed myself to be a witness. It was surprising so I thought of recording them in order to watch as a neutral observer later. The moment I shut my eyes, the rhythmic movements would start of their own. I think the energy meridians try to get into alignment with the energy frequency around me. I suppose that's how the yogic movements were revealed to the mediators. They try to bring the body in alignment with the larger energy meridians. One feels light like air, almost flying. I think the conscious mind takes a backseat during these moments, opening the portal to the subconscious, which further builds up the possibility for entry into the corridors of cosmic consciousness. I think *pranayam* and yoga postures are a means of opening the portal to the subconscious.

In any case, I feel very sad about the fact that he has abandoned such a lovely, peaceful place. I prayed to his guru to bring him back to the hut. I prayed because I feel the decision was taken in anger, and he should come back to resolve this little chaos of negative energy that got unleashed due to those uncontrolled moments. I clearly feel that he has developed a lot of energy at the place, which will help him in his journey.

We have been so well primed for apathy and moral degradation that anything contrary to the above seems off-the-cuff-remark, an inopportune adventure. Mother earth looks imploringly while it gets pestered with more smoke and fire. Uncomely, unsightly behavior. Perilous phantasmagoria. Hideous pomposities. A gnashing, unvarying sarcasm. Smutty, fetid, filthy, unwholesome plot. Avaricious. Putrescence.

Bombs, fire and smoke in the name of nationhood; industrial smoke in the name of inimical, coarse industrialism; more smoke in the name of lisping, detestable festivities; smoke arising with derision from farm fires. Gibberish, egotistic, debased haze. The metallic haze spreading like a colossal giantess. A roguish varnish that eats the colors of evenings. The evening colors melting in subservience.

A sluggard and idle saunterer, I'm walking witnessing this heartrending chastisement of mother nature by Her own child. There is swarming joy in adding more smoke to the poisoned air. The new world leader, Trump, doesn't believe in climate cause. More smoke in the middle east; more bombs and explosions in Ukraine; more smog born of farm fires; more marriage celebration firecrackers gleaming in the maelstrom of smoke.

I'm walking on my solitary trail between the canals holding a crooked staff, a knotted and thorny stick, smoky exhausts hitting my eyes, nose, lungs with suffocating digression. The smoked air impregnated with the smog of hate and apathy. I squint and spot a flock of goats in the smoky distance on the trail. An insurmountable enormity of survival among beaten brambles and bushes.

The goats move slowly nibbling at the beaten grass. The shepherds are two gouty old men bravely holding their crooked baton of life in the gloomy, sooty parody. They are in their seventies, move with a monkish disposition, carrying decades of depositories on their soiled clothes in the form of poverty and low social status.

One is at the front of the herd, the other (still older) manning the back end. There are lots of baby goats and they gallop with childish verve, which seems so mismatching with the two old goatherds. But these little playful ones can't escape on the sides because of the canals. It makes it possible for the old shepherds to manage the herd at this age. The slower their steps, the more time the goats get in nibbling the grass. In between they can take sips of water from the canals on the sides.

The front herder raises his hand in greeting as I approach them. We raise hands exactly at the same moment. I had seen him a year back. He has aged quite significantly since then. His eyesight has further deteriorated. He mistakes me for a farmer who has a little plot of land by the canal. The farmer is a bachelor and stays with his old mother. He was once drinking by the canal and invited them to share drinks. They chatted for a long time once relaxed by the cheap liquor. Such solemn reminiscences! I can feel the traces of appreciation in his eyes for that farmer.

The smoky gaieties have been grafted on the evening colors. It's an early twilight. They are confused about time. They have to walk another kilometer to reach their village. He asks what time it is. 'It's ten minutes to five,' I tell him.

Smoke has advanced the twilight by more than an hour. We know the obvious and ignore the listless fact. Instead he boosts his spirits by an enlivening talk about the farmer with whom they shared drinks. We talk about the economy of goat-herding, the sadness of vanishing grass and their sun-setting life story.

A human touch, acknowledging a fellow life's existence with respect. 'Well, it has been a good time-spending activity at least,' the herder says about their occupation. 'It's an honest, honorable job,' I reply. It brings light to his old feeble eyes.

The older herder doesn't speak much but he smiles a lot, the wrinkles coming to life with wisdom. 'What will we take with us?! It's just greetings and smiles. Who knows whether we meet again or not! So it's better to greet each other with a smile!' he smiles again. My smoked self is relieved. I watch them slowly melting into the metallic haze on the trail. I pray that we meet again even if it's on such a smoggy evening next winter because human life and smiles are precious despite all the hate and anger in the world.

The fog with adulterous traces to turn noxious smog. A chilly mid-November morning. Whom do we call the dimwits? The ones whom we couldn't fraternize for forgery and cheatings required to outsmart others on a routine basis in daily life; who unquestionably can't be turned shrewd like the smart majority; who have a void somewhere wherein the inherent innocence tranquilly stays in a safe chamber. Bc is more or less the same as I remember him during his boyhood. He has grown in body but the child inside is ageless, beyond societal spoliation. He must be carrying some nerves that despoil the spoiling agents'—the agents that ensure the transformation of innocence into shrewdness—best efforts.

Bo is a big man in his early forties. He can smoke as many *beedis* as you can manage to offer him. This is a foggy, smoggy, chilly morning. I see him working on his brain, performing a kind of exercise. He has spread his palms against a wall and hitting his forehead, gently with nice rhythm, against the plaster. He then shifts gears and hits the side of his head, then the other one, followed by the back of the head. Maybe he is shaking his nerves from the spell of irresolution, probably born of hangover caused by country liquor.

Normally he breezes past you with triumphal air without even looking at you even if you greet him with a wide grin and huge bouquet. Sometimes he startles you with '*kya haal hai*' when you are least expecting it. But today after these soft penitent plummets at his head, he seems to have discovered some socializing fibers in his nerves. 'How are you?' he *says*. He doesn't seem to *ask* because 'how I feel' hardly means anything to him in this off-course, uniquely poised state of being. Well all of us have our own peculiarities and eccentricities. He has his own. But I take it as a good omen when he speaks. I'm eager to reply to his statement but he has already moved on before I can send him my first word.

My friend gets diabetic retinopathy treatment at an eye hospital in Dwarka, Delhi. It's a long treatment involving frequent visits to the hospital for routine check-ups and retina injections. On the days when his eye gets an injection, it needs to be patched under a dressing for a few hours, so he isn't able to drive back to the town. On such occasions usually I drive him to the hospital in his car.

He understands that I prefer to use my time in reading and writing. So keeping me away from my study table for a whole day makes him embarrassed sometimes. That shouldn't be a problem at both ends because what else is friendship. If someone can't do even this much then he is a mere acquaintance. And helping someone continue reading the lovely book of life is always better than reading a few more pages in a book.

It's a big, glass-fronted hospital, imposing like a corporate office. Rich people come here for treatment as one can guess from the series of big cars parked in the parking lot.

The other day we reached there early in the morning. He has an early appointment; before the normal opening time. The parking lot has a few cars, the rest of parking slots defined by yellow lines are vacant. There is a big car parked wrongly covering two slots. Many slots are empty on both its sides. I know the value of space—there are fights over parking space in Delhi, which sometimes result in people killing each other—so I'm parking by its side, leaving about three feet space between the cars.

The parking guard is frantically waving hands trying to guide me to park the car within the next slot because by adjusting to the first mistake I'm adding to the series of wrongly parked cars partially occupying their slots and transgressing into the next.

In my opinion lines don't matter as long as there isn't too much or too less space between two cars parked side by side. So I park the car as I deem it fit—partially occupying two slots, in balance with the first mistake, even though there is just three feet space between the two.

As I come out I see a big cloud of disappointment on the guard's face. I tell him that if I park the car in the next slot, it will leave many feet of space between the cars and this space isn't sufficient for any car so it will be a loss of space. The same will be the case on the other side. It means one car will occupy two slots leaving big gaps on both sides.

'I understand but in this way the entire series will be broken,' he points to the rows of yellow lines, 'and they,' he points to the people high up there on the swanky floors above, 'have big issues with it. They say I can't get even the cars parked properly.'

'O come on, it hardly matters… such a small issue,' it casually escapes from my mouth. I try to smile at him and cheer him up but he doesn't smile, instead I can feel utter helplessness blanketing him.

My friend's car is a big one and incidentally I'm wearing formals today. He thinks I'm a *bada admi* with a big business or job. I sense that he is trying hard to take in a big draught of belittling insult; a situation where a better placed person can defy his little authority in his small job space in the parking lot. 'That's how it is! Who cares? Big cars, big people!' he sighs resignedly.

My friend's appointment time is nearing fast. Just a couple of minutes left. And before that the paperwork has to be completed at the reception. So we just rush in leaving him there in a sad mood.

Leaving my friend in the care of doctors, I come out. I see the guard sitting on his chair. A short, very frail man in mid fifties. I flash him a smile. He doesn't smile back. Probably he thinks that I'm mocking at him from my position of a more privileged guy.

Usually I'm in my shabby track pants, rumpled shirts and worn out slippers. When they see me in my small dented car, the parking guards are very confident in handling me and show me the right path as if thinking, 'He isn't a *bada admi*…must be someone almost equal to us.' Here *bada admi* means a rich man only. What other definition a poor man can have? But today the car is big and I'm wearing decent clothes. So he thinks I'm a *bada admi* teasing him after showing him his lowly *aukat*.

I go to him and say, 'Sorry, we were in a hurry! Now we have all the time to do it exactly the way you want it.' He is surprised a bit but gets onto his feet with a nice sense of duty to his job. I feel respect for this man as we walk towards the wrongly parked car to correct things. He is doing his job with dignity and commitment.

This time I follow all his instructions. A parking guard has a nice manner of moving his hands giving you instructions about directions. You have to trust him. His hand movement has confidence now. I park the car exactly the way he wants. And this time when I smile at him he smiles back. Who would withhold your earnings from your smile?

It feels so good to bring a smile to someone. In hurrying I had given him a grimace. Now I'm lucky to bring the smile back. What a dedicated man—parking cars exactly between the lines!

We rarely accept love as the inevitable part of our life. We take it casually and lose it. Result: the old lovers becoming new enemies. A dark, sad cloud of pain settling on one's soul. Then we do what comes naturally to us. We bury the pain to prove a point.

But once you bury the pain sadness settles firmly. Dark, festering subsurface air takes possession of your lungs; soaks your once fresh-aired vitality. In such moments, all we need is to unbury the pain and face its decaying corpse.

There is an art and craft of unburying the pain. Exhumation. To bring light to the maggots eating the rotten corpse. It is about digging a hole, emptying yourself of the rotten flesh. Dig, dig, dig. Unbury the coffin of pain. It's a surgery of the soul to regain the rain, the sunshine, the fresh air, the open sky—the treasure.

You can't add anything to a full vessel. The empty jar has the potential to receive. So dig a hole and exhume the corpse of pain, which would otherwise take decades to decay and still its bones will remain like sharp needles in the flesh of one's soul.

Unbury. Pry it open. Lay it bare under the fresh-aired churning of the surroundings. It'll disintegrate, scatter and spread out; no longer claiming you as the porter, the miserable carrier. It'll break into tiny pieces and the inviting wholeness will absorb it. You—the empty hole—will then be filled with fresh prospects of joy.

8

YOU feel better once you step into a metro train in the national capital—if it isn't too crowded of course. It's a respite from the polluted pestilence outside. You set up a type of narrative privilege if you are lucky to grab a seat. Then beyond the clutches of the outside chaos, the time elapses in peace. Traffic-born hassles seem superfluous. The train moves with sagacity. I have a seat and feeling quite at ease with life despite the smog outside.

Two women board the coach with their children. Both of them carry infants in their arms. A boy and a girl walk alongside. A man immediately gets up to give his seat to the ladies. The ladies settle in the vacant space. The man stands near the boy and the little girl. It's not a casual, principled offer of seat. It's something very human in nature. He is a Hindu bearing a *tilak* on his forehead. They are Muslims.

There is such a huge chasm between the two communities currently; the fissure nurtured for political gains in the communalized air. One can feel these invisible fault-lines at public places even when things look normal with the common people carrying on their routine life. It's a livewire, invisible though most of the time. You can feel its slow pulse in people's looks, gestures and words. But he is a very good man. He allays the tension. He playfully chats with the little boy and the tiny girl. It turns into a very friendly conversation involving common people beyond the wars on religions. The children become relaxed in his presence; their mothers feel comfortable after the initial signs of slight tension.

They deboard a few stations down the line. He gets back his seat—in fact, earned his relaxation time after this kind deed. The boy and the girl look from the window as they walk on the platform. He waves them a bye. They smile. He has given them a priceless memory that will help them in becoming better human beings when they grow up.

Just before the doors would slide shut, a girl rushes from the aisle and drops the crushed cups and bowls in the narrow gap between the platform and the train. Well-aimed, clean drop of garbage by an educated girl. She has been eating with her friend onboard. They are modern girls clad in tight jeans and revealing tops, all decked up with freedom, the freedom to spread litter on a metro station. Look at the contrast: the man groomed a rosebud for humanity and the girls spread litter. Such contrasting characters so nearby! Well, that's what makes metro rides quite interesting.

The state roadways bus is lurching with archetypical languor. There is someone who catches one's eye with conjecturing vivacity. A wrinkled, flabby old man is gawking at the person with open-mouthed, gap-toothed leer. His pinched, shriveled wife watching with repugnance. A skinny, bony adolescent boy is caught in a motley of hormonal storms. He seems curious and seeking answers to the questions that will plague him during this build-up of youth regarding sexuality, gender and more in the domain.

The bus conductor up-heaves his effort; he denounces the melodramatic passenger's denial to pay the bus fare. 'We're entitled to travel free!' the adamant passenger rebuffs in a bristling, vagrant tone. The tone has effulgence to drown the conductor's stern professional pitch. 'No!

You have to take ticket and pay!' the conductor is sticking to his point.

The passenger has the artifice and classical eloquence to catapult the arrows of maidenhood from behind subtle masculine ramparts. The passenger is a handsome-pretty eunuch clad in a yellow and orange shimmering *shrara*. The uncouth notes in the conductor's voice don't appear to be considerate enough to give her a free ride. She strikes her palms accompanied with a little bit of oratorical violence. The gestural escalade fails to perturb and slim down the conductor's rotund demand. He is a Muslim man. She greets him with '*salaam aalekum*' to make some friendly bridge over the torrid flow of his duty. He is unfazed. She again gets into a rebuking tempest. 'I will take off my clothes and turn naked here in the bus!' she threatens. The *kinnars* view this act as the hammer of revolt against all social prejudices against them. 'Do it if you want,' he isn't repulsed by the threat.

Despite all the male-female interpolations and undulations in her persona, there is an imperturbable streak of friendliness in her. She is young, her face an exquisite mix of handsomeness and prettiness. She has hennaed hands; bangles on masculine wrists; lovely, gentle, big eyes under boyish eyebrows; the jaw-line is manly but lips are lovely like a young girl; the hair having feminine elements of style on masculine girth. She turns coquettishly cheeky and cuddles him on the cheek. All this while she looks at other passengers and involves us for a sort of free entertainment. I am sitting across the aisle from her seat. She winks at me after making a mischievous comment.

She is no abashed wretch. She is joyful. Such setbacks—like the conductor insisting on taking the bus fare—are easily taken in a playful stride. After all, one has to trample such tiny heartburns to survive in a world structured on male-female binary; where all possibilities of love, profession, education and social standing are customized in the routine gender duality. It's a calamitous contingency to have an off-beat gender. The mainstream society takes them to be foredoomed from the beginning. They have to claw their way into the main thoroughfare to survive.

She won't allow him the entire way. 'I'll give only hundred rupees,' she relents, calculating the conductor's defensive portals. The fare is 120 rupees. 'Twenty rupees on you *raja*,' she teases him. She gives him 100 rupees. While he is making her ticket, she looks back at the passengers, makes a face and says, 'I'm his wife. See, how unkind he is to me.' The passengers laugh. She feels the malignant notes in the old woman, the wife of the oldie who has been leering at her with drool in his mouth. '*Radhe-radhe mataji*!' she greets her. The old woman can barely shake her head in greeting back.

She has already won many hearts with her banter and friendliness. 'O *raja*, I'll reimburse the loss within no time,' she defiantly says to the bus conductor and sets out on making up for the loss. I give her ten rupees and she affectionately pats my cheek because I have been nodding and laughing in support of her. She collects 80 rupees within two minutes from the moving bus. 'Lost just 20 rupees,' she says almost triumphantly. She goes to the conductor and asks his share of donation. He angrily shakes his head in a firm no. She pats his cheek. The passengers laugh.

She has two smartphones. Her Instagram account is full of her luscious photos and vibrant musical videos. She plays them for the young man by her side to watch. Then turns back to show them to me. 'You look like a heroine,' I compliment. 'I was in Bombay for three years,' she says with nostalgia. Photos and videos in sunshades, strappy bras, revealing tops, sexy leggings. She opens the keypad of her phone and moves it to me, asking me to dial my number. She has mistaken my support for her cause as my interest in off-beat sexuality. I look at her with a *straight* face and then smile and gently say no with respect. She understands that my interest in her is born of respect, curiosity and sympathy and not sexuality. And then she smiles a normal smile.

All life-forms on earth are seeking a home; a safe and cozy home that makes you feel at ease; where you can drop your guard, rest, recuperate and rejuvenate. I *feel* that our garden houses nests of tailorbirds, oriental white-eyes, doves, silverbills, squirrels and flycatchers. They, on their part, *feel* that their nest houses our home. That's why they raise such a ruckus when we humans happen to be near their nests. So basically, the feeling of ownership is a matter of perception only.

Most of the garden lizards have their houses among the leaves of flowers, shrubs and trees. They make their skin dull colored and sprawl on sunlit leaves, just like we humans warm our bones on sunlit terraces in winter. But one garden lizard has a unique house. A multi-paneled window faces the garden; its lower portion flanked by *tulsi* plants and above looms the clustered canopy of *champa*, *chandni*, *parijat*, guava and *kari patta*. The window shutters stay closed from the other side behind the iron grills. There is a narrow slab projecting over the window. On the upper end there is an abandoned potter-wasp's mud house sticking to the grill. And here the garden lizard has made its home. An abandoned house turning into a home; the little shelter possessed so warmly by a cold-blooded little reptile.

It seems a stoic lizard. At noontime, for an hour and a half, sunrays engulf its house in their warm, embracing fluidity. The house owner sprawls in peace. It puts its chin on top of the oblong mud shelter, closes eyes and soaks as much warmth as possible to beat the December chill. At night it sneaks into the little space between the mud nest and the wood of the closed window, a space just enough to hide its main body. Its tail is visible from outside curled around the mud nest. I have seen it occupying its property for the past many weeks. I usually go and tease it, standing just a couple of feet away, peering into its eyes. It's a shy one and closes its eyes to the uninvited guest.

It looks a very stable and contended guy: the same look, the same routine, the same acceptance of the uncontrollable factors of life. The stable chap doesn't experiment much with life, which is a prudent thing to do for a reptile in the winters. Possibly it's an introvert one and is happy in its little world, just comfortable to be what it is. I wish him good hibernation during the winters. Best of luck garden lizard! Given your stoic patience, the three winter months seem a cakewalk. Then one fine day lovely spring will arrive. You will then come out, get colors on your skin taking inspiration from the blooming flowers. You will then reclaim that much of life, which you missed in the winters. There would be colors, love, food, hunting, escaping, getting hunted, or call it flirtations with life and death. That will all come with the spring. Happy hibernation until then!

I do a little exercise. When I'm not on my writing desk, I usually write on little scraps of paper like bills, receipts, pamphlets and flyers. Just random thoughts. Later these develop into some piece of poetry, a passage or an article. Then I take the little scrawled upon slips, put them in a tiny heap and burn. It gives a strange feeling; something that bloomed, came into existence, served a purpose and turns to ashes. It's like a holy ritual to me—a tiny replica of the dance of life and death, being and nonbeing. When the tiny pyre burns, the ash eating the words, I hum the beautiful Hindi film song '*khilte hain gul yahaan*', whose translation comes to be: the flowers bloom here to be happily scattered to pieces.

If you find yourself praying for someone, take my word you are doing well my friend. This lovely urge to pray for others is a sign of divinity itself. Don't hold any doubts about its effect. It's effective and one need not find any proof of its effects. The mere reason that one does it is a proof of its effect. You need no validation by others in the form of effect or result. The mere fact that you do it is sufficient. And your prayers always have a positive effect in subtle dimensions, irrespective of whether you know these or not because such beautiful fine-tuning of positive vibrations will have its positive effect. It's simple cause and effect, simple science.

Further, we can avoid comparing the extent and reach of our prayers. All prayers are lofty. They are equal. They are beyond the physical structures that can be compared. Whispering prayers for someone in the lovely chamber of your kind heart is a great spiritual exercise.

The liberal, mystic scent of Sufism was buried in an unknown grave. So was the fate of a Sufi *shahjada*, Dara Shikhon, who lies buried in an unidentified grave in Humayun tomb complex situated in Delhi.

Humayun's tomb was built by his wife Hamida Bano Begum. I like this emperor because he died in his library, not a bloodied battlefield. And his mausoleum is a beautiful precursor to the great Taj Mahal. The grand beauty of Taj Mahal doesn't stand in abstract and doesn't sprout on its own. This modestly grand tomb is the inspiration behind the majestic Taj. You can say it's Taj Mahal in infancy.

Made mostly of red sand stone, with thin marble inlays, it contains many structures (containing about 150 graves in 60 chambers) within the sprawling complex. It's a mosaic of architectural styles blending Rajput and Iranian styles such as *jharokhe* (windows), projections of the entrance, arches having elephant trunks and circular medallions. Interestingly, there is a structure named Bu Halima, probably named after a famous Arab dancer.

Had Dara Shikhon, the Sufi *shahjada*, become the emperor of India, he would have been a great Sufi, philosopher and king combined in the rarest of a rare personality blend. To understand the Upanishads and translate them in Persian one has to be the master of soul as well as languages. I'm mesmerized looking at his massive commentary on the Upanishads displayed at the museum. This is something phenomenal; simply out of this world.

His life is a testament to the fact that it's possible to be 'a prince with esteemed spiritual values'. A unique royal personality, he tried to walk on the unorthodox bridge between the royal palace and the Sufi *khanqah*. He possessed keen interest in Hindu thought and philosophy and in pursuit of that interest he commissioned translation of many Hindu sacred texts into Persian.

A prolific writer he chronicled the life of 400 Sufi saints in his work *Sufinat-ul-Aulia*. In another work named *Risala-i-Haq Nama* he sets up a treatise on the path to the divine. In *Hasanat-ul-Arifin* he delves into Hindu thought through Ramayana and Krishna stories. Most importantly, his translation of Upanishads into Persian shows the depth of his soul and vastness of his mind. The beloved prince of the masses believed that Sufis and Hindus share the essential core of mystical truth.

Had he become the emperor of India, it would have been a different India altogether. But he was killed by his Islamic zealot brother Aurangzeb who ruled with sword on hardcore communal Islamic principles. The latter left enough communal mud for the current Hindu nationalists to wallow in it for political gains. The voice of sanity and secularism lies buried in one of the dozens of graves in the Humayun tomb complex, unrecognized, unsung.

Auragzeb was very punitive towards his secular brother. He buried him in an unknown grave. The historians haven't so far been able to recognize the Sufi prince's cenotaph. I think his grave should be discovered and a separate memorial should be built in memory of this great philosopher prince whose life symbolizes our composite culture.

The impressive museum on the tomb premises gives a nostalgic peek into the poets who scented the society with their sweet emotions about eight centuries back. It's an overpowering feeling to look at their works at the museum. The great poet Amir Khusro's works displayed at the museum whisper to you, conveying the message of love and peace.

Amir Khusro's *Shirin-o-Khusro* (1298-1301) deals with the tragic love story of Emperor Khusro and Armenian princess Shirin. It's a grand feeling to look at a copy at the museum. The ancient book decorated with gold borders in *nastaliq* calligraphy by a master calligrapher and containing many illustrations by a master painter.

Imagine Rumi's 25,000 couplets drenched with universality of love and compassion. That was the time when Sufism, the jewel in the crown of Islam, was at its peak. Sufism that stood for the unity of faith across various religions; Sufism that was liberal; Sufism that was mystical Islam's loveliest prayer to the Almighty. Unfortunately Sufism too was buried in an unknown grave like Prince Dara by the hardcore, fundamentalist followers of Islam. It would have been a different world had Sufism become the public face of Islam.

Do you know the significance of a solitary trail? All of us have a solitary trail, our very own secluded path where we are face-to-face with ourselves. Where the small worldly self walks with the larger Self. Where each step is a quantum jump in evolution. Where the destination doesn't hark you, rather you become your own destination. You inhale wellness, you spread your wings, you float. Where you get a causeless smile. This trail is available wherever you are situated, even in densely populated cities. You just need to feel it and then follow its alluring call. Seek your solitary trail, own it, stamp your love on it. Then walk in solitary leisure and divine pleasure.

Fight for a kingdom and be a king. That's your 'right' beyond the debate of moralistic right or wrong. But remember kingdoms have their consequences. It's very natural for the kings to be killed by their own sons. Just a natural consequence. You hand over the lust for unrestricted power to your son. He will be a worthy inheritor of your legacy and would dethrone you on the chessboard of power when he comes of age.

In the same vein, if you have been lucky to have official powers and privileges—for which you get paid and are expected to do your service strictly as per the contract— you will sometimes get an itch to set-up a mini-kingdom by going out of your domain and misuse your power and privileges for unjustified gains. That of course is also your right. But remember your son will inherit the same mini-kingdom of misuse of your privileges beyond your official domain. He will dethrone you when his time comes. He will also kill you to occupy the little throne that you have set up by inflicting injustice through the misuse of your powers and capabilities. He may not slit your throat directly but will definitely do it indirectly. He won't respect you, he would be undisciplined and you will see your little kingdom falling apart under his erratic lifestyle. That is as good as a son killing his father. Again it's not about right or wrong. Simply cause and effect.

The more you 'make' as an angry, arrogant and violent person, the more you expose yourself to be 'broken' by the bigger forces of similar nature. And the rot begins at home, remember this. Again, simple cause and effect. Nature doesn't operate on moralistic principles. It's only about what you are doing at what frequency. Life will give you back a hundredfold of exactly what you are investing in the same currency. If it's arrogance, ego and greed that propels you, the trajectory of your life will be defined by the same factors. Keep fighting. When will you ever stop? And if petty, tyrannical fights of this nature make you feel like a soldier, it's a nice cover for the demons inside to be decorated with honorable military dress.

If you see yourself in this write-up and get angry then I'm sorry. As a writer, I just hold a mirror in front of the reader. What you see in that is your own making, your own labor. If you don't like the image that stares back at you, change it. If not, keep the angry fight till your last breath. You may achieve anything but not peace.

Tibetan Buddhism is one of the most pristinely preserved belief systems. There was a time when every Tibetan family had a full monk or nun devoted to keep the lineage going. Tibet had more monks than soldiers. Imagine the spiritual depth of this vast land during those times. Then tragedy struck. Atheist China put a big challenge for the Tibetans to preserve their unique culture and religion. Scattered over different countries in tiny communities, Tibetans still hold onto their faith with devotional perseverance.

I know a few lovely Tibetan Buddhist *sadhaks*, one of them a deeply, spiritually imbued woman *sadhak*. She is a good friend. She was out of radar for the last three years and I was worried about her. But the other day it came as a relief to know that she was fine. She was in a remote cave in a totally uninhabited part of Ladakh. Faith makes you quite daring on the path and pushed by the same force she carried her basic provisions on six pack horses and trekked for one full day to reach a remote cave. She meditated here for three years in complete isolation.

I am amazed at the spiritual passion of the Tibetan Buddhists to maintain their legacy. It's a vast domain of esoteric, mystical practices. I myself don't believe in extreme austerity on the path of religion and feel comfortable with Buddha's middle path, but I respect such honest seeking by someone on the path of realizing the true Self.

She is back to her east Asian country at the moment and sends me a mesmerizing collection of pictures. The pictures from her spiritual hideout somewhere in Zanskar, Ladakh are unbelievably grand, almost mythically exciting.

It was a little cave-cum-room away from a remote hamlet in Zanskar, beyond the glutinous knick-knacks of crowded worldliness; in unmoored, unfettered, uncontrolled, untouched, unmoved, untrammeled barren hills; among stones and a few wild streams. Using her woman's skills to mold her surroundings in the colors of her aesthetic sense, she covered the tiny hovel with colorful Buddhist murals, cloth paintings and carpets covering the entire walls. And there trying to come out of the zigzag course of follies, she—surrounded by the colorful syrupy souvenirs of faith—sits down to meditate to realize the straight, simple path to wisdom.

Emptiness here is clearly defined by miles of barren brown canvas, pristine blue of the sky, pure white of the clouds, a rippling stream in the gorge down the slope and howling mountain gales. Here she would look into the distances, witnessing the nature's avatar as a serrated knife on the one end and a wisp of wool on the other. As she sat exploring the miles of emptiness in her heart, the cutting mountain wind went harping on the sturdiest stones and the clouds melted in the pristine blue.

In winter she would sit down under the falling snow on the frozen banks of the once gurgling stream. The rushing blue liquid in a thin line between the frozen banks. Her maroon great cape cradling her physical body while the soul kissed the snows on the slopes around.

Mother nature slowly filled its few colors on the almost empty canvas. Brown fire on sunlit slopes. Blue snows on the shadowed slopes. Massive boulders beaten and shaped by the wind stood like ferocious demonic sentries protecting her isolated haunt. The sentinels of this isolation singing with the mountain winds. A leafless bush standing like a torn banner of summers; but still holding up the hopes for a revival. The subdued murmur of the thin stream between frozen banks carrying the prayers alive to burst forth with the songs of summer some day.

Her neighbor would be a tiny sparrow peeping with curiosity from the makeshift window sill, wonderstruck at the tiny cocoon of colors inside.

She would muse over a rainbow above the chocolate brown hills against dark grey clouds, its arc vanishing into the clouds suspended like hanging waterfalls of wool. Then the summer would have sparse grass and wild little flowers. She would hold a flower and muse over the irresistible force that life is always fighting to come out of snows and stones; the iron will of a little seed to stay under the snows and burst forth with joy as the summer sun melted the snow sheets.

She would peek into the sky where the little fluffs of clouds floated in a mauve sea of tranquility. And all this would again transform into iciness, all cloaked in thick snows, just a few very steep snowless slopes visible. A perfect sun beating on a blinding blizzard of white. The sky flawlessly dark blue, not a speck of cloud. With the warmth of her faith cloaked in her maroon woolen cape she would sit to meditate on the snow. A drop of pious blood of life on the white icy face of death.

A few fluffy sparrows would sit meditatively with eyes closed on the little grain bowl. The snowy desolation making it feel remoter; the deep blue of the sky condensing the mystery even further, but drawing it still nearer to the soul. The strings of prayer flags hanging languidly with their sagged but discernible multiple colors: an effort of putting meaningful colors among the binary of white and blue prevailing around.

A flock of dozens of pigeons busy in searching among the partially visible dead grass on the frozen slope below her window, picking the grains of life, to fly, to play. Like an excited girl, catching to some innocent strand of harmless fun that she had in childhood, to see their fluttering flight in a flock, to play like a girl, to feel the excitement of the flight of the pigeons, she would move the creaking window. A lovely little prank with the birds in that snowy wilderness. And they would lift with a flutter and swoop down the valley.

Her only neighbors the birds playing on the snow-beaten dry grass, chirping to keep warm, grabbing some grass seed, some wisp of food for preserving life in this cold desert. Sometimes she saw flocks of gorals, the muscled, nimble essence of what the barren stones have to offer in the form of the beaten grass.

Then one day right in the middle of meditation two policeman arrived bearing a letter signed by the Senior

Superintendent of Police-cum-FRO, district Kargil, copied to the SHO police station Zanskar. It accused her of illegally overstaying at Shadey village (for this was the nearest village) in Zanskar after the expiry of e-visa which had been extended by one year after the expiry of the initial one. The extension visa had expired six months ago. In her innocence she had even forgotten that boundaries existed in this divided world. She thought they would just forget her. So she hadn't applied for further extension. The notice directed her to leave the country within ten days.

The policemen said, 'Please leave India because your visa expired long ago.' They were gentle people, didn't scare her, so she served them tea and thought maybe she could mollify them. She replied, 'I'm not going because I'm just meditating here and playing with animals. I am not meeting anyone, not doing anything bad against India.' They laughed at her elementary schoolgirl's pure innocence. How she wished there were no borders!

With a heavy heart she had to say a goodbye to the lovely pink colors of a dawn peeping over the dark brown hills as the day arrived.

I had been sending her one-liner messages to know any update about her on Facebook and WhatsApp for the last three years. No response. The messages stood undelivered. Then she surfaced.

'Hello, it's me. I just finished a three year retreat in the mountains, everything is fine! Don't worry! I will keep in touch with you,' she assures me about her safety.

'I'm glad mother existence gave you these golden hours of silence and seclusion. Let your path be showered with sunshine of awareness,' I'm relieved that this nice woman, who reads my books and whom I met at Majnu Ka Tila Tibetan colony in Delhi over Tibetan tea and *tsampa* bread, is safe and well on her path to self realization.

'I wanted to do a retreat for three years but now my visa is expired, so I have come back to Hanoi. So many wonderful experiences. I will tell you later. Now I am taking another five months of meditation and practicing speaking again. I have not spoken for almost three years now. Sometimes I will. Will send messages to you,' she wrote.

She seemed to be gingerly tottering back to the worldly clatter after that near perfect peace in the Himalayas. We had a deep exchange of messages over the coming week, I as a curious seeker and she as someone who is already at a very stable frequency.

'You were in India all this time?! Vow... I was in Ladakh for two weeks this summer. Had I known I would have come to meet you,' I'm excited like a child.

'It would have been very difficult for you to access my hideout. I had to use six horses to carry my things and walk for a day to reach my hideout,' she is very excited about this feat of isolating herself in an alien environment.

'Are you into secret *tantrik* mystical Tibetan Buddhist practices?' I ask because I feel that maybe she is into something very esoteric in nature.

'I can't tell you all. But I'm back home. The Indian police moved me, asking me to leave India immediately because my visa expired six months ago,' I can feel traces of sadness in her messages. Why do the borders exist for such sincere mediators, I wonder.

'Kindly share the wonderful experiences when you have time. I can try writing on these,' I request.

'It is difficult to talk about my experiences during my days of retreat in the Himalayas. My mind was completely empty and there was only a gentle joy in enjoying everything around me. If you want to write something about it you must send me a list of your questions, because I do not know where to start and cannot describe to you my nameless joy. My meditation hours were always consecutive but did not put pressure on me. I did not use language but communicated by communion with the environment and the animals. Silence for me did not become heavy but a sweet absorption of stillness. I communed with the sound of the wind, of the river and the birds, the howling of wolves when the snow came. Each and every sound went straight to my heart and was very gentle. I can talk about my feelings all day long but for you to write it down you have to give me your list of questions, because I cannot tell you my experience in solid bullet points. I can only tell you that peace in emptiness always takes over me,' her soul feels satiated with joy. I can feel this in each of her words.

I take closer looks at the pictures sent by her. It's simply incredible. Even in virtual two dimensions they speak countless volumes about some mammoth dimension redolent with unbound peace and joy.

'This is paradise… a spiritual charging port for the willing person who is aware of this openness… beautiful… thanks a ton for sharing… I enjoyed watching these… So is it like charging the self, like we charge the batteries? But the batteries get discharged, so we get them plugged again for charging? So does your *self* also crave for charging after spending time in the city and hence you seek solitude again? It's a lovely craving if it's so…but how is it fundamentally different from other common cravings of the common people like me? Craving seems to be craving, even though it seems a holy one, but isn't it still a need?

'Do you expect to reach a stage where you feel the same serenity and peace which you feel in Zanskar in Hanoi itself? I mean an awareness when one is at peace even in outside chaos… like a steady lamp even among winds,' my logical mind is full of questions.

'Any mystical experience? I mean that would give some logical validation to the skeptics? Did you have any experience with entities and disembodied beings?' my questions are endless.

The vacuum that she created in solitude is now spontaneously getting filled with explanatory words. This is very surprising because she has been very reserved during our interactions and hardly speaks during meetings, just silently listens to you. But now she has many words.

'Yes, I agree with you that true peace is when you are as comfortable in the middle of the market as you are in the mountains. Your emotions and awareness are not affected or get changed. But you also know that this is really difficult if you have not experienced true peace, and to achieve this you need to change your familiar living environment to clearly see how your mind and body work and how you recognize the entanglements from your mind. Being addicted to something cannot achieve true bliss. Sometimes you have to separate yourself from your familiar environment and experience different things.

'I am not saying that living in the mountains will give you enlightenment or a super wisdom but I am saying that your experience with different living environments is important because only then you can separate yourself and observe how your mind works.

'For me living alone in the mountains is not a challenge but a gift, I do not need to make any effort and when I return to the city I will have objective experiences when observing life in the city.

'I want to experience contrasting ways of living so that I can observe how my mind works. That is my purpose when I withdraw from society and live fully with nature. Then I return to society and test myself.'

She is very clear about this lovely urge to merge with solitude on her solitary trail.

'I can experience the mystical even when I live in the cities. It happens to me all the time, but living in the Himalayan environment and practicing silence there, it is always magical. I easily communicate with invisible beings and *dakinis* or angels. I can communicate with them mentally or I can see their manifestations through their transparent bodies. I can hear their music and smell their mystical scents. In short, I communicate with them as sentient beings with bodies. When I sing prayer songs in the mountains, sometimes they join me and sometimes I dance with them on the snow.

'To others it may seem miraculous but to me it is normal communication. When you open your heart and immerse yourself in bliss you can easily feel the joy or suffering of all beings in other realms.

'When you live in the mountains this is a great place for you to penetrate and communicate without words. This communication is completely different from verbal communication. You can easily understand every animal, every invisible being who wants to communicate with you and you can talk to them by opening your mind and heart to them. They will easily understand you.'

She expresses it beautifully. Yes, one's experience is beyond words because words are fragments and are limited to our interpretation. But when we tell others, we are bound by words to convey what one has felt. But I have a questioning mind and I'm seeking answers on the plane where I have perceived things myself. She is talking of a different plane but she is graceful enough to try to make a bridge so that she can convey a portion of what she experienced there.

I'm trying to interpret her experience in my dimension, 'You are right about the significance of exposing the self to different environments. It definitely enlarges the perspectives, gives additional dimensions of awareness and perception. So you mean basically it's about exploring the mind, its ways, its patterns and impulsive structure. But can't the mind *mind* its own business? The entire body is mind, each cell has memory and function and millions of spontaneous actions keep going without our conscious effort. So why should we *mind* the mind so much? Every thought, emotion, pattern, feeling, fluctuation is inherently part of the over-all cosmic pool of cosmic intelligence. So why should we just filter out a particular state to be better than the others, when mother existence is willing and ready to have the so-called worldly elements in its *leela*? You mean we *mind* the mind to that extent that we go beyond the patterns of impulsive thoughts and random changes in our feelings?

'A very strong mind can manifest its beliefs. They say at the quantum level, there is no abstract reality without the observer. And the observed and the observer are interlinked. Tibetan Buddhism has concepts of *dakinis* and with conscious effort you manifest that reality. Maybe in that very pristine environment some Muslim or some tribal shaman from Africa or a Hindu devotee will manifest their deities and entities mentioned in their faith. Have you ever seen anything which is absolutely not related in shape or feeling to the *dakinis* mentioned in Tibetan Buddhism? Do they have strong likes and dislikes?

'In India there is this story of Ramakrishna Paramhansa and Swami Totapuri. It tells to what extent Ramakrishna had taken his faith. He had taken it to the extent of seeing mother Kali alive in the idol at the temple where he stayed. He worshipped mother Kali, a prominent Hindu deity. And he was stuck up with that beautiful mind construct, the image of Ma Kali. He needed to be convinced to stop manifesting this reality at the quantum level—the observed is always related to the observer. Swami Totapuri could feel that Ramakrishna is stuck up in the holy chains of his mind construct (attachment to the deity) and needs to be set free. Using the same mental construct, he guided Ramakrishna to behead that image. Mother wanted him to grow beyond Her image. To become mature, to grow into a highly spiritual man, a true son of the divine mother. Dense perception, dense concept, dense focus create a too solid image. It also somehow restricts one's flow. In infinity there is no final limit. All remains to be known even despite knowing all.'

I have my counter logic inspired by what the quantum physicists say about the ultimate nature of reality.

Logic is insatiable. No point was ever proved by the sword of logic. Ever. Because each and every logic has a counter logic. But sweet is the addiction to logic, the bane of modern man, so I'm still on my logical fusillade, 'Those who know that they don't know and can't know all despite being seen to know very much, will say there is nothing miraculous. What we take as miraculous is a simple cause and effect in its own dimension, just that we don't understand and feel it. In its own field, the apparent miracle stands like a normal existence of a flower in my domain of existence. So I very much believe in your lived reality. It's a cosmic soup, infinitely layered with potential for self-manifestation of its *self* through various means, for example through a gentle, highly aware peaceful being. And that includes you as well. So I don't have any doubt about it. Yes, I might have a vague feel of it myself—the words of the wordless, the language of silence. Everything manifests in the womb of nothingness. This is what I felt in Ladakh myself.

'In moderate climate you have luxuriant manifestation of life forms. But there is emptiness and sheer sense of nothingness in harsh Ladakh climate. No tree, just stones, open skies, distances redolent with the possibility for the emptiness to unfold miles after miles. As you move towards Ladakh, you are moving from dense manmade manifestations in the cities to naturally produced forests in middle Himalayas to the lofty barrenness in high Himalayas... from collective pool of struggling frequencies, we are moving to more harmonized layers of energies. No wonder, we feel relaxed in open forests. Here, mother earth is responding to favorable weather elements, trees, meadows, grass. It's more evolved type of manifestation than the cluttered cities, but it's still manifestation... under the burden of *being* so... in trees you have the game of life, natural noise, romantic and poetic... but still there is some heaviness, simply because there is a struggle for survival in this manifestation.

'In Ladakh, on the other hand, it is almost empty. It feels like we are moving from the manifest to the unmanifest in that pure, lucid stony high-altitude desert. One feels even more relaxed and peaceful… it's beyond the game of manifestation… just open iciness… the open forces of nature, unbridled, untouched by competing frequencies… a still picture… the frozen moments of just *being* so… so near to the unmanifest on the roof of the world. There have been so many *sadhus* and *sadhaks* who could feel the joy of just being so.'

She knows the value of silence. A logical talk about what can only be conveyed through a wordless smile can only be met with silence—a nice, courteous full stop. She doesn't reply.

I acknowledge it, 'Your "silence" is the best answer to a "chatterbox" like me. Words can never give answers. Mere pointers they are. But yes, by being relaxed and at peace one adds to the beauty around. A peaceful mind is like a honey drop in this bitter world. Lighted be your path to peace and joy!'

Now she knows that laughter is the best answer in this situation, 'Haa haa.' I visualize her laughing; her lovely, narrow eyes closing with childish mirth. 'Don't worry, I'm just a little busy and I'll reply to everything for a talkative person like you.'

A spiritual person can easily laugh off such minor irritants like talkative persons. I'm amused that *silence* here was *work*, 'If you have the time to waste then most welcome because the more I speak and write, the more I know how irrelevant and illusionary all this is.'

I find typing too limited to carry on with such a profound discussion, so I propose why not we talk on the issue.

'I really have difficulty listening and speaking after three years in silence and solitude, so please write to me what you want to say,' she is comfortable with typing.

'It has been a long time since I spoke and heard human voices. Yup, everything written and spoken is a product of the mind and being a product of the mind it is an illusionary thing.

'When I write down my feelings to send to you and then I read them again, I still feel like I haven't said anything, what I want to convey to you is still far away.

'You asked me "but can't the mind *mind* its own business? The entire body is mind, each cell has memory and function and millions of spontaneous actions keep going without our conscious effort." Yes, the mind is not capable of doing that, because the nature of the mind is always fluctuating and uncertain. It cannot take care of the peace of each of us, but it is only an expert in creating fake problems and dragging us into them, so recognizing and observing the mind is extremely important for each practitioner.

'The mind cannot be spontaneous, only emotions from our heart or from our body can be spontaneous.

'The mind operates from our conditioning of knowledge and it habitually dominates all our perceptions and gives us the illusion that we perceive from our own spontaneity.

'The intelligent universe is not present in the mind but in the cells that make up our body.

'Buddhism has the concept that the mind is the greatest obstacle that every practitioner must face and recognize his mind and not identify himself with the mind. If we are not controlled by the mind, no practice will be needed and religion is unnecessary. As you know, in primitive societies when people were innocent and lived naturally with themselves and there were no laws to control people, religion was unnecessary.

'It is very important that practitioners today are always interested in methods to recognize and control the mind because we have lost our innocence and we have overvalued knowledge over real life experience.

'The masters have spoken a truth: outside of the mind there is no Buddha, god or devil. Our mind creates heaven and creates hell.

'So if you are a Buddhist then the visualizations like *dakinis* will correspond to your Buddhist perception and if you are a Hindu then your mind will always have images or symbols of Krishna, Mahakali. There is no fixed or standard religious or demonic image, all images will appear corresponding to your mind.

'There are so many religions in the world today because we have so many different types of minds.

'You asked "have you ever seen anything which is absolutely not related in shape or feeling to *dakinis* mentioned in Tibetan Buddhism? Do they have strong likes and dislikes?"

'This is impossible because you can only see them through your mind, if any form is outside your trained mind you cannot see it. So when I tell you that I communicate with invisible entities like *dakinis*, they all come from my Buddhist mind.

'Now I've said it, any questions you have I will continue to answer until eternity.'

Words are the limited waves that temporarily surface on the ultimate sea of realization of the truth. She is very confident of creating more waves to make me feel the uselessness of wordy waves in getting profound answers.

'You have problem in talking and listening. I have mine of typing because I am typing on my laptop most of the time and feel saturated with typing. All of us have our comfort zones. But yes that's how one feels when ego melts and one feels like a small medium for the expression of a few things,' a person with theoretical knowledge of the experiential matters is a very irritating rival in a spiritual discussion.

Since she has given me a free hand in wordy discussion by saying that she is willing to talk till eternity to answer my questions I carry on with my queries.

'What exactly is the mind? The concept of mind itself is our creation and what we have created can't be an entity in abstract from our biological operation. Mind is a very vague concept, a wonderful creation of our brain operation. To me mind is the entire body. And what matters is a balanced body functioning. This in turn will create a balanced output at the operational level and for convenience we can say it is to have a balanced mind,' I ask the question and give my answer for the same.

She answers, 'In my experience there is never a balanced mind, we can only have a balance between mind and body. Mind can never be the whole body. Mind is a big illusion of ours, it does not really exist, it is a creation of the karma accumulated from our body. Mind exists because body exists, when you lose this body the mind also disappears. Our whole world is created by mind, that is why the masters say that the world is Maya.'

The subject of mind has always been very significant for me, so my counter comes readily.

'Whatever you have written about mind arises from an assumption of mind as an abstract entity, something having a separate dimension from the body. It isn't. The concept of mind is merely a total summary for the way our biological systems operate in entirety. This extreme focus on mind is the root cause of all the problems. Why give it that much importance to erect an entire system of theology, religion and meditation practices? Why not accept one's reality at the natural level without the concept of mind? An existence in totality, like the rest of the species.

'First we create an entire mountain of the complexity of mind, give it a name, assign it a problematic domain and then we set out to cut it down. It's very easy to live at ease, in totality, in the moment without giving too much attention to this concept of mind. I don't look at myself as a mind struggling with the rest of me. It's just me, pure me—my flesh, my energy, my thoughts, my feelings. I don't segregate and first visualize a mammoth entity like mind that's putting hurdles in my evolution or enlightenment. I see myself as something very normal, an animal like a cat or dog, weak in my areas and strong in some zones. Simple. And the more balanced is the body operation, one need not get haunted by the ghost of mind.

'Sorry I don't agree. There is no separate zone between mind and body. I accept them as one. Then one need not fight for balance.

'You say "mind exists because body exists." Yes this is what I mean. Mind is a human-devised concept to indicate the operational output of our biological systems.'

My kind and loving mediator friend now realizes the futility of words and also that one cannot answer till *eternity* to curious, argumentative people like me. I feel she is irritated a bit and feel sorry for triggering this unorthodox reaction in her.

'The difficulty is that you have never had an experience outside of your mind and you are talking to me from your mind, this will be very difficult for me to explain to you clearly,' she is coming near to accepting the futility of taking about mind, the ways to dismantle it using the mind itself.

But the whirlpools of conceptual mind have taken me in. I'm rather fighting my own battle with the concept of mind, 'Why create a false enemy first and then create a huge system of religion to defeat the enemy. To me there is no adversary mind to tame it and balance it with body. To me it's merely a thought, a thought about mind, a mere output of my biological existence.

'I have had my own experiences of the so-called mystical things but I don't overvalue these and leave them as something that's not yet comprehensible to me at this stage. I think you too are merely talking from mind because you are just centered around the concept of mind'

She seems to *mind* the talk of no-mind through the concept of mind, 'Yes, you said "is no adversary mind to tame it and balance it with body... to me it's merely a thought." So what are all your questions for? What are all those books you've written for?'

She has a point here. I try to revalidate my position, 'Mind is a beautiful thought but still just creation of our operational system at the levels of body and energies. It's very easy to say to someone that you have never experienced anything beyond mind but I can say the same to someone that you haven't experienced God, so you won't understand.'

'Yes. This is the destination where we use our minds to talk to each other, when we use our minds to talk or argue we can only go to this destination,' she seems resigned to the futility of discussion about the mind.

Nonetheless I clarify my point, 'I'm not asking you questions to understand mind. I just asked about your experiences as a fellow seeker. It's you who said you will talk through questions and answers format. I just wanted to ask about your experiences like I would ask another friend who went to Thailand and I would say how was it. Just that. I didn't mean to experience more about the mind or God through questions. It was your interpretation. I am just about experiences. And all the books that I have written aren't meant to seek some meaning of the ultimate truth. They are written as a form of wonder, curiosity, acceptance of this game of life, in its entirety... just an expression... without any purpose... simple. It feels good to be in wonderment and trying to express my small view about this endless game.

'I flow with life. I am not erecting check dams of mind to tame it and divert the flow to take myself to divinity. I accept the present, the way it's... in totality. And when I feel totality, there is no mind, no body... just being so. That's why I don't find them contradictory in nature to be battled out for balancing them. We have to fight to balance them because we ourselves have conceptually set them as adversarial entities. To me they are one and I don't find myself wedged between body and mind. I just feel the way it's, something that's just me beyond body and mind bifurcation.'

A smilie from her side.

I fill in the blanks, 'Joyful be your battle with mind. Let's meet over coffee sometime in India. I will try to speak less. Do you read these days? Or just meditate?'

'I took a break from reading and just meditated and watched birds and flowers. I think I will read again in six months,' she says.

'Vow that's lovely! You have a very interesting way of managing your life. If I may ask, when was the last time you had an erotic dream? And what could have caused it? Extra energy born of food, or surroundings, or memories, or plain old habits of the mind?' the stream of my questions hasn't yet dried out, especially about this unsolved puzzle about sex and spirituality.

She is very honest and open about it, 'This happens on my monthly periods. It doesn't happen usually. It's not regular but if it happens it's usually on those days. And I think it happens because the old habits have not been fully purified and because a women's body and mind are strongly influenced by the lunar cycles. This is a big obstacle for the women on the path of practice, but if you have full observation at the times when it happens, you can turn this obstacle into an opportunity to come out of it completely.'

I know a woman is best placed to talk about it but I take it still in flow with the previous discussion, 'So we can accept it as a natural thing influenced by uncontrollable elements like lunar cycles which have a cause and effect on our biological systems, right?

She agrees, 'Accept with observation and understanding. Accept with observation and awareness and grasp the cycles of its occurrence.'

But my doubts won't stop barging in, 'Why should it then be taken as an obstacle? Something so natural. Isn't it like taking gravity as an obstacle because it is a hindrance in our urge to fly? Because we are evolved to walk? And if we nurture a pious end to fly, then even gravity is a hindrance! Should we then get into hard core *tantrik* mystical practices to levitate? Why can't be just staying natural be pious? Why is it taken as an obstacle? Something so natural as walking under the force of gravity. I mean why can't we be at ease and restful with what we are? Why try to be something different?'

'It is only an obstacle if we do not observe and grasp it, but if we observe and understand it, it will be the door for us to transcend the physical. Your question is answered. Yes if you can be at peace with it, there will be no need for any question or any practice. If you can accept your whole body and mind as it is then you have come to ultimate enlightenment. Otherwise you have to search,' she seems at a very stable frequency.

But mine is a speedy stream of questions and curiosities, 'Why do we consider the physical urge to be a bondage? So as to transcend it. Why can't we just accept the way we are? Just like a tree does. Is it the human destiny to try to be something else from what he is? Humans try to be scientists, artists, sports people, wealthy businessmen, politicians, stars. And just in the same flow, some of us try to be pious and holy and transcend the physical dimension. Isn't it the same striving? To be something else.

'I'm asking from your perspective, out of curiosity, because I hardly feel the requirement to know and be something else than what I am. It's like just a child's play to me. All this reading, writing, questioning are just in sync with what I already am; not something aimed at changing myself fundamentally.'

She takes a nice, cute, innocent jibe, 'Yes, so you have attained the state of supreme enlightenment and I have not, so I have to search.'

I firmly deny this, 'No. I don't have the concept-bound mind regarding attaining supreme enlightenment. I just am. And while I search, seek, read, write, ask questions or give answers, all this is just like a child plays; for the sheer fun of it; not to become something extraordinary or supernatural. Ask a child why does he play? He doesn't play to become something else; he just plays.

'O my Tibetan friend, take me just as an argumentative Indian and meditate in peace. Joyful be your day!'

Then she used the best language befitting argumentative Indians. The language of silence. I believe she went into another long silent retreat. I just added to the noise around.

We carry a weird-shaped emptiness inside us; something we have hardly any clue about. And we keep filling it now with a dream, then some relationship, some desire the other time or some ambition or some man or woman or a friend.

We try filling it with some external shape, one after the other. But it never gets filled up, never gets a perfect shape to cover its emptiness.

A strange vacancy. Empty corners always stay, making the filling objects and people unsatisfactory after the trial at fitting. We just seek something appropriate to fill it up. The everlasting quest. Hence the restlessness.

9

IN a passenger train starting around midnight from New Delhi. Just a couple of passengers per coach on average. Chilly air gushing into the almost open carriages. An eerie emptiness in the absence of jostling crowds. An empty passenger train, which is usually crammed to the ceiling, seems weird as it battles past the dark countryside. A *sadhu* settles on the floor by the wide open doors. He feels comfortable to sit cross-legged even though there are empty seats around. An educated person is holding discussion with him about God, ethics, religion and spirituality.

You need safety in an empty train at night. A *burqa*-clad woman comes scanning for a safe spot. She sees three of us in the coach and sits on a corner seat. The gentleman disembarks at the next station. The *sadhu* prepares to call it a day. He isn't interested in occupying any of the empty seats. He spreads his cloth on the floor near the wide door-less entries on both sides. At the next station, a group of about a dozen adolescent boys comes rushing. They create a lot of turbulence. Crack lewd jokes, fake loud orgasms, imitate sadistic moans, dangle from the hand-support handles and shout with vulgar merriment.

The *burqa*-clad woman leaves in a hurry to find some other harmless corner in some other compartment where she can smell some harmless, protective human presence. The *sadhu* gets up and sits with eyes closed, trying to bear the disrespectful remarks, not hurled at him directly, but offensive generally just with their existence in his ascetic presence.

209

'Shakeel… Ahmad… Waseem…' The words acquire identity in the chilly night air. Now I get their religious identity. Razor sharp knife of polarization comes cutting the chilly dark air with silvery sparks of glee. Communal polarization. The Hindus feel victims due to the misdeeds committed during the Islamic rule in the medieval period of Indian history. The Muslims feel marginalized and pushed into a corner in the present nationalistic, hyperbole-ridden air. The future looks dangerous. I can feel that the Muslims as a community perceive themselves to be on the back-foot presently.

These boys must have heard lots of discussions about partiality against their community at home. The empty train gives them a space to pour out all the scorn. They do it with a rancid sense of taking revenge against the system. We keep mum. They seem primed for crime. The slightest reaction might flare up vagrant passions. It might start a chain reaction leading to a big communal fire. Only the common people burn in a communal churn. It's wise not to jump into the fire; the fire that fattens the big and the mighty.

What happened in the past was relevant, if not altogether apparently good. It involved some learning, some evolution that needed some closed setup within challenging situations. And as you came out and took tentative steps towards healing, it was also good—a flow after the stay and stagnation. All was well; all is well; all that will happen will also be good. The tough episodes are mother nature's indirect means to give us a gentle shove to nudge us to step out of the situational and psychological constraints and see more of life and living in this beautiful, exotic chaos of cosmos where we have to fix a few random pieces to make a meaningful life, to feel relevant, to be loved, to love, to live.

Go and pick the pieces of your sovereign choice; make anything you want. That's your making, your independent free will. The random pieces lying around have infinite permutations and combinations and hence you have the limitless potential to create. As a maker of something lovely, specific and beautiful, you serve as an arm of God even though you are His children. Run on the beach of creation and play in the sands and give shape to all your imaginations: a castle, a house, animals, birds, machines, vehicles, anything for that matter. It will be there as you play with childlike joy. Of course, Father Sea will surge and arrive with His waves to wipe it clean for all the future children to play on a clean sandy beach. But till the high tide washes you and your creations into the bosom of the sea, play you have to with full enthusiasm.

Capitalism was one of the hands—that too indirectly—which pulled the strings of the puppet of democracy. Of late, the capitalists have begun to pull the strings—directly. Individual powerful capitalists now are a parallel force in the world's largest and strongest democracies. Democracy is now more or less capitalist democracy. Well, when the entire world becomes a bazaar, and tariffs and profiteering become the major geostrategic forces, the world will have major upheavals. Other democracies will be stretched thin in the wake of this reshaping of the two major democracies: India and the USA.

Against this background, communist capitalism will be viewed in new light. It might be viewed as far more normal than it has been so far by the world outside the iron curtain. It will no longer be an anathema merely on ideological grounds. Democracies will possibly lose the high moral platform from where they have been taking potshots at communist China. There will be more practical judgment of China and its system of governance. Basically, the greed for power, money and authority carries the same muscles, bones and tissues under the varying skins of political ideologies and systems.

Now the sun of blind profiteering will tan all types of skins in the same color.

We get bored with what we have possessed for a long time. So don't get too surprised if the equations get reversed in future: democracies taking to communism and communists trying democracy for a change.

The crowded Jammu Mail at Subzi Mandi station in Delhi. There are many passengers waiting to board at ten in the night. The train has just three general compartments. These are already crammed to the gills. But surprisingly almost hundred more people squeeze and force themselves into its steely guts. Passengers everywhere. These are mostly migrant laborers with huge bundles and large families. You consider yourself lucky if you can stand on your toes somewhere.

A *sardarji* is standing, reclining rather in the sinewy opportunity available to fix his fat body in the twisting shapes of crammed space. His wife has a seat by the window. The children are perched on the upper berths. At every new station more people force in. Then a spicy *chana daal* seller arrives. The father gets a paper cone of spicy *daal* for his children. Onion, lemon, grams, chili. Mouthwatering. It lets loose a heady smell. It can tickle the water-buds even on the tongue of the most reserved elderly eater. His daughter eats with relish and he smiles forgetting that he is almost getting crushed by the bodies around him. The seller has to squeeze through the wall of bodies.

The tea seller has it easy though. 'Boiling hot tea! Will burn your skin! So make space!' he comes hollering the warning. And people further squeeze their limbs, making a safe passage for him.

A woman dozes off for many long minutes sitting on the floor. A poor woman. Then sleep overpowers her and she sprawls her body among the feet. Some people stand on one leg to keep the sanctity of a female body sleeping among boots and shoes.

A slim boy has fitted himself along the back of a seat behind multiplicity of bums. Some have forcibly occupied the entire upper birth and lie pretending to sleep so that nobody asks them to sit up allowing others to give rest to their bums in the freed space.

In such a tight situation, one can expect anything from the best to the worst. The same with the night. It has its own ways. As it moves towards midnight, the bodies relax, become less rigid, pliable and they flow to acquire whatever weirdly warped space is available among the mass of bodies. A strange solemnity creeps in silence.

Me and my brother decide to take a shared Eco van from Agra to Fatehpur Sikri. It's a well-worn, thoroughly used vehicle. The owner driver is named Lehri Singh Faujdar, a dark man with *pan-gutka*-painted red teeth. He flashes them with great effect with a smile. 'I usually take 14 passengers,' he forestalls any logical protest as me and my brother find ourselves bundled in the front sheet. 'There are no more passengers today, otherwise I would have put one by your side,' he informs me. The gear shaft between my thighs, tightly squeezed between him and my brother, I watch in dismay as he pulls the gear, pushing and prodding almost in my groins.

I start praying that let there be no more passengers on the way. My prayers are heard. He sees an old woman waiting by the road. Obviously she can't be stuffed by our side in the front seat. She protests that there is no space in the vehicle and she will take some other convenience. Her protests fall on deaf ears. He has to have one more passenger to make up for having one less on the main middle seat. I thank god for sending this old woman as a passenger. The six passengers on the two side seats at the back moan with agony. He puts her heavy sack on the roof. The load lands with a thump and the roof bulges down a bit in the middle. He secures the load using tight ropes with expert hands. Then the six passengers at the back are pushed and shoved and the old woman is dumped among them. The back door is forced shut. It's for them to adjust the old woman in any cubic meter of space available. They won't fall. With jolts their bodies will acquire the most feasible shape to fill the space, settling down more comfortably.

The main middle seat is not cumbered much with human weight. A patient is lying here, his legs folded, nose taped and a nasal pipe still in it. He probably got discharged from hospital. He is seriously ill. The patient is accompanied by a man and a lady in *burqa*. Sitting at both ends of the long middle seat, they are holding the patient between them.

I take the van owner to be any other passenger-hunting transporter. He cracks his point—beyond which you can't say much—flashes his red teeth with a challenging smile. 'How many times you ply between Agra and Sikri in a day?' I ask. I think that he is so passenger hungry that he must be relentlessly plying on the route till night. 'I do just two rounds in a day,' he says. Then he naughtily slaps his palm on the battered dashboard and says, 'Irrespective of how many rounds I make up in a day, she will give survival crumbs only. More rounds won't mean a big mansion. So just two for me. Two, four, six or eight will give just enough to see through the month. So why torture oneself?' he again flashes his red teeth and gums.

By the turn outside Sikri he stops by another rental shared van, opens the sliding middle door and helps the sick man to be transferred to the other vehicle for the onward journey. I can see that it's not just about fare. The fare would mean just stopping there, leaving the sick man's wards to take care of the transfer.

I feel big respect for this man. We talk to him and then as promised he takes us nearest to the fort's gate, gives us instructions regarding the return journey, warns us to stay cautious about tout guides who act as middlemen for the chador and flower sellers and cajole people into buying high-priced items to get their commission later. We have talked to him like friends and he reciprocates as a well-wisher. It has been a good experience with him. A good man, soiled under the dust of daily survival. You have to give a friendly swipe at the dust to see goodness in someone.

We have reached Fatehpur Sikri through a very decent mode—a good man under rough outer bearing due to the tough battle for survival on a daily basis. Before entering its grand courts, complexes and step wells another piece of kind welcome awaits us—the omelet served by the Muslim woman. The court complex is primarily in red sandstone—trabeated construction; designs evincing composite culture under the Mughals. It's an open and airy luxury involving many arched facades (multiple-arch deep) and bulbous domes crowned by lotus petals and *kalash* finials. The imposing masonry walls, huge pillared halls, coquettish archways, sensuously carved pillars with inlaid designs, arched prayer chambers, the king's tower (*jhorakha darshan*), sturdy battlements, geometric symmetry and aesthetic frame take you to ancient times. It's redolent with multiple layers of history.

It's advisable to visit the monuments of past—belonging to any dynasty, be it Hindu, Muslim, Sikh, Christian or Buddhist—with an open mind and restful heart. It helps us to learn, to grow, to understand things better. I just look around, when I'm at such places, with a sense of wonder carried by a little student.

The *petha* sellers of Agra think they carry a reputatious virtue, which makes them so bold and aggressive in soliciting your attention to their sweet shop that it literally makes them look like marauders ready to kidnap you and forcibly make you buy their *mithai*. Your courteous denials finally bid you bye and you start saying 'NO' in sour notes.

For a few hundred meters facing Taj Mahal's eastern gate there is a lovely tiled walkway, flanked by trees, shops and restaurants. The lights are screened behind tall square columns of slab-stones. A subtle, subdued light emerges from the patterned holes in the screens. It builds a healthy prelude to your next day's early morning visit to the monument of love. You might be lost in myriad tunes of history emanating from *veena's* soulful notes of the past. But the shopkeepers will keep crying an encore, keep throwing their verbal bouquets, which finally begin assaulting you like bricks. It keeps pulling you down from the paramount constellation of emotions about the embodiment of living soul in white marble.

The present's popular caricature boosted by consumerism is too noisy for poetic sentiments about Taj Mahal in the markets surrounding it like a tight noose. A sort of irreverent drabness sizzling through the grand monument's mythical dimensions. I have been trying to keep focused on the crystallized voracity of romance etched in stones while being bombarded with almost kidnapping calls of *autowallahas* and sweet-makers. They look ready to force you into accepting their services.

Me and my brother have been walking on the Taj Nature Walk boulevard. At every step we have to say 'no' to an *autowallah, petha* seller or some hawker. Saying 'no' hundreds of times makes us hungry and finally we give into the insistence of a short but smart looking young man. They are all on the younger side in this dining establishment. We hardly expect the dinner to be anything but ordinary. I'm still baffled with my decision to agree to enter this restaurant. We sit and wait for our order to be served.

The establishment is garishly decorated. Not much footfall, we being the only customers at the moment. We can't expect the food to be delicious. We just pray that please god let it be fresh at least, however bland it might turn out to be. Then the young man arrives with our order. The salad pieces are nicely arranged in circles. The mix-veg is no random assemblage of parts taken from other recipes. It's prepared individually. The *makka roti* is lovingly laced with butter. The hubbub and helter-skelter of doubt vanishes.

We thoroughly enjoy the dinner. 'It's delicious food!' we compliment and share our feedback. He isn't used to hearing words of appreciation. The customers basically cringe and complain when they don't like something. Criticism sits on their tongue-tips. But they turn misers and dumb while praising someone's goods or services. As our feedback pours out abundantly and positively, he stands absorbing this unique experience. It stirs emotions in him. Tears are on the verge of toppling down from his eyelashes. Looking at his eyes, our eyes also get their share of moisture.

It's a beautiful feeling. This human touch. I can feel these words of appreciation mean so much to him. There is usually an inundation of critical stuff from family, friends, peers, customers. The words of appreciation can bring new light and life in someone's eyes.

Who knows what problems in career and family this young man has been facing. But our words of appreciation give him some hope and pride in his profession. Shivam Pandit is his name. We leave him more in love with his work.

Earlier in the day, I had given compliment to a woman in similar circumstances. Her husband managed the front end of the shop, selling tea, coffee and snacks. She ran the small kitchen at the back with a few tables and chairs in between. A Muslim woman used to work in the shadows, she prepared the omelet with ease and care. The taste was good. But the way it was served was unique—cut in little pieces, just big enough so that you can take it with a fork in one bite. Served with care. 'Your omelet is really good!' I said as we got up to leave. She was sitting in a corner chair looking at us eating, her eyes trying to gauze the standard of her cooking from our manner of eating and talking.

The people won't praise when it's good. But they will say a lot when they don't like it. She was visibly surprised at the compliment. Maybe it was the first time a customer expressed his good words. It was a new experience to her and she didn't know how to handle it. She just nodded with a little hesitant, shy smile. But I'm sure she will have enough time to digest this new encouraging pill. Won't she find her work meaningful and feel proud of it? She will. Kind words of appreciation give people hope. Who knows what testing situations they are facing. And a few positive words can brighten someone's gloomy day. She will find her cooking more meaningful. Just like Shivam would be happier the next day while manning his establishment.

You need not shower people with wealth, benefits or favors to make them happier. That's asking too much from yourself. Making others happy comes without any cost at your end. Just give them the credit that they deserve on account of their product or service. Just this much. When someone's karma is appreciated with contentment and joy, it dispels darkness and doubts from that person. It opens a little ray of hope. And even if you are a pessimist and don't think it's too substantial change maker in someone's life, even then you have to accept that at least that moment is freshly lit when you deliver that feedback. Even that's sufficient. Because NOW is all that matters.

Taj Mahal Nature Walk street facing the eastern gate. We have to go to Agra Fort. The *autowallahas* are asking 150 rupees. It's seven or eight kilometers they say. I see an elderly Muslim rickshaw puller going at a decent pace down the lane towards the Taj. It's a slight descent and his rickshaw rolls with a song. I hark, 'O rickshaw!' He puts breaks. He says 40 rupees to the destination for the two of us. The *autowallah* is hovering nearby. He grunts and snorts accusatively as if the rickshaw puller has stolen his clients.

Autos are not allowed beyond the barricade about 200 meters from where we board the rickshaw. So they have to take a detour through the congested city to reach the fort. The rickshaw puller takes a chance. If he is allowed to cross the barricade and move along the Taj's outer boundaries, he will need to pedal for just two and half kilometers.

He is going at a nice pace along the gentle slope. 'O *miyanji*, turn back! As if you don't know that rickshaws aren't allowed beyond this point!' one of the policemen manning the barricade hollers. The rickshaw puller gives a broad smile and takes an instant sharp U-turn. In fact he answers just through a broad smile to most of your words. He seems to take everything impersonally—nothing personal. He turns back with ease as he would turn around when faced with a wall.

So his shortcut has been belied—for which he asked just 40 rupees—and the only route left is the long-cut which the autos have to take. It means, as per the changed equation, he will have to heave the rickshaw for almost eight kilometers for just 40 rupees. For a person who takes things personally this calculation would immediately suck out fuel from his pedaling legs. But not this man. His smile doesn't go. It was his offer. The route choice isn't in his hands now. But he won't back out from his word. So without any hint of disappointment or complain or any inclination to redraw the deal due to the changed route he focuses on pulling the load up the slope.

It's a heavy pull. The rickshaw is crawling slowly. You can argue with someone who grumbles, frets about the loss-making deed. He isn't affected in mind due to the changed situation. We feel his physical exertion. We have no doubt that he will continue pulling for all these eight kilometers without complaining or asking extra money. Such honesty and integrity to one's word makes you sensitive to the situation. More than him, we feel the weight of his almost unrewarding assignment. His legs would possibly bear the weight to take us all the way for just 40 rupees. But our conscience won't allow it. We feel the extent of his loss-making assignment.

He is all focused on pulling the rickshaw. 'Shouldn't we take an auto because it's quite far from this side,' we start discussing, expecting him to agree and propose it himself. But he doesn't say anything. Just silently pulls. Then we ask him, 'Shouldn't we take an auto?' 'That also is ok,' he says casually with a smile. His smile is unaffected by all considerations of the amount of fare, distance plied, weight, etc. He halts. We give him 20 rupees. He accepts it with another beaming smile. The very same smile. He is simply at ease with himself. With that ease of being, the outer flutter of leaves hardly disturbs the inner lamp.

Our spirits uplifted by this gentle brush with a tender and honest soul, giving us a lovely starter for the aesthetic senses, here we are at the Agra fort welcoming us with a marvelous dining prospects of medieval architecture. It's a vast palace complex involving spacious courts with mansions around; designed brackets supporting the *chhajas* and lintels; large assembly halls with flat ceilings; glazed tiling and stucco along with ornamental stone carving; harem complex once guarded by chaste women and trustworthy officers. The past pulls you with musty but welcoming force.

Humayun was coronated at Agra fort overlooking river Yamuna. It has double ramparts with massive circular bastions; a broad deep moat, bearing drawbridges, in a semi-circle; four gates in different directions. You feel special while standing in *Diwan-i-Am* (hall of public audience) with its pillared halls with cusped engrailed arches on the façade and grand columns in triple-aisle deep complexes plastered with white shell lime (over red sand stone). The imperial *jharokha* (throne) chamber still has enough luxuriance, even after the dusty layers of centuries covering it, to give you an idea of aristocratic opulence. There is a private marble mosque for the harem ladies, enclosed for *purdah*. You can't help but appreciate the water tank with cascade and the *shahi hamam* with its impressive water supply system—closed complex of octagonal halls, interconnected by corridors with *jali* openings on the river side. Then there is the chain of justice, the regal bell tied to a chain which could be pulled by the commonest of the common to seek justice by directly appealing to the emperor. How I hope that justice was as easily and directly available to the modern citizens; that we had some direct means of being saved from injustice instead of spending our entire lives in the unsurpassable judicial corridors. There are so many things I want to shout. I feel like pulling the chain but it's not accessible to the visitors; just there for viewing.

And among all this grandeur, the sadness of the historical fact that Shah Jahan spent eight years at Agra fort as a prisoner looking at his soulful salutation to love, Taj Mahal, on the other side of Yamuna.

The early December morning sun beating on the monument of love. Its beauty ablaze in full floral glory. The wonder in white marble with inlay ornamentation, carved plant motifs, inlaid creeper designs; silver and gold work on the ceilings; Persian inscriptions carved in ornamental cartouches; repetitive stylized creepers inlaid on borders; marble and precious stone inlay. How much your aesthetic sense can take in under the pleasant onslaught on your senses! The arches, windows, cupolas, panels with ornamental cartouches, incised painting in multiple colors... Keep watching and trying to have a knowledge of all these details. Then you give up. Not possible. It's a sea of beauty, only there to be felt. So you surrender to the seductive arrows of beauty and then you simply feel it, bask in this white beauty.

Here you feel that stones have a soul, a dancing one. Go to Taj Mahal to see it and feel it. Tourists are loitering in awe on the spacious plinth around the shrine of love. With soaring spirits people look up to the Taj, lost in its majesty. This is pure appreciation. But there is someone who has crossed the threshold of appreciation, built upon it to achieve something more substantial—reverence. To him it's a living temple of beauty and he the priest. The elderly white gentleman is in love with the deity, beauty. He is performing rituals. He has some physical disability which makes him walk with a slight droop on mildly moon-walking legs. He lights a lamp of love in obeisance to the shrine. As he and his friend move around clicking pictures, he stoops down to pick little pieces of paper and patches of green shoe covers which the tourists have to wear while going into the tomb of love. It's his business to

222

keep it clean, safe, at least as long as he is here; to contribute his effort in maintaining the sanctity of this place.

The tourists are simply clicking pictures, chatting, laughing, enjoying the proximity to this wonder of the world. But this man is in awe of the beauty in marble. Any scrap of paper is a stigma to the splendor of the shrine of love. It's heartening to see him going slowly with his cleaning job. It shows the depths of his feelings for this wonder of the world. A girl hops onto a ledge on the monument from the platform. Her boyfriend starts clicking pictures. The shoe covers would spoil the picture. She removes them. The Taj might be spoilt but not the picture. The gentleman walks to her and reminds her that it's forbidden to do so We Indians don't care about such things. They ignore him. He reminds her twice and then finding her to be inconsiderate enough to commit this illegality, he sadly walks away.

I would term him as the best tourist visiting Taj Mahal on this particular day; someone who felt the definition of love etched in its grand design, beautiful patterns and relief pictures. Every square inch on the beautiful memorial is a complete story of perfection and flawless faith to make something unparalleled. Every little flower, leaf or geometrical pattern shows the endless hours of artistic passion. You are lost in a maze of beauty.

The sanctum-sanctorum of love, bearing the graves of the emperor and his beloved queen, lies under the main dome. The lofty vault enclosing a rich history of love and pain. Every inch carved with chisels drenched with tears of ecstasy. It's a sea. One can't grab its immensity. So the casual tourist, clueless how to appreciate it or say anything, settles down to the base-level appreciation. The main high-vaulted chamber echoes with voices. So they shout their names and feel pleased to hear them echoed in the unbelievably lovely interior. Little do they realize that stones have petalous souls and these shouts count as pollution doing damage to this grand creation. If at all you have to say something, say the name of the person whom you have really loved and hear its echo.

It's a UP state roadways bus plying between Agra and Delhi. The conductor is a woman in black; short, stocky but pretty in face and impressive in limbs. She is extremely efficient and confident about her duties. The tone is bold. She needs it to deal with unruly passengers. She manages it with impressive effect, keeps eyes on each seat to be filled, ensures each passenger pays the fare, guides and gives instructions about the further journey once the passengers deboard the bus in the puzzling maze of the Delhi NCR.

The bus reaches the boarding point outside Agra to take the Expressway. There is a slight misunderstanding. The driver has allowed a young man to board thinking there is one seat vacant. The boyish man panics when he finds there is no seat available. He finds it a betrayal. His father is some official in the roadways. He feels he has been wronged terribly in not being offered a seat. He calls his father on phone. A real papa's boy. When will you grow up, you crying sissy? He gives the phone to the conductor. The father talks to the lady conductor. She expresses her inability to get a seat vacant for his dear son. The father official gets offended, feels insulted that his very own son has to travel standing. Shameful and unpardonable. What is the use of his position then? He fires on all authoritative cylinders.

There are checking officials waiting at the next toll gates. The bus is raided. The boyish man looks with an authoritative leer. They surround the lady conductor as if she has been caught smuggling banned items. They bombard her with accusations—the rules that have been broken in the episode. One of them is enlisting the

224

probable actions that will be taken against her. She defends her position confidently. But they are like hounds. The very same patriarchal mindset. The lady conductor starts crying. A woman passenger seems to be trying to mollify the raiding flying squad.

It's taking a bad shape for the woman conductor. She needs more people on her side. Me and my brother get down. Both of us engage two staffers and straightway get into accusations that they have delayed the bus, that we paid the luxury bus far to catch our train (there was no scheduled train to catch), bla bla. My brother looks like a six-feet tall wing commander in military style cargos. Imitating him even I'm smartly clad today. They think that even we have connections to be so full of confidence in confronting them. They turn defensive. They ask us to board the bus as if the issue is settled.

When I feel they are no longer on the front foot, I give them my sermon on women empowerment: 'She is a very efficient conductor, manages it really well. Far better than scores of male conductors I have seen. She is a working woman. Don't harass her in the name of performing your duties!' I speak loudly at the mustachioed man, the most rascally looking in the group. The boyish man is puzzled. The lady conductor is shedding tears. We raise a ruckus. The penalties are forgotten. They find it advisable to stop the matter from taking an uglier form. The bus starts again. After half an hour we see that she is her normal professional self again. It's good to help someone in having a normal day.

Who am I? Or what am I? Just a common *sadhak*, a seeker of a bit more than I know or understand or feel. Or not even a *sadhak* because I don't follow any particular path. What exactly I'm, I'm yet to know. I consciously know the identities given to me by others, but at a subtle level I know I'm not any of these. I feel just like a little bird flying on its own path, wondering about all this *maya* scattered around; curious, full of wonder, observant; just a bird of its own type like the rest are. Or maybe, a tiny humming bird, to be more specific; flitting among different flowers of faith; taking small sips of the nectar of truth from various-colored flowers; taking little independent sorties while going from one flower to the other; belonging to all and none at the same time; loving and being loved by all.

Enlightenment is a mere word, and like all words, it's an indicator of some fraction of reality. So it's practical to use the word 'enlightened' for the ones who are in a joyful flow of life. According to me, an enlightened one is someone who, in the real sense, 'knows' that he doesn't and can't know. Because existence is ever transforming (and the so-called knowledge is simply a skill born of the operational part of our brain, i.e., mind; a mere capability like any other skill that helps us survive). To know that one doesn't know brings a grace and flow to one's life. It gets one in peaceful sync with what is. It in turn gives a joyful being, almost unconditional.

We deboard the bus and stand on the outskirts of Mahadev's land. To reach the famous Banaras *ghats* we need an auto. Waseem the kind *autowallah* agrees to take us for 150 rupees while others charge more than 250 rupees. Political *Hindutva* is very aggressive. We can feel that he, as

226

part of the minority community, is on the back foot. A biker bearing a big *tilak* on his forehead misbehaves. It's his mistake but instead of apologizing he unleashes a sharp reprimand through his *gutka*-filled mouth. Almost hisses. At a crossing a *carwallah* almost bangs into the auto and carries on with his aggression through his obscene tongue. We came so near to a collision—his rash driving being the cause—that I closed my eyes. Waseem doesn't argue. He just moves on with his business: to earn bread and butter for his family.

There seems to a tacit understanding that as UP Muslims they have to play safe. We brothers try to give an impression that India is still reasonably secure. We chat with him in a polite, friendly way. We ask him about the famous eating points in the city. So still on the way there we are sharing a lovely, mouthwatering delicacy with him at Bengal Chat Bhandar. Further on, we all three have tea at a place of his liking. He comes out of his shell, talks happily and shares his personal story. He used to work in Delhi but Corona epidemic forced him to move to his native place. It's difficult to provide for his three children. 'Corona took away everything… wife, Delhi job!' he says with sadness. He remarried for the sake of his children but his second wife won't love and take care of the children. To avoid the daily drama he decided to separate. Now his mother takes care of the children.

I think the key to unlock the treasure chest of goodness in someone is smile and kind words. The same applies to another auto driver Suresh. Give them respect and generally people would go out of their way to reciprocate on the same frequency. He tries to do his best to show us the beauty of his city. Like an expert guide he points out the famous landmarks falling on the way. The people are looking to share their stories with sympathetic souls. Very soon he is telling us about his family. He praises his wife because she takes care of his ailing parents. He is in gratitude to Mahadev that his daughter is lucky to get married in a good family.

On the *ghats* we come across a Tamil *baba* with an imposing *danda* draped in saffron cloth. He asks for *chai*, which means 10 rupees. He is very happy to get clicked. The frank *baba* is very honest about sharing his personal information. He takes drinks liquor two-three times a week, eats one vegetarian meal in a day, is not addicted to ganja but happily takes a few draughts of weed when offered by someone. He is very pleased to see his pictures on my mobile, gives his friend's number and asks me to forward them to his friend on WhatsApp. The *baba* is joyful that his latest pictures have landed in his friend's phone far away in Tamil Nadu and points to small gulls following boats in Ma Ganga and says, 'I fly like those birds. I feel very light!'

Two *babas* in black with ash-smeared faces. You click their picture. Give us *chai*, they demand. One *baba* in orange with a carefully painted face is sipping tea. 'Pay for my tea,' he says while I click his picture. I don't have change. The tea seller doesn't accept digital payment. The *baba* gets angry and throws a cuss word. I hurry away lest he beats me because he seems capable of doing that. A *baba* with a long tower of hair braids is reclining on a platform. He naughtily waves at two white women. 'How do you feel looking at them?' we innocently ask. He gets offended and flares up, 'All bitches have the same thing.' He fumes. We placate him with gentle words and 10 rupees for *chai*. One ash-smeared *baba* is sitting on a stone bench right in the middle of the crowded bazaar opposite Daswamedh *ghat*. I raise my phone to click him. He brandishes a warning finger. 'Then why are you sitting in this crowd with all this make-up?' I feel like asking but think better of it because they have a right to beat anyone without any provocation. It's good that common people have the patience to take their slaps as blessings.

The *ghats* are crowded and polluted under the throes of spiritual business. Ma Ganga is polluted beyond reparation point. The water is muddy green. I miss Her bright blue and green waters that one sees at Rishikesh. Touts literally drag you by force into the boats sadly chugging in the polluted holy river. The evening *arti* is elaborate in operations involving chanting of hymns, big prayer lamps and expensive rituals. A *naga sadhu* angrily shoves a few Brahmins roaming in the crowd with plates bearing *arti* lamps and receiving charity money. The ash-smeared *naga* seems angry and pushes the Brahmins to gather the donations himself. Most of the ash-smeared *babas* are very intimidating. They take it as their right to collect money and bathe first in the holy river.

The burning pyres of Manikarnika *ghats* have multiple pyres burning on big mounds of ash. It's a chilly mid-December windy night. Standing near the burning pyres gives you warmth and the realization of death hugs you from very near quarters. The next day is *Purnima* and thousands of poor women from the villages are jutted against each other along the *ghats* amid stinking urine smell to take bath early in the morning next day on the auspicious full moon occasion. They huddle like a flock of sheep, taking warmth from each other under an open sky on this chilly night. Many are singing folklore songs and dancing. That's how they will spend this cold night. The power of faith is warming their souls.

The renovated Mahakal temple complex is mythically grand and lofty in spiritual stature. Gyanvapi mosque built on the same complex is clearly an Islamic dome set up on a pre-existing Hindu temple. It's as clear as anything else in broad daylight. Why do they even need archeological digging to prove it? The lower part clearly shows a temple structure and pillars. It doesn't need expert digging by the Archaeological Survey of India to prove that a temple was vandalized to erect a mosque's dome on top of it.

We have taken a mediocre hotel near the *ghats*. The hotel owner is an old gentleman. He doesn't like Modi and angrily says, 'We have been voting for him but he just tells *jumlas*, doesn't work on his promises and this time was simply lucky to win from here through…' I remember the honorable prime minister's claims that he will make Kashi clean like Kyoto. But Banaras is stinking with pollution. I can hardly see any improvement apart from the temple corridor.

Banaras is so congested that going to Sarnath, just a dozen kilometers away, gives a totally new and refreshing experience. It's almost opposite to the pleasantly chaotic, noisy Banaras *ghats*. The place seems very symbolic of the historical truth: peaceful Buddhism was churned out of the chaotic, noisy, hyper-ritualistic storm of Hinduism. One can clearly feel it.

Chaukhandi and Sarnath *stupas* bear testimony to the mythical whisper of silence and peace. Rows of east Asian monks going chanting mantras around the *stupas*. The sprawling lawns around the *stupas* still carry the layers of peace and tranquility that Buddha spread here centuries ago with his first sermon. The museum is full of grand Buddha statues dating back to many ancient centuries. There was a time when this land had millions of Buddha statues, temples and monasteries. Was it wiped out of India by force? Or did it naturally fade out? Or was it assimilated into Hinduism again? I believe it was a slow, almost natural process involving all these factors. Also, there are reasons to believe that aggressive Brahmanism helped in systematically dismantling it by force, cajoling and even spreading rumors.

Naresh is a small, gentle, patient guy selling Buddha souvenirs. He allows you to check his items even if you are clearly doing a free eye shopping. He even plays the instruments to give us information about them including a big conch which he plays with nice skills. He seems to be soaked in Buddha spirit and is happy to get whatever lands in his purse at the end of the day. A small conversation with him is sufficient to make you feel that he is a good human being.

Ashokan pillar is a 15.25 meter monolithic pillar of polished *chunar* sandstone with a tapering cylindrical shaft. It was once surmounted by an adorned lion capital which serves as our national emblem. The shaft is lying in the lawn around the *stupa*, the national emblem in the museum. The pillar's broken lower shaft bearing some fragments in Maurayan Brahmi script warning the monks and nuns against schism in the *sangha*.

Chaukhandi stupa is a four-armed terraced brick structure. It was here that Buddha met his five disciples. The outer walls of the terraces are ornamented with niches having Buddha images. A brick tower, bearing an Arabic inscription, erected by Raja Todar Mal's son to commemorate Humayun's visit, stands on the top of the *stupa*.

Dhamekh *stupa* (Dharma Chakra Stupa) commemorates the place where Buddha gave his first sermon. It's a solid brick-made cylindrical tower around 40 meter high. The circular stone drum at the base topped with a cylindrical mass of brickwork looks sturdy against the winds of time. Carved stones with geometric designs of swastika, leaf and floral patterns, birds and human figures create an aesthetic nostalgia for the ancient past. The East Asian tourists and monks are chanting hymns on the peaceful lawns and many are doing *parikrama* around the stupa. It's wonderful to share the peace of this place, the place where the seed of Buddhism was sown from where it grew into a massive tree spreading the shade of its faith to far flung countries in the east.

Sarnath is a lovely open small town, its peace palpable as if drawn from the Buddhist sutras of love, kindness, peace and joy. There is a sad-looking Chinese Buddhist temple here. It was made in 1939 by an abbot from Beijing. It bears the traditional Chinese temple feature of entrance gate pagoda. The *Boddhisattva* hall has double pagoda roof and a monastery around a central courtyard. The walls are adorned with Chinese motifs. Hieun Tsang's journey is pictorially depicted in attractive murals. The temple's land was owned by China. Now a lone monk with hennaed goatee looks suspiciously at the visitors. He has central Asian mongoloid Muslim features. An interesting character, has shifty eyes and looks anything but a monk. He tells me that he is from Delhi and is taking care of the temple for the last decade. 'A Thai monk is in charge of this place. He planned for the construction of a grand stupa. But he hasn't returned after Corona. I myself almost died of gall bladder stone. Nobody cares,' he is angry and sullen. I can clearly feel that there is more to it than he shares. After all, the complex is built on 12 acres of land. So definitely there are property issues.

Angarika Dharampala (born 1864, Sri Lanka) found the Buddhist sites in a deplorable condition. He established Mahabodhi society to rebuild Buddhist holy sites and restore sacred places linked to Buddha. The Bodhi tree's branch cutting was taken to Sri Lanka by Ashoka's son and daughter and planted at Anurudhpura. In 1931, a branch from the same tree was planted here by Dharampala to commemorate the place where Buddhism was born. Sarnath deer park, housing a few deer, is mobbed by some students on a trip. It was here that the first sermon was given. The first sermon of *Sakyamuni* Buddha, the seed, has germinated quite well and the mammoth tree of Buddhism is now luxuriantly spreading its branches for global peace and harmony. The tree is the grandson of the Mahabodhi tree at Gaya where Buddha attained enlightenment. I collect a few dry leaves that have fallen on the ground. I touch them with love and care—for inspiration to be on the middle path. I feel that I have a small connection with Buddhism for being born on Buddha *Purnima*.

Mid February. An adamant winter giving a gentle, pleasant rebuff to the summer slowly treading ahead. The mornings dawn condescendingly on the vegetable market at the town, the town that's itching with urban lust to become a city, then a metropolis and finally merge with some mammoth urban megalith. The clutter and chaos going up with the rising sun. There is an ineradicable typical smell of a vegetable market in a town. The seasons change but this smell remains the same. A myriad-colored smell—the smell of fresh vegetables entwining with decaying organic discards, mud and dung. It unleashes its assault on your olfactory senses with a squinting spurt. The dealers and sellers shouting hoarsely. The monkeys nimbly crawling on the wires, doing antics and jumping down to run away with something eatable, or at least fir for giving it a try to chew at.

A bleak, pathogenic, primordial smell pervading the congestion. Paddlers and roaming hawkers arriving with their carts to buy vegetables wholesale and sell them in the streets in the neighboring villages. Householders, directed by their budget-calculating wives, arriving on bikes and cars to buy a week or ten days of vegetables in one go and store them in refrigerators and thus save money. An economizing tussle.

Life trying to ward off death. A dreadful chasm between the two. There are many who have fallen in it. The outcasts, born in hideous circumstances. Their faces speckled with haunting melancholy. The broken pot shards that feel they can still hold water in their shallow curves defined by jagged, broken, sharp edges. A soundless cry on their dark, unwashed faces. It's a group of children. They walk around with imperious timidity. They compete with cows in salvaging the castaway fragments of stale vegetables from dirt heaps.

Are they Rohingyas, or Bangladeshis, or some tribals from India itself? Whoever they are, they carry the same passport of misery. Their eyes full of innocent but still vile determination to beat the stray cows and bulls in salvaging the castaway, stale, spoiled chunks of unusable vegetables. It's a childhood copiously fed on spoonfuls of sorrows. Their lightless serious eyes furtively darting around on the filthy ground looking for their treasure hunt. *Aaah*, poverty the depraved seducer! The dung-smeared bulls move around with a sleepy enchantment and languor. Emphatically moody monkeys crawling over cables, jumping on the tin sheds with clang-bang jocularity.

Furiously flaming frenzy of survival. Harassing, haunting, gnawing, devouring. Horrible paroxysms of the will to live—an eternal tenderness beating somewhere deep down in the womb of worldly garbage. The ground-sloggers amidst rack and ruin. The hawkers and middlemen shouting with burbling, stinging energy. The capricious coax of currencies mollifying all vileness and crossness faced on the path.

It's a bearable world as long as you can sell your stale vegetables dabbed in acidified colored water to make them gleaming fresh with false promises of health and nourishment. Consumerism sets forth lynching questions. The bloodhound is baying for your blood in the tumult. Scuddling along, it's always sniffing at your strained smell. Its bestial fangs ever-present, ever-lasting. You have to keep abreast of its swift trot. Either you eat someone's chance to life through adulteration, giving them a slow dose of poison—your buyer whom you give such a nice welcoming smile—or get bitten by the spiteful hound and find yourself in death throes.

Hard-driven by destiny, withstanding the shameless stumbles, spirits all cheerless and discharmed, absorbing the acute pangs, you try to emancipate the sour most morsels with some weird dignity. Destiny dastardly debased. The migrants pulled in by the delightful roar and potent frenzy of the bazaar. Running away from the monstrosities of life drooling at their native places. The frenzied, spasmodic, sobbing circumstances swatting them away like a gunshot pierces through the fabric of peace in a forest and scares away a flock of sparrows. Running away from nightmarish tormentors of deprived life, they land at a distant place and try to cope with the ingenious cruelty unfolding at the new place. Miseries hop along with a frenzied scampering.

They squat on a little space in the open area in front of the vegetable sellers. With a groaning and grinding effort, like the persistent rub of a rope leaving a mark on a stone, they wriggle, relentlessly haggled by the rival claimants, to get a foothold—their self-marked space to set up a temporary establishment in the morning. There is no legal right to it. It can be swiped away like any garbage heap on the market compound. They also have to pay some monthly money—some kind of protection money to the neighborhood bully who controls the unofficial market affairs—to further cement their claim. Then they have to fight with the visitors who come to purchase vegetables and park their vehicles exactly on top of their little space where they have been cleaning the ground before setting up their shop. They sell cheap clothes, utensils, groceries to the people who are exactly like them but are struggling to survive through some other means.

They have to arrive early, lest someone takes their marked place, necessitating a brawl. They carry a swaggered dark, grimy look in order to ward off any competitor to the space just with a mere look. They arrive with huge bundles of their wares—clothes, groceries, toys, utensils—heaped on carrier rickshaws, pulling in with purpose. It takes about an hour to clean the dirty floor, pitch poles, draw strings and ropes, put their products in presentable order. They do it with a strained and flustered expression. They count upon the footfall of their own types who work as laborers in factories and farms.

Two little boys, aged six and eight at the most, confront the falsehood and misery of life. Their father has pulled the heavy sacks of clothes laden on their carrier rickshaw early in the morning. He has left them to set up the shop and gone to attend some other task that will add some more bucks to their meager purse. The boys are clad in their school uniforms. They perform the task masterfully. Setting up poles in the cemented holes, cleaning the ground, drawing ropes, spreading a tarpaulin sheet, laying shirts, pants, jeans, shorts, socks, caps, hankies and belts in nicely segregated order. The other day it's their mother who pulls into the ground with the cart and does all the stuff by herself. She has a dull and drowsy look on her weather-beaten face having fine features.

A thickset short old woman sells peanuts, *gazak*, grams and colored rice crunchies. She scans the passersby with one eye; with the other she tracks the monkeys who rob her at the slightest lapse in concentration. She holds a big stick to ward off the robbery. She says that her son has betrayed her for his wife. To further worsen the already strained relations, he operates a rival stall nearby. Her husband is partially paralyzed. He moves dragging his left foot. Another paralyzed man operates a tea stall. It's a tiny sheet iron box on a mobile cart.

Young shop helpers are rubbing potatoes in sawdust to give them a freshly dug look after dousing them in acidified water. These are then sold as fresh arrivals from the fields. All the sellers are looking to sneak in a percentage of stale products into the fresh ones to increase profit. While the monkeys scamper around to cut that profit by a little margin.

Father's death anniversary falls on March 1. Me and my brother go to a *gaushala* for donation. Here things are challenging and cramped for *gaumata*. But something is better than nothing. Hundreds of cows get food and shelter at least. And we can think of improving the conditions as long as cow shelters exist.

There is a bull whose front leg is broken from the joint leaving it as a crooked and unusable stump. It's a sad sight. The caretaker is from Bihar. He has been working here for the last five years. He holds a scrubber in hand to give them a nice scrubbing. He tells the story how the bull got injured. The villagers bring their cows for mating. This cow was in heat and was tied at a distance. The farmer then untied the bull. It ran too fast in excitement. Love is blinding after all. Risky. The bull slipped on the uneven brick flooring in the compound and met a nasty fall. It broke its leg. Now it's a very difficult handicapped life.

Golu, another bull is standing nearby. It has won many prizes at cattle fairs. The last was a first prize of 51,000 rupees at Kurukshetra cattle fair. There are far more bigger and muscular looking bulls at the cow shelter. But Golu has beaten all of them here and at other shelters because it has a huge hump which gives it the USP and the top prize. Thus Golu is a revenue maker. One can feel that it carriers extra confidence in comparison to other bulls.

If you feel all the layers of sorrow spread around, you might feel gutted and minced with wet earth. Or you may see the light of love—sharp, pointed, clear, a shiny spot on the fabric of darkness. A white dot on the blackboard. The blackboard perspective. Or you can have the whiteboard view—feeling the joy that oozes from everything around. The dot of pain on this will be like a tiny dark well that sips little rays, eats them in fact. The whiteness having a black hole; the darkness having a white hole. They sustain each other. We have to accept them.

When things are 'wrong' at socio-economic (and politics as a result), you have the far 'right' taking over, claiming to be the remedy for all that's wrong. I'm right, I'm right, I'm right it says and everything else is wrong. When things go 'very wrong' at the socio-economic and political fronts, you have far 'left' taking over to bloodily undo all that has gone wrong by unleashing still bigger wrongs. The best political representatives for a stable society are the centrists on both sides giving each other tolerable, within-limits, bound-by-law punches.

High in Uttarakhand mountains, in a little hamlet situated in seclusion of one kilometer steep climb from the nearest road, a native *Bhutia* dog has reached the ripe age of twenty. Earlier it was a common dog owned by the entire hamlet. A common asset for vigilance against *langoors* and bears tearing the bark of apple trees. But for the last two or three years it has stayed at my friend's house. Almost blind, most of the teeth gone, stiff weak joints. The dog has become a perfect representative for old age.

They say that for the last few seasons they have been expecting the old dog to call it a day. It would appear almost dying. But it has always sprung a surprise by coming back to life. They say the reason for this is that the dog has a good appetite and doesn't stop eating even when it looks taking its last breaths. The black dog with rheumy eyes and long shabby fur soaks sunrays during the day and gives a proof of its good digestion by eating thrice a day.

They have another dog, a golden retriever. It's very moody about eating and is all focused on playing and socializing. The old dog keeps sleeping even while the young one is jumping over it. In human terms, it's as old as someone at least 125 years old or even more than that. I'm saying him bye, 'Please be here when I come back again!' The old dog can't see properly. The old canine gentleman looks deeply at me, and having failed to see me clearly with its almost blind eyes, twitches its muzzle to smell the sense of what I say. It then shakes it old, bushy tail. Maybe it understood what I said and felt happy about it. Again it raises its muzzle in my direction and inhales the smell of the well-wisher who is expecting it to survive another season. Maybe it has clearly understood what I'm saying. I won't be surprised if it understands human language after spending two decades with them.

My friend's wife laughs loudly to hear my wishes for the old dog. But she is very positive about her responsibilities and I'm sure the old dog will get proper care as long as it is alive.

There are people, lot many in fact, who have already died to almost everyone around, long before their soul leaves this body. The dead-alive or alive-dead, I call them. They are already buried under earth. Their existence just a little mound, a tiny bump—an unnecessary interjection on the landscape. Once in a while someone stumbles upon the tiny protrudation, pauses briefly, tries to find some familiarity, recognition or relatedness. But just a little earthen mound it is. He or she simply passes over.

There are so many graves of the living dead on the footpaths and in the slums. The least one can do is to acknowledge their life, their existence and hence save them from a complete death long before they shed this body. A smile, a greeting, a slight bit of acceptance of the little space they occupy is all that is needed to confirm their living status. That is a ray of hope, light and love—a tiny beam of light let into the grave. It saves the still living corpse from rottening.

Nurture life. This much you can do if you are lucky to be still alive to those around you. You save them from getting eaten alive by the worms in the feed trough of oblivion by temporarily unifying your lucky existence with the unlucky ones to give them a momentarily enhanced being. It's healing in nature. They get a little respite from the rupture, fracture and parting from the living part of social fabric.

They have a hope in their heart struggling to meet the light outside. Their heart under a layer of dust forming a hard cake of dirt between the two. By pausing and acknowledging their existence, even by as small a gesture as a kind look, you let out a whiff of air from your mouth to remove the dust. Even that is sufficient.

Wounds are the cut marks but portals for new opportunities, new saplings, new shoots to grow—like a stream of life raising it little head from a branch grafting. They are an avenue for growth. Their—the living dead—entire existence is a big wound. The sun in your eyes and the compassion in your heart, just by a little gentle friendly brush with them, might help them in growing a tiny shoot.

10

FEBRUARY 25, a visit to the Mahakumbh *mela*. The more we feel the pangs of profligacy, the more we feel the need of rituals awaiting antiseptically to treat the germs of guilt born of an inner feeling about our wrongs in actual deeds, thoughts and emotions. The growing spasm between the set of moral values that we worship and our actual deeds is impulsively held tight under our instinctive dive into the pool of rituals. No wonder we have a buxom blossoming of rituals even in the modern age. Sullied with sins, we take holy dips to absolve the self from sins.

Even tragic news are attractive. Many holy-bath aspirants have died in stampedes. But instead of deterring the people, it's attracting still bigger crowds. The government of course has a political agenda, which is its right just like any other political party, in publicizing the event. Millions throng a limited space on a daily basis. Irrespective of untoward instances, the arrangement is commendable.

Since it's the *shahi snan* on Mahakumbh's concluding day, there is extra rush to Prayagraj. The bus starting from the town is full. There are many old people. A group of young revelers on the last seat in great festive spirit. They shout Lord Shiva's name in not so decent slang, raise a ruckus, shout, play cards, drink alcohol secretively mixed in coke bottles.

A man is travelling with his wife. He finds the drunk din rising from the last seat offensive. There is an argument. A policeman—in civil clothes—is also going to purify his body and soul. I ask him to intervene. The couple is offered a seat in the front section, away from the din. The party at the back goes as before.

By the time the bus stops at a rundown *dhaba* for dinner an old man is moving on unsteady legs. He is clearly drunk but still has a quarter left. He buys a small coke bottle, empties half of it as an offering to mother earth and refills it again with the contents of liquor from the other bottle. He was the most sober voice when the brawl took place earlier in the journey. He had spoken like an elderly sage, 'Brothers you should mind the fact that he is traveling with his wife. With a woman of course one would have less digestion for such fun and cry. Even you would have found it offensive if you were in his place instead of being the merrymakers on the last seat.'

Two farming women seem to be really loyal to their bedtime. There they lie to sleep in the narrow aisle, shaken to sleep by the rattling tin cradle. About 80 km from the destination the clutch system of the bus gives in. One can see smoke near the driver seat and a burnt smell fills the bus. The engine stops. Now is the time to chant Shiva's name with pure intensity. The older passengers remain inside. The rest of us get down to push the bus. The driver has given up hope and wants us to push it to a patrol station a few hundred meters away, visible with its hazy mercury light. He intends to park it there. And then allow the things to take their own course. But surprisingly the engine flutters to life after a few meters of pushing. It continues to run till 100 meters from the Nehru parking, the final destination. We are happy to reach despite the technical snag. I have been chanting *Mahamrityunjay mantra* all along the journey. So I take it as my reward for my chanting the Lord's name with focus and dedication.

They are minting money at Prayagraj. From Nehru parking, we ride a bike (200 rupees/passenger), travel for 12 km across the post-midnight mercury-bathed sleepy holy town and get dropped about 3 km from the *sangam ghat*. It's about two in the morning and a huge crowd is merging on the point of salvation. It's a *shahi snan* day and everyone must be having the thought of stampede deaths that occurred a month back. One can feel nervous air around the mass of pilgrims.

Millions of people have been visiting daily for the last month and a half. The facilities have been stretched thin, almost to the breaking point. Temporary toilet boxes are literally gas chambers They can blow you off your senses. A person with delicate nature will surely faint within a minute if locked inside. Most of the *babas* have gone to Banaras to pay homage to Lord Shiva at Kashi Vishwanath temple. It feels good. The probability of being beaten by an irate *naga sadhu* without any provocation is very less now. Many videos have gone viral showing the *nagas* abusing and hitting people without any reason. They seem to be enjoying the show like little children. It's good that most of the people take the beatings as blessings.

The crowd moves carrying a hum of faith, almost sleepwalking into the arms of divinity. Me and my friend take many dips. Millions of Her children have dumped their sins in the stream of Holiness. The water is murky. But it hardly matters to anyone. It's about being here with openness and acceptance. Emptying yourself of your strong sense of ego and Her blessings flow in like water filling an empty vessel.

Thousands of more pilgrims arrive with each passing minute. The administration is tense. There is a public announcement going on asking the pilgrims to leave immediately after taking holy dips to avoid overcrowding. As we get out of the bathing area, thousands are moving with us, humming with happiness for having taken the holy dip.

Again a bike ride to the parking lot. And just as we reach the spot, a UP Roadways bus to Delhi is waiting to be filled. We get the last seat. The suspension system looks rudimentary. It bumps up and down like a cart even on the smooth road. The jolts put the intestines in a knotted, defensive posture. It makes the task of forgetting the morning's call of nature quite easy. The bowl movement gets driven out of rhythm. It shuts off its operations to deal with the jolting emergency. Because in such a crisis the intestines have to save themselves first. Performance is secondary. It helps though, because there is hardly any usable toilet all along the journey. The system would stabilize only after a night's rest.

I'm happy that I went for this holy bath. It had been playing in my mind for the last many weeks. It's better to let the desires flow out instead of letting them stay in your system in a twisted form.

A perfect spring day in the first week of March. An utterly wonderful day poised between contrariness of hot and cold creating a tremulous ceasefire between the two. The sun unceasingly bright with a steady radiance. A cold wind cutting the warm fabric of sunshine. Mother nature crossing the fords to bloom fully. An idealized conception between hot and cold. A lovely liaison between father sun and mother earth. A pulsation of procreation. The balance lying in a mystery box teasing with tender inaccessibility. The sky bright blue shimmering with celestial wholesomeness. Restarting of a frozen flow; a blooming up after the winters. The air carrying courtesy, cordiality, felicity.

New leaves emerging with easeful proficiency. Buds opening fascinatingly, artfully. Flowers blooming as angelic personification of some cosmic urge to smile. The butterflies will soon arrive with the message that life is all beauty and honey. A sort of fullness flooding a rose as it maximizes its potential to bloom and happily scatter its petals to a gust of wind—a painless dissolution. A flower smiling rapturously with youth. The trees waving their branches with stately majesty in the wind. A leaf fluttering tremulously.

The squeaky falsetto of a purple sunbird. Maybe the female prodding the male with questions. Plentiful squeals of a tailorbird. Bewildering, chit-chatty sonority of sparrows as a flock. Velvety, marvelous smile on a maiden freshest with love. The shambling gallop of an old dog feeling young in spirit. At the zenith of their resolution, the trees and plants having survived the winters, now getting rewarded with new shoots and saplings. Mother nature watching with methodical magnanimity. Everyone looking up to the future having ridden themselves of the lacerating recollections of the past. Enlivening. Invigorating.

Self-loath is the genesis of all the hatred pouring out of us. It's the seed that lies deep in us nurtured by the manure of guilt, sense of failure, shortcomings, and the things that make us feel incomplete. It grows and acquires its domain over those around us. We can't hate anyone unless we ourselves hate a part of us. We just project it on others. The others just make us realize the existence of that hate deep in us.

In the same vein, those deeply in self-love will be able to carry it over to others. Otherwise, we are just trying to forget our own self-loath for some time in the form of a relationship. So fall in love with yourself. Go so deep that you become all love. Then your relationships won't be a mere need. They become natural bonds like the sunlight has with a flower.

This is something in celebration of the Taoists. The great sage Lao Tzu maintained that real knowing is to know that the unknowable can't be known. It leaves one with a clean slate at every instant, despite all the knowledge, information and analysis accumulated so far. It makes one an eternal learner, not learned. One flows with the flow. There is so much to learn at every instant, still one stays empty—an empty vessel where mother existence pours down a fraction of existence and a lovely unique manifestation happens. I'm glad that there are people who are in harmony with the Tao even in this post-modernist clatter and chatter!

Mid-March musings in celebration of colorful Holi spirit. Mother nature itself busy in springtime festivity of flowers, fresh shoots, verdant leaves.

Can you ever give something that you don't possess to someone? No. To give a coin to someone, you first need to have it in your possession. We can really give something to someone only if we have it. Otherwise, we just pretend to give and such fake offerings are laid bare sooner or later.

How will one give love, joy, companionship, peace, support and guidance to someone unless he/she already possesses them? So own these things first and then offer them to someone. In relationships we assume that we are there to give these things to the other person. While mostly we ourselves don't possess them. So we pretend that we are a real giver. While in reality we are in need of these very things. Imagine a situation where two takers are pretending to be givers.

An honest taker is better than a false giver. So be an honest taker, full of gratitude and acceptance, while you work on the lovely stock of joy and peace in your possession. And then one fine day offer it to someone in the form of a relationship. If you still have some surplus left with you, it will flow out of you in the form of grand emotions, art, poetry, healing words. Or say, your presence itself will become a conduit for the outflow of peace and harmony around you.

So blossom the colorful orchard of fragrant flowers within your *self* first. That is what Holi is about. Once we have the lovely garden in our persona, the bees and butterflies will come kissing the smell riding the air. Wish you all the vibrant, natural colors of humanity in your persona! Happy Holi!

The democratic world is in a crisis. The concept of freedom is warping due to the tug-of-war between liberals and conservatives within the democracies. As per the latest trends, the far-right radicals are targeting the leftist liberals as if they are the scourge of democracy.

Radical conservatives are becoming more popular. The conservative leaders are basically the showmen playing with the jugglery of rightist ideologies. Their swashbuckling hysterics create excitement and passion among the masses on the basis of religion, nationality, immigration, or anything that can create insecurity and false pride in the masses. They sell dreams in hyperbolic terms. Jingoism. Drama. Lots of noise. Nothing much is done on the ground. But in shouting, yelling and raising banners, the people think they are contributing to make their nation great.

The leftist liberals accomplish far more things at a natural pace, bring out real change. But all this may go down as nonperformance given their subdued intonation. A classic example is the work style of PM Manmohan Singh and PM Modi. The former with his unassuming persona actually brought about real effective change on the surface. The latter has built a high-pitched public avatar of himself, which is disproportionally too big for the little change that has actually happened on the ground for the common man.

The major world democracies are shifting to radical rightist control under powerful monopolist leaders who find democratic institutions and consensual obligations too limited and confining to operate. They are pushing at the edges of democracy to give it a new shape. They are spreading their cult to the fringes of electoral autocracy. The spirit of democracy is seriously strained. The far right conservatives are looking to melt the democratic iron fence and take their newly created space to meet China-type communist authoritarianism.

These macho leaders feel suffocated by the checks and balances of democratic institutions. They find the leftist liberals bigger enemies even than the non-democratic authoritarian rulers. No wonder, one can feel that Trump and Modi are more at ease with Xi and Putin.

Democracy seems like a bloated amoeba. A part of it (the rightist conservatives) is trying to cut itself off from the main body and merge with the authoritarian regime. And in countries where this is happening, the people are slowly getting habituated to a new set-up. They still believe that it's the very same old democracy. It's out of habit that they still believe that nothing has changed even though so many things have changed gradually just in a decade. The fundamental character of once autonomous institutions is slowly giving way to a new normal where their political misuse is the new norm.

Oligarchs—in both democratic and authoritarian world—are in close brotherhood across the ideological divides. They are like a dismembered amoeba, having different limbs in different countries but still sharing the same soul even though there is no physical contact. They are a great cementing bond between the far right democratic politicians and the dictators in shadow regimes. Oligarchs would always prefer a closed, manipulated politico-economic system. It's beneficial to their unique regime. No wonder they would naturally support and finance radical, rightist authoritarian leaders who will mold the economic environment for oligarchy's smooth passage.

Here are a few snippets from Shekhar's illustrious life. In school the best piece of writing he accomplished (far better than any exam he wrote) was a letter he wrote to his armyman father. His illiterate mother dictated the contents. The basic idea was about conveying his undisciplined, errant ways that were in reverse direction to all that was taught at the village school. It was to be concluded with a request to give him a spanking when his father arrived for his annual vacations.

He was ten or eleven at that time. She thought he wasn't smart enough to temper with the contents at such a delicate age. But she was mistaken. Shekhar remembered at least the essence of antonyms taught at the school. So he wrote the opposite stating he was a good boy giving details of his obedient ways in school and nice helping tasks he performed at home. And all this, the letter concluded, entitles him to a prize, a cricket bat. So a couple of months later his proud father arrived with a cricket bat. But first it was used on his bum once he came to know about the truth.

Shekhar possessed great treasurer qualities. His clay moneybox full of coins, he was looking for the safest place to keep it hidden from his siblings and other thieves prowling the village streets. At dusk he went to the shrubbery outside the village, serving as open public toilet, dug a hole, put the treasure inside, placed the soil back, padded it quite firmly and put the locker of his defecation on the top as a firm seal of inviolable property.

He loved money and even at a delicate age understood that it takes lots of efforts to earn wealth. Ajit was a few years elder to him. He was tossing a one rupee coin with malicious glee. He was testing the money-making guts of the village brats. He pointed out a farmer's big heap of defecation and challenged anyone to strike it down with a fist blow and earn the top prize.

Even the most rascally ones gave in. Not Shekhar. He made a ball of fist with his left hand, kissed the curled little finger at the base and struck with purpose and force, with enough power so that there was no space for the bet-maker to cry foul. The heap was flattened. He had a dirty left hand. 'In any case it does the same every morning!' he consoled the shocked group of brats around. After that he bathed in the village pond for half an hour holding the prize money in his right hand.

Apart from running his barber shop he manages a tiny dairy unit. It involves three or four cows whose milk his wife sells to get her share of pocket money to feel economically independent. There are plenty of *gau* and *nandi shalas* in the countryside where the farmers leave the surplus calves. It was a male calf that Shekhar had to leave at the cow shelter. Named Sanda, the baby bull was much pampered by Shekhar's family.

Shekhar was very sad to leave it in the cramped space full of bulls of all sizes ranging from Hercules to motes. From behind the grills, they competed to eat donated chapattis, jaggery and other cattle feed. After a fortnight Shekhar committed the mistake of crossing over into the yard and call Sanda affectionately with a piece of jaggery in his hand. It recognized him and ran like a child rushing to meet his father. But a huge-horned bull got offended and as if accusing him of favoritism ran after him. When he jumped over the wall he felt a rough graze of cattle horn on his bum. It was a close save.

'Nothing' wants to be 'something'. The eternal emptiness is forever seeking to be impregnated with something (temporary). The endless flow of emptiness (eternal) briefly sparkles as a stream of water. Carrying its fluid independence, shaped by circumstances, moving without any ego constraints, following the natural free-flowing law of its mother, the stream of eternal emptiness. The line of water also has a smaller empty womb pregnant with a broad set of possibilities (but still limited in comparison to the eternal mother). It sires a still limited manifestation of the free eternal flow—a snake. The snake is a more conscious replica of its mother stream having flesh and bones. It's still further away from the free flow (water), just like water itself is away from the mother stream of eternal emptiness. The fluidity and freedom of its crawl is curtailed by the impulsive fears and struggle for survival because it has to maintain its structural elements.

Similarly, from the eternal empty float of 'nothingness', the air manifests with smaller freedoms than its mother. Out of air the birds manifest and fly with still lesser free flow than the mother component. The grandchildren of the grand eternal 'nothing' have lesser and lesser element of free flow with the coming of new generations. The eternal simplicity turning more and more complex.

The eternal 'nothing' becomes earth, the earth becomes trees. From the eternal grand simplicity to a structural sophistication in each new generation. But this drive towards sophisticated manifestation—from eternal emptiness to rudimentary elemental structuring to complex restructuring further down the line—is like setting up check-dams of restraint upon the infinite force of eternal 'nothing'. It's a channelization for smaller streams.

An evolutionary path: the Big Bang, galaxies collapsing, black holes eating stars up the stream to a small wild flower and a honeybee hovering over it down the line. The blinding fury of the infinite now channelized to a beautiful little fragrant stream. The species like humans—who have a relatively bigger capability to channelize the little streams—have a special responsibility to take it further down the path of lovelier manifestations. A human blooming flowers is far more in symmetry with the eternal flow than the human who is making nuclear bombs to create more destructive forces. It's like going back to the primal age of infinitely destructive forces.

This existence has already seen too many explosions happening of its own in faraway galaxies. It can definitely do without our little childish firecrackers. Evolution is to take us more and more away from the destructive forces. Because we have started from super-massive galactic bangs. Making weapons to create more death and destruction instead of helping evolve more and more beauty is like going back into the fire we started from. Let's add to the beauty. Let there be sunshine on the layers of foggy illusions. Let there be more flowers and trees. Let there be a heaven on the earth where callused hands enjoy delicious fresh food and exquisite wine. Let's accept that wisdom is basically about silence and just a tiny fraction of essential words. Let's accept the commonality, our shared being. Let's acknowledge the entangled roots that we have. Let's be sensitive to the perceptible and imperceptible flow of pain in our veins. We carry the joys and sorrows of our ancestor forests in our body. Let's feel it and be aware of it. That's the soil that nurtured us.

Superstitions will have easy takers among the people of different nationalities, races, religions, ethnicities, classes, castes. We will easily fight over different gods and geographies. But when it comes to superstitions we drop the guard. A Hindu will take Muslim superstitions to ward off the evil eye. Because all of us carry the same primal fear. In the brotherhood of fear, we are just the same little children. It's the same reaction. Like a well-organized and tidy person of any religion or nationality winces with the same reaction after cutting on the soft inside of his cheek.

I'm walking on my solitary. A lot has changed in the last three-four years. Then it was a little ribbon of wilderness running through agricultural fields, flanked by two canals and the foot track overgrown with trees, reeds, shrubs and bushes. It gave the feeling of a forest walk. To ease the removal of silt from the canals the trees have been cut, the reeds and grass mowed down. Just a few big trees remain. So now it's like walking on a big field embankment. The blasting human population is finding it increasingly difficult to find more resources.

It's late March. The wheat crop has a golden hue and moving fast towards harvesting. The evening heat seems to be stewing a fragrance of grass and wild flowers. Heaps of silt have been dredged from the canals and line the trail like March flowers once used to dot the path. The sand and silt is a lucrative business. The wild flowers just inspire some poems in a poet. I accept the change, the inevitable master of earthly ceremonies. I smell the lovely fragrance of whatever is left. A heady smell of honey sweetens the mood. Some lone honeycomb nearby on a *peepal* tree!

And there stands the mourning tree. It was once a huge, luxurious *semal* (silk cotton tree). In March and April it used to smile with big, red, luscious flowers. Then the sand mafia came. Greedy for the river silt piled around the tree, they scraped away earth, cutting its big roots. The tree survived somehow. But it hasn't smiled even once, not a single flower, during the last two years. And now when the spring is at its peak and flowers are abloom on uninjured *semal* trees somewhere else, this sad tree stands without even a single leaf, forget about flowers. It's its way of showing its mourning over the loss. It still greets me with its sad barren silhouette. I feel its pain. With a little extension of our sensitivity, we can feel and be aware of the joys and sorrows of the non-human component of life on earth. The flowers are their smiles. The blobs of sap oozing from the cuts on the bark are their tears. Their luxurious canopy swaying to the winds is their dance. The ripe fruits, shadow and fresh air is their kindness. It's all there. We just need to be aware of it.

I put my hand on its hard bark. A handshake. An acknowledgment of the humans' rapacious ways. I feel sorry from the side of the humans. 'Don't worry, I am trying to smile with flowers and one fine day I will welcome you on this solitary trail with my red blooms!' it seems to say. Well, best of luck you fighter tree. You are injured but big and strong. Keep your faith alive. Let's hope for the best during the next spring. And till then our handshakes and greetings continue. Let this friendship stay fresh in my heart and your wooden tissues. It's a lovely friendship and I'm honored to be your friend, privileged to feel your pain and would be joyous in sharing your spring smiles.

Rashe Ram smokes weed. Eats lots of chapattis. Works like a beast as a daily wage earner. On top of that he hasn't got a mind bugged with over-thinking. So he is hefty and relaxed. There are many in the village who share his weed-filled *beedis* for free. He gets it from the slum areas in Bawana and after meeting his personal needs sells the extra stuff at a very small margin of profit. If we take into account what others smoke for free from him, it's a no profit no loss venture. Still he is a weed seller in the eyes of law.

Someone informs upon him. The police pick him up. The cops basically beat the vagrants, giving prodigious pain to body as well as ego. They enjoy both. They love taking bribe as well and let out the beaten guy after making his wallet weightless. But in the case of Rashe Ram they instantly realize that there is hardly anything to be drawn out of his wallet. So this source of pleasure is gone. They take recourse to the other—beating. Normally, in case of routine offenders, it gives the policemen a sadistic pleasure to see their ego melting and identity crumbling. But unluckily for the police, Rashe Ram's detached self is beyond the bruises of ego. So as they thrash him, very soon they realize there is hardly any fun in beating this guy. Just plain wastage of energy. It's like hitting a wall, or some street bull at the most. They can feel that their strikes aren't penetrating beyond his thick skin. It feels like they have been beating a big heap of sack cloth. The policemen feel cheated. They just throw him out to get rid of him.

Bookish guys are usually lazy. Poetic in a practical world; grandly aloof, musing over time's mossy transience. So I find myself congratulating India for its digital platforms to provide online financial and administrative services. I'm elated the moment I come to know that I need not go to the district court premises to get my driving license (DL) renewed. It can be done online. It feels like a gift. Wow! So I apply in high spirits. I pay the fees and upload all the required documents. Now I just have to wait for a brand new DL. I keep checking for the latest status of my application. But the process doesn't move ahead. It shows the same 'document scrutiny' stage for more than three weeks. So I go to the district mini-secretariat with all my application printouts in a file, just like one does in an offline application.

As I'm walking towards the e-Disha Kendra, located on the sprawling district secretariat campus, a man comes running. 'Bumblebees are here! They are attacking people!' he shouts a warning to me. I see big bumblebees reconnoitering the air for human enemies. I take a turn and start moving away by the side of the block towards the more crowded place of steno kiosks, notaries and lawyer chambers. The ratio of the enemies per bee would be high there. They have targeted a man. He is crying for help, flailing his arms to ward them off. They are biting him with more force in greater numbers. It's like getting stuck in a quagmire. The more you flail your limbs, the more you get stung.

Someone has started a smoky fire to deter the natural drone attackers, known for their volatile temper and painful stings. Two soldier bees are stuck in my hair on top of head on the right side. They furiously buzz their wings. I know the rule. Never move your hands to ward them off. If you do so, you are instantly locked as the target and hundreds of bee fighters would attack you. So I walk like Dr. Manmohan Singh, keeping my arms stuck to my sides, not moving my torso in any direction or angle. The disciplined, non-threatening walk of an academician.

I can hear the man who has been attacked shouting, '*Hai* they are eating me, please save me!' You can hardly do anything to help someone in this situation even with the best of your philanthropic emotions. The bees in my hair are angrily buzzing but I keep my arms jutted to my sides. Dozens are hovering around me. The moment I swipe my hand to get the bees off my head, they will pin me down as the next target. When I feel that I'm safe in a narrow corridor I start brushing with a soft hand, my fingertips barely touching the hair, to get the bees away. They unleash the entire stock in their weaponry on my head. Bumblebees sting very painfully. For an instant I go numb with pain. But I'm successful in getting rid of them. Thankfully I haven't been spotted striking their soldier friends by the other bees.

I hastily cross a narrow strip of lawn between the blocks to move towards another section, the older blocks which aren't spacious and airy like the one that I have just crossed. It's an old, claustrophobic, musty, rusty maze. It makes me feel more secure as I move into its outer corridor.

An old man and an old woman, husband and wife visiting the courts for some official work, emerge from the new, spacious block. The bees have entered its main lobby. The old couple has broken the rule. They are panicked and vigorously waving their hands above their head and around their face to keep the bees off. Hundreds are hovering around them attacking and stinging at free will. To make it still worse for the man (in comparison to his wife, who is waving just hands), he is forcefully waving a cloth in the air around him. It invites bigger attacks. The woman shouts feeble cries for help. The man is simply focused on beating with the piece of cloth. They are tired. They walk a few steps and sit on the ground almost giving into the bees.

Everyone is at a loss about what to do. I shout and ask them to keep moving towards our side. The man seems to have surrendered. He can barely walk. The woman performs slightly better. She keeps pleading in a helpless tone, 'Pour water! Pour water on us!' But where is water? I feel utterly helpless. What to do? I can feel their pain but what to do. A young man comes rushing out from the new block. He is waving a black piece of cloth around him to avoid getting stung. He has a mosquito repellent spray bottle in hand. The bees attack him also. He is spraying clouds of mosquito repellent around the old man. But it's almost ineffective.

Our family has a history of death due to bumblebee stings. My great grandfather was attacked by an entire swarm of bumblebees while returning from the fields after a hard day of tilling land. It was early 1890s and there was hardly any medical facility in the village at that time. He died because of excessive swelling which the village *hakeem* couldn't manage. I feel on the upper right side of my head. There are two lumps. The crown of my head is numb.

The faces of the old couple are blood red due to multiple stings. By this time they seem to have given up to fate. You want to help but how? There must surely be better and more efficient ways of managing a bumblebee attack. At least I don't have any clue. Neither has the district administration.

It's a weighty fact that someone can be almost drawn to the portals of death right there in the middle of district administration centre, the axis of local police, judiciary and bureaucracy. Where you have the district collector, police superintendent, magistrates and judges. But the powerful authority is clueless as to how to help an old couple getting painfully stung by hundreds of bumblebees, crying for help while slowly moving from one block to the other. The response is just to watch, wait and allow the bees to stop stinging. Big cars, sirens, gun-toting guards, arrogance, systematic loot and plunder. All helpless in the face of a bee attack. The officers, judges and magistrates must be watching from safe, sealed windows.

The bees keep attacking the old man even while he has reached the crowded notary stalls. Finally the attacking squad dissipates. Someone takes the old couple to the hospital. I hope they have injections against bee bites. A thin plume of smoke is splaying the air as disaster management response.

I enter the block where my file needs to be submitted. There I stand with two lumps on my head holding an offline folder as a follow-up to the online application. I complain why wasn't document verification done since I have uploaded all the required documents and the website says I need not visit the office physically. 'Because you didn't submit the file,' the woman tells my curtly. 'Then what's the difference between offline application and online application?' I'm about to ask. But I think the better of it. She might get offended and raise some unnecessary issue about the file, requiring more visits. So I keep mum and enjoy the offline process after having completed the digital version.

A bookish stilt in my attitudional accent. It's a precarious poetic perch. Spirits dampened with driftless destiny. Exasperating decadence strewn around. The world lost in the lore of gladiatorial guts and bloody gore. Thankfully my yard and small garden possess a stageful dignity; a small world having its deference-deserving dust.

The brown and yellow striped cat is commodiously pregnant. The would-be mother is relaxing with a rotund belly. A cat has exemplary excellence in the art of relaxation, almost perfect ease. And from this arises an esteemed sense of alertness. A sepulchral silence out of which are born swift darts at the prey. Extremely relaxed, extremely alert. Latching onto the productive strains of providence whenever the slightest chance opens.

The flycatcher voicing frilly thoughts; convulsive nerves of the tailorbird; churlishly blinkering babblers. They see the cat relaxing. It has lost its agility but it needs to eat till the day of delivery. For its kittens. Lackadaisical attitude won't do. Aha the eminent rhythms of motherhood! And there it jumps up suddenly and runs across the courtyard towards the garden, galloping with a stately mix of firmness and gentleness. It has undertaken eight or ten such runs to catch some lazy bird or squirrel. It wants some meaty delicacy which we can't offer.

Chapattis and milk it doesn't prefer, a feral cat it's after all. So it wants to hunt for its kittens in its belly.

When you see a pregnant female, across all species, it breeds natural respect for her. You might not be actually aware of it, but when you give a look of respect, or hold out a helping hand, or get up from your seat to offer it to her, you are performing a deeply religious act. It's almost like a holy ritual. Usually when I see a bird or cat after a prey, I impulsively intervene from the prey's side. But not this time. Scaring her away from her hunting pursuit in such a heavily pregnant state feels like something unholy. I just leave it to fate and watch it as it unfolds.

Nostradamus… Baba Venga… What to say about their predictions? In my humble opinion, which is inspired by what great Osho said on the subject, it's about recognizing the cyclic pattern of major types of events and the chief types of characters involved in them. It would obviously fit with later events and the people involved in bringing them into effect.

See, there is a cyclical pattern in wars, like small wars occurring after so many years and bigger wars happening after roughly a particular number of smaller cycles of time. And all the violent leaders have a particular type of personality, which can be easily guessed because all of them are cut from the same fabric.

So these so-called future forecasters, they don't have godly insights to see things in advance. They have practical knowledge of the cyclical pattern of major types of events and the mind and personality types of the leaders who get engaged in these events. So obviously what they forecast in advance will have some matching with the events that follow and the leaders involved in them. It's a very practical art or rather skill.

The same goes for all astrologers and the science of astrology.

I go and pick-up my niece from the university hostel over the weekends. The last spring was a special one on the campus. The head gardener was a man who loved his job—the result was a beautiful flowery world; rows and rows of healthy, well-cared flowers. The flowers danced, smiled, grew old and died under the merciless April sun that followed the short north Indian spring.

I picked up many varieties of dry flowers to store and use them as seeds during the next season. My little garden is overloaded with plants and trees. The only space available was in the pots of rose plants, about a dozen of them. This January I mixed the seeds with soil and dung manure and layered them in the pots having single rose plants. There they came out heralding a lovely spring.

Hundreds of chamomiles, a daisy like small flower with little white petals around a yellow core, waved at me in February and March. Chamomile is a lovely flower, which is used as flavoring agent in food and beverages. There were so many of them in the crowded little space in the pots. The space was limited but they gave their best. They couldn't grow to full length but even the tiniest ones among them smiled and offered a flower to some lone bee or butterfly. The chamomiles had beaten all other varieties to bloom as a colony.

The present university gardener doesn't seem too sincere about his job as can be guessed from the absence of flowers save for some marigolds. I think the chamomile angels attracted the fancy of a poet and carried the survival of their colony in his little yard. I saw some honeybees among the chamomiles. At least some tiny honeycomb somewhere not too far!

The chamomiles dazzled for almost two months and died under hot April sun, their withering looks asking me to preserve their seeds for the next season. I did as asked.

I pull out the dry stalks carefully avoiding injuring the stunted growth of *gaillardia grandiflora* (blanket flower) which had been trying to seek a way out of the dense crop of chamomiles. There we have the runner up. A few green leafy sprouts of blanket flowers now growing hurriedly to make the most of whatever the season has to offer. Their soft leafy sprouts had been struggling to come out and kiss the air above and dazzle their smiles.

Within a week of the clearing around them one of them smiled its ornamental orange red smile. So they occupy the second position. It's a hybrid plant in the sunflower family. I have put the pots under the shade to allow dozens of them to smile even in this heat. These are brave flowers.

I hope some lone flower of some other variety will also blossom up to claim the third position. Sometimes just being there earns you a standing among the top three. So come on you some lone ranger, plow your way up!

It's a tailorbird boy. I remember it tagging around its parents among the garden plants, its parents shouting the moment you stepped into the zone where it was hiding. That was during the winters and it was really smart of them to keep their chick out of the dining table of the brown female feral cat that sunned itself on the premises. Now in this early May heat I think the adolescent tailorbird chick is on its own. I don't think it goes out of the garden walls. It has enough among the plants and trees in the yard to meet its dietary requirements.

The boy tailorbird has chosen an interesting place to sleep during the night. There is an iron hook in the once barn wall—now housing my dented old car instead of mother's buffalos and cows—about five feet from the ground. From it hangs a dusted polybag having dried flowers meant to be used as seeds next spring and a couple of thin rubber tubes hanging in loops. And in one loop there it perches for the night.

The birdie boy retires early for the day, when it's still bright enough to see it sitting at its place. It doesn't mind our moving around the perch on our normal routine tasks. But it has almost crashed into my nose a couple of times when I inadvertently went too close to its house.

At night it almost mixes with the surroundings by raising its fluffy fur and drawing itself into a little ball. Since it's an adolescent boy, it'll be a dashing handsome man by the time the monsoons arrive a couple of months down the line. I hope by that time it will be grown enough to have a partner.

The *champa* shrub—though I prefer to call it a tiny tree—is squeezed between a wall and a domineering *parijat*. But even in the limited space the tiny tree with green stems and mossy-green long and sturdy leaves gave its best and sprung many lateral shoots. But the monkeys would love to break the green stems. Maybe they love the distinct juicy thudding sound when the stem or branch snaps. It's quite distinct from the breaking sound of any other tree's branch, which is high-pitched and tangy in feel.

So the plant grew slim and shot through the narrow opening between the *parijat* and the wall. It has a little canopy now, and in harmony with surprisingly plenty May rains, it's redolent with seven bunches of lovely white flowers having a scented yellow core. They have a very gently, yet quite effective, wafting smell. Shaken by the wind the flowers keep falling through the day. Each time I pick a flower it seems like a gift. When I'm feeling lethargic I put a few of them on my palm and inhale the smell from close quarters. It changes the mood drastically, making me clear headed instantly.

The *parijat* has shed all its leaves. It looks forlorn with dry seedpods at the end of dead fringes of dried branches and boughs. A death before getting reborn. The hardworking *champa* has shown enough resilience in blossoming so many smiles despite the challenges it has faced. It deserves a reward. A reward for staying there as an optimist despite monkey mischief and limited space.

I clear a few dry twigs and branches on the *parijat* to give a little bit of extra open sky to the lovely sprinkler of smiles. Well, if you keep trying to bloom and grow despite the roadblocks, you reach a point where someone or something will be there to help you. But for that to happen you have to keep going and reach that point.

When I'm near Gaga Ma I somehow go footloose. Walking on Her banks or on the landscapes shaped by Her torrential flow becomes my meditation, my ritual, my *tapasya*. I just find myself keep walking. The pent-up energies, emotions, karmic entanglements all start flowing as if pushed by Her blessing shove. I just walk. Gently. In a fine flow with myself. No destination. No goal. She does what is supposed to be done; what is needed for Her child's growth.

This is late April and I'm staying at Dharali. I'm here to walk with Ma Ganga Doli Yatra from Mukwa to Gangotri—the colorful procession starting from Her winter abode to culminate at Her summer home. It's a soulful procession, full of colors, redolent with local hill people's unquestionable faith in Ma Ganga. No words can describe the feeling. The participants in the procession caught in a devotional frenzy. I walk with them and simply keep looking at Her beautiful, kind, pious face visible through the small opening in the little silver shrine being carried by the bearers. I'm just filling myself with as much *darshan* as possible. Plundering the divine *prasad* actually. Greedily. Copiously.

It's a lovely little trek lasting about 22 km. When the procession reaches Gangotri, the entire little pilgrimage town lines up to welcome their mother. The place is as good as nonexistent without Her. No wonder, it's abandoned during the winter months when the mother is away at Mukwa.

There is a suspension bridge over Ganga Ma linking Dharali on this side to Mukwa on the opposite hill. During nights I keep walking from this end of the bridge to the other. The hill people usually stay indoors after the dark, so I have the bridge all to myself for meditative walks. It's a spiritually heady cocktail of elements: the mountain wind rushing through the valley, Ma Ganga's roar, my seeking self and the pristine open starry sky above. All the elements forming a tiny intersection defining my path.

I keep asking people whether they know some real saint to recommend for a meeting. Almost all of them say—with helplessness—that presently it's all about money, power, authority, perks and privileges; religion is more or less a big business and a political tool now; the *babas* are powerful and do liaisoning work facilitating big interests of powerful people. But when was it not so? The ritualistic part has always engaged with worldly matters more or less on the base frequency.

I'm more into spirituality. Moreover, this is *kaliyuga*— the age of darkness. And expecting *satyuga* purity in *kaliyuga* sages would be asking too much. To me it's pretty simple. Earlier in pure climate you had massive trees lasting centuries; now we have lesser trees struggling to survive in the changed climate. The same is the case with the sages in the changed, degraded social climate. They are also the stunted version of the lofty mythical sages of the ancient times. But at least they are carrying the lineage and deserve respect for that. So I'm not too judgmental and usually try to have *satsang* with *kaliyuga* saints.

Mahesh, the gentle and kind hotelier, is a thorough gentleman; always ready to do something for the *babas* and *matajis* of the entire area from his place to Gangotri. I ask him about any serious *baba*. He also says with sadness that it's all business now. 'But you can try meeting this *avadhuta*. But it depends on his mood. Usually he asks the visitors to leave within a couple of minutes or straightaway refuses to meet,' he tells me.

This *babaji* stays at the other end of the bridge towards Mukwa. As you emerge on the other end of the bridge, the main steep climb goes to Mukwa up the hill. The *baba* has a tiny hut of planks and tin fixed against a rockface on the left side a few meters above Ma Ganga's stream. To reach his ramshackle little gate, one has to walk under the bridge along the bank and cross over to the other side of the bridge's base.

As I reach the tiny indicator of the start of a human's domain in free wilderness, I see a stocky figure sitting under a tree on a platform in front of the hut. I gently hark his attention from the gate. He waves his hand asking me to come in. I walk gingerly. I'm extra cautious, full of additional politeness in order not to disturb him. As I come near, with a swift action he throws a small *durri* piece on a beaten down wooden chair near him. I touch his feet and sit at the chair's edge with folded hands.

'I'm sorry if I'm disturbing you *swami ji*. I just wanted to see you. I simply come as an empty vessel. Ready to accept whatever you bless me with,' I cautiously approach with respect and acceptance of his graceful presence. He laughs with childlike innocence.

I keep my promise of being an empty vessel and just listen. The *baba* talks. I'm lucky that he is feeling happy to talk today. He is a Begali *baba* initiated into Ramakrishna mission. But he found the ashrams too binding and has been on his own for the last six decades, most of which he has spent in this area near Ma Ganga including the last 37 years here at this place. Earlier he stayed in a cave about one kilometer up the stream for some years and before that at Gangotri.

He speaks with a cute Bangla accent. Quite hale and hearty for his 77 years. The *baba* is happy to share his life story and even tells me about his family. It's a nice *satsang* for an hour and fifteen minutes. He is quite vocal about a *sadhak* keeping the vow of celibacy. I have my opinion on this but I know he knows more than me and I must listen to him.

'O *narayan ji*, why are you unnecessarily entangled in this worldly *maya*? Leave it. Quit,' he says it very naturally like he feels that's what I should do now. 'Sit for *sadhna*. You can sit in my former cave some distance from here. I'll ask the villagers to help you initially. In any case, what does a *sanyasi* need? The basic needs are met by mother nature. So you need not worry about that,' the *baba* is quite optimistic about me taking full *sanyas* and abandon all worldly connections.

'Can't one achieve peace even while staying in the world with its issues?' I ask. He says a firm 'no' and doesn't explain it further than this. I have arguments in my talkative mind but I don't say anything.

Even Kaka *Maharaj* who stays outside my village, asked me to abandon everything and sit for *sadhna* somewhere by the canal in the area where he has been staying for the last many decades. In fact, my brother laughs that I have been offered two penthouses by two *babajis*. But I know I'm not for complete severance of worldly ties. I'm for a balanced life in all matters. More than that, I believe in reading and writing and that I will do till my last breath. I'm not worried even if that creates situations not conducive to absolute peace. No problem.

'If you don't quit, the God will force you to leave all this worldliness, which stops one from enjoying the grace of absolute peace,' the *baba* says emphatically. I just clear my throat apologetically.

As I take leave and stoop down to touch his feet, the *baba* puts his loving, kind hand on my head and gently pats my back saying, 'Peace be with you! Peace be with you!' He gives me two apples, a bit stale, dejuiced, somewhat shriveled. Actually all his apples are like that. He isn't bothered about freshness of fruits. But the fruits are fresh with divine grace.

During our interaction the *baba* gets a firm idea, and rightly so, that I'm a bookworm. He opens a bundle of soiled cloth and from a stack of very old books randomly picks a part of an old, dog-eared book. 'Read it! But reading scriptures is like using a thorn to take out the thorn in one's flesh. After taking out the thorn both thorns have to be discarded,' he says. The *baba* knows the utility and futility of knowledge. He is after all a graduate himself.

There I walk back after hitting the jackpot—*satsang* with a saint, two apples and an old book about the lamp of knowledge. The rumpled, crumpled book has been thoroughly thumbed; possibly during his former knowledge-seeking days. The thorn of knowledge which he used to pull out the thorn of ignorance. The pages bear extensive markings, underlines, sidenotes and scrawls in Bangla to give me an idea how extensively *babaji* has gone through this book. He seems to have gone into depths over each world and phrase on the banks of Ganga Ma over the decades.

This is a prized catch—in worldly lingo. I might not be able to read it as extensively as the *baba* but its mere presence among my books is enough to dispel the dark corners of ignorance in my study. It's enlightening just by its presence. How it can't be? After all, it has stayed in the hands of such a longtime *sadhak* who has definitely attained a joyful state. I feel that joyfulness in my head now. A feeling of ease. Palpable. Not many ideas swimming in the brainy pool. Just an emptiness. I feel the grace of his peaceful touch as I walk back.

Yea, missed to tell it. The *baba* listens with the cute excitement of a child listening to fairy tales. I was telling him the story of a Zen monk and he looked and listened in rapt attention, a childlike smile on his face all along the narration.

A thin film of distrust deposited like limescale on the taphead; yellowness on the teeth; moss on a shadowed musty stone; stains on a toilet seat; permanent smudge of holy paste on an idol's forehead.

It was coming up slowly, stealthily, the thin film. Then you see it someday—cropped up like fungus on dead wood. You and your partner see it but won't speak about it. But it's quite distinct, palpable now. The thin film gets under dust and then with more coatings of dirt turns to a solid concrete wall—the partners working like masons busy in laying their share of bricks, erecting walls. The hard boundaries come into being. Separation. The division of that unity. Fracture.

The wall could have been avoided had both of them done a little bit of daily scrubbing, de-scaling, polishing, rubbing and de-staining to keep it decently clean if not spotlessly clean altogether.

We keep pseudo-patriotism on our tongues. The shouters; the culinary rationalists tasting the exciting dish of hate, leering with misplaced, mouthwatering pride.

As the super-species ruling the planet, we have created a hierarchy of pain, rights and entitlements. The pain and rights of the non-human manifestations of life are secondary, almost inconsequential, and are taken as the means to fulfill our needs.

No wonder the balance is gone. It's unsustainable. The birds, plants and animals are rightless. Their loss is meaningless. It opens the way for their destruction. But the fire won't stop there. It will then start eating we humans. The non-human part of nature is in fact the shield against this fire.

Poetry is a medium for the expression of truth, love, peace, joy, one's deep pain, hope and dreams. It's never meant for conveying falsehoods. Falsehoods can be sustained to an extent through prose by going into logical arguments. It comes from the smaller *self*, the insecure animal trying to survive. But poetry comes from the bigger *self*, from the soul and its representative, heart. It bypasses the mind. If one conveys falsehoods through poetry that'll be mere prose written in rhyme.

As the insecure minds unleash wars world over, a poet will keep praying and hope that a soft bud of peace starts to open as the war hysteria touches its peak and would inevitably slide down onwards. Then will bloom a small fragrant flower somewhere among the charms of highland mists.

11

TWO brothers can make a very useful, helpful and convenient travelling pair. There are limits drawn which avoid things from taking an ugly shape. In addition, the assurance that they will be going to the same house again provides an openness and vast space for both the good and bad to unfold naturally. There are no protocols to follow, no rules of friendship to abide by to keep things going. You are at your natural self. You don't have an image to keep that fits in the mold of friendship. No wonder, travelling becomes very enjoyable in such a scenario. To cash all the above benefits, me and my brother usually go out on trips a few times every year. He is younger to me and the Indian tradition of seniority and respect falling in the kitty of the elder brother makes it advantageous for me. This time we are bound for Ladakh.

We can say that earth is completely owned by the humans by now. The rest, everything from the animals, birds, reptiles, insects, trees, plants, stones and even plain dust seem to be the mere means to the question of how far the humans can stretch, elongate and further their desires. We have been plainly greedy; not ingenious in the least.

We are too crowded in mind, body and soul. When it becomes unbearable, and if we can afford it in terms of time and money, we set out to the hills to feel less loaded and burdened among open hill forests. Earth is covered with human-made concrete megaliths in the plains. However, the stamp of mankind shows a gradual dilution from the congested lanes of old Delhi to the hill forests. The hill forests in turn give the baton to alpine meadows and grasses. The alpine grasses then change to barren waste and cold desert adorned with snow-covered peaks.

Ladakh is a beautiful empty vessel where one can dive into the vast wilderness stretched from horizon to horizon. The bus from Delhi to Leh is making a big buzz on the social media. It starts from Delhi at noontime, reaches Keylong in the wee hours and after a few hours halt proceeds to Leh, plying on the toughest and highest motorable passes to reach Leh by nine at night if everything stays normal in terms of weather and roads.

There are enough challenging and exciting jolts on the road journey from Keylong to Leh, so we avoid this first phase of the journey by the HRTC bus from Delhi and board a luxury Volvo bus to reach Keylong. From there onwards one doesn't have an option apart from the HRTC Delhi-Leh bus.

The plains are burning in the June heat as we board the Volvo bus to Manali. There is T20 cricket final between India and South Africa played in the Caribbean islands. A group of youngsters is watching live streaming of the match on some OTT platform. There are expert comments, gesticulations, guffaws of agony, ecstasy, *hoos* and *haas*. We Indians have lots of cricketing sense at least. All this overshadows Sidhu's hyperbolic, rhetorical commentary in the stadium. The youngsters are engaged in such a dissecting analysis of each ball, each run, each moment that it feels like one is watching the match live. It was a very exciting match. The entire bus full of tension. When India won the match, one chap shouted at the top of his voice, '*Bharat Mata ki jai*!' We had to rally behind his chorus in our varying capacities to shout.

We reach Manali in early morning and immediately walk to catch a bus to Keylong. Once you come out of the Atal tunnel (9 km long) cutting across the guts of a mammoth wall of mountain, thus avoiding the difficult Rohtang pass, you arrive in a new geological structure of mountains. The trees slowly vanish as you move along the torrential stream of Chenab river. Alpine meadows and wild flowers try to cover the hard, bare craggy base of the mountains. *Rosa webbiana* (Himalayan wild rose) is a beautiful sight by the road. It's a lovely wild flower that blooms in the grassy meadows on craggy slopes. Yellow oriental hawk weed acorns the alpine grass trying to cover the stony nudity. From Keylong to Leh, mother nature slowly opens to stony nudity, innocence, purity and emptiness.

We reach Keylong at noon after the nightlong journey and decide to stay at the quaint peaceful town for a day and then catch the early morning bus that arrives from Delhi.

Little scenic Keylong is situated in the valley of Bhaga river that roars past to meet Chenab river down the stream. Beautiful snowy peaks overlook the small town. Two of these are quite popular: Lady of Keylong peak (6016 m) and the Saptarishi peaks. There are many myths and legends linked to these peaks.

Lady of Keylong peak was earlier called '*Churail*' by the locals. The Europeans gave it a nicer name and now it's a popular trekking point in the area. It is the bare face of a cliff that looks like a hill woman holding a scythe and a baby tied to her back against the background of pristine white ice sheet of the glacier around it. I'm glad that now she is called the Lady of Keylong, not *Churail*. She inspires many trekkers to take the challenge to go and look at her from close quarters.

The Saptarishi peaks at Keylong are a series of seven beautiful peaks on the top of a high ridge. The name *Saptarishi* connotes seven sages (Marichi, Atri, Angira, Pulaha, Kratu, Pulastya and Vasishtha) in Hindu cosmology.

The small budget hotel, Khandorling Guest House, gives a heartening view of pastures on the lower slopes and glaciers in the upper reaches. I can see a little monastery on the opposite hill. Fluffs of snow-white clouds hang languidly in the pristine blue sky. The wind plays with the prayer flags. The Buddhists believe that as the flags move in the wind, they spread the message of love and peace for the entire world. Bhaga river is audible with its rigorous sound in the valley below. From the terrace I can have the entire view of the lazily sprawled out bus station. I inhale big breaths of unruffled peace.

There are a few eateries. Lama *dhaba* is run by an old gracious Tibetan Buddhist lady. I mention HH Dalai Lama and tell her that I have been lucky to meet him and hold his hand and put it to my forehead. Immediately her eyes get filled with tears of reverence. I tell her that His hand feels boneless on touch, almost like a newborn's soft contact, the touch of divinity. She listens to it like she is listening to hymns in a monastery. He is their God King. Her father came to India with Him and later settled in Nepal. Making the ends meet is very tough, she says. The monthly rent for the shop is 8,000 rupees per month.

Her neighboring outlets are named Kathmandu *dhaba* and Sherpa *dhaba*. Mostly women run these tiny food establishments. These little hotels and restaurants offer tea, coffee, omelets, maggi, noodles, cold drinks, cigarettes, *namkeen*, chips, *rotis*, *rajma chawal*. The family stays in a part of the same block. The eating points are mostly run by the Nepalese and the Tibetans. The hotels are owned by the locals. Most of them go to Manali during the snowbound months of winter and return in summer. The menfolk work as casual laborers, but mostly the women pull the domestic economic cart.

As I have mentioned, there is just one bus from Keylong to Leh, the Delhi-Leh Himachal roadways bus that has an early morning halt here before moving onto the final destination in the land of mountain passes. Most of it is full with tourists from Delhi itself. At Keylong the bus depot changes and a smaller bus takes over for the further journey on treacherous roads cutting across high Himalayas. At Keylong about two dozen tourists have to fight for three-four odd seats available at this point. If the seats aren't available, many still decide to board the bus and travel standing in the aisle. We talk to the driver who has driven the bus from Leh. He is a decent chap and proves a nice Himachali host to we plainsmen. We compliment him on his good nature. Then we share our problem with him. He gives his word that he will try his level best to get us seats the next day. Pay some sincere compliments to someone and he or she will always reciprocate. We have a chance to get seats in the early morning bus next day. Till then Keylong has enough peace to cordially shower upon us.

We go to the old Buddhist woman's small eatery for dinner and not feeling hungry ask for maggi. She makes a face. 'Maggi for dinner! That's not healthy,' she says. If you talk nicely and give respect to people, you create a human touch. She is concerned about the quality of our food. So Mrs. Lama convinces us to eat a proper dinner and lovingly makes *rotis* and *sabzi* like a mother. If food is served with joy, it feels very fulfilling. The appetite returns and we eat to our full without even realizing it.

After the nice dinner as we lie down to sleep, Bhaga river's gurgling murmurs sing a lullaby to get us into the folds of a restful sleep. Early next morning, the driver we talked to yesterday remembers us and gets us seats among the rush of many claimants for the few odd seats. The bus moves with an excited load of the plainsmen looking forward to enjoy the road trip across the highest motorable mountain passes, glacial lakes, deep valleys and scores of snowy dazzlement. There are mesmerizing landscapes of Jispa and Sarchu leading to Nakka La.

The most adventurous and tough stretch is called Gata loops at 16,800 feet. There are creepy, spooky stories about the treacherous series of these hairpin bends going one after the other. Gata loops stretch for about 10 km, involving 21 hairpin bends leading to Nakka La. A myth says that the dangerously loopy stretch is haunted by a spirit. They say a man in shawl appears suddenly asking for cigarettes or water thus scaring the drivers. So the people pay a respectful tribute to the spirit to pass safely to the other side by offering bottles of mineral water and cigarette packets. You have this big pile of offerings to the spirit on the nineteenth bend. There is a small stone structure built here and it contains a human skull in it.

The story of the spirit of Gata loops is based on an event happening a few decades back. Those were the days when there was no Atal Tunnel to provide year-around passage for traffic to this side of Rohtang La pass. The narrow, rugged road had to take Rohtang La pass, which was snowbound for many months in a year. A truck driver and his helper started from Manali almost on the date when the road was being closed for the winter months. So probably they were the only vehicle on the road from Manali to Leh. The snow was already making it difficult at many stretches. Their truck gave in at Gata loops. There was no help and no mobile phones to contact anyone during those days. In order to seek help, the driver walked back, leaving the helper with the truck. He reached a human habitation about 40-50 km down the road. But before he could start back on the journey with men and material for help, there were more landslides and snowfall preventing them from moving ahead. The poor helper died after two or three days. So the people say his spirit sometimes appears by the side of a vehicle asking for *beedis* or water.

The bus ride is adventurous at many levels: leading to lovely rich barrenness with its sandy hills, splendid golden plains, yaks, sheep, goats and some rare nomadic tent that one may come across. The fabulous, aloof, unadorned, beautiful face of mother nature. Travelling on the rugged road you feel like a child running into the open arms of freely playing childhood. As the bus struggled on the top of mountains, slowly chugging ahead, some passengers faced breathing problems born of mountain sickness. But thankfully all the plainsmen reached to the other side with reasonable safety.

As the bus moves to Leh, at full speed through the plains leading to the capital, one feels freedom and openness in the sandy plains spread on both sides of the road. It feels like there are no boundaries. One feels like flying. It seems like an earthly version of cosmic freedom. These are Moore plains, a plateau spread out in brown majesty along the last phase of the Manali-Leh highway. In Tibetan it means a plain where the wild ass doesn't find water. It covers an amazing 40 km stretch between Pang and Leh. Nomadic population has shrunk dramatically. But still you can spot some nomadic settlement with their tents, sheep, goats and yaks in enclosures. The yaks are becoming fewer and fewer. Almost all individual nomadic families have a pick-up truck parked by their tent-side. I could spot just one yak during the journey. Ladakh without the yaks doesn't sound fitting. But the camps by the smooth road, even with their pick-up trucks, still carry enough touristy charisma for the visitors. To provide some more lease to my hopes of the survival of the wildlife, I was lucky to see some herds of wild ass and *bhralls* on the craggy slopes by the road.

The average elevation of the Moore plains is about 4800 m. Some portions along Lungpa river create stunning sand and rock formations. After the challenges of the previous mountain pass (Tanglang pass), the bikers love this stretch as they speed at a high speed towards Leh. If you are lucky you can see a little sand tornado travelling across the road or along the sides. It's arid, rocky, scenic. The road is smooth here and it feels like your back is getting a massage after the jolts of unpaved, uneven roads over the mountain passes.

Leh feels congested and very hot. The effects of tourists and climate change obviously. A ribbon of ancient culture tightly squeezed by the commercial forces trying to encash the old; to mint new gold. Bare, craggy hills surrounding the small houses sprawled with a strange mixture of the old and the new, but still somehow feeling on the ancient side. The Indus river gives a small chance to plant life in the valley. Poplars and willows stand out like green brushstrokes on the brown, barren canvas. The ornate, artistic Buddhist architecture is like a soft whisper, a prayer, an artistic muse. The sound and sights of Buddhist rituals, mystique of murals, monastic gateways, intriguing carvings, rich forte of ritualistic practices in monasteries, souvenir shops, prayer wheels, prayer flags— all fluttering for life among barren stones.

Enter a monastery and you are enveloped in a world infused with an intermixing of spirituality and artistry. You feel like stones have as vibrant a heart as the lush green trees. Prayer flags fluttering in the evening breeze and the message of love and peace floating up, rising in the air and kiss the golden yellow on the tops of brown hills. Small white lime-washed houses having multi-paneled glass windows look at you with unhurried demeanor. Clouds hung lazily in the azure blue. Touristy hustle and bustle in the bazaars. Leh is the base camp for the wanderlust tourists seeking the higher meaning of life among the unparalleled landscapes of Ladakh. There is no destination, you move and make a fresh path; a lively destination, the journey itself.

Before you take more arduous journeys across the length and breadth of this amazing landmass, it's advisable to stay at Leh and enjoy the local places for at least a couple of days. We do the same and visit the nearby places in Leh.

The *shanti stupa* is a white-domed, two-level *stupa* on a hilltop. Built by a Japanese, Bhikshu Gyomyo Nakamura, in 1991, it holds the Buddha's relics, serving as the foundations of the spiritual heritage of Buddhism, at its base which were enshrined by HH Dalai Lama. The place is adorned with panoramic surroundings. Ladakhi Buddhists offered voluntary labor and the Japanese

Buddhists provided money and technical knowhow to build this monument of peace. Like most of the Buddhist monuments, it's built to promote world peace and harmony. Beautiful golden Buddha image stands as a spiritual patron. Around the dome you have relief pictures of auspicious symbols, *dharmachakra* (turning the wheel of dharma), Buddha's birth and death events, Buddha defeating the devils and many meditating Buddha *mudras.*

Leh palace is a lovely legacy set in mud, stone and poplar and willow wood. The palace overlooks Leh from the top of the Namgyal hill. It was built by Sengge Namgyal around 1600 AD. It has nine floors. The upper floors housed the royal family and the lower floors served for the soldiers apart from providing space for stables and stores. There are beautiful Tibetan *thanka* paintings and colorful murals made of crushed gems and stones. The murals depict sacred Buddhist themes, symbols and mythical deities. One has to have patience to get a real sense of the marvelously intricate details of these paintings. The palace is a splendid piece of heritage constructed on the lines of Potala Palace. It was deserted after Dogra commander Zorawar Singh captured Ladakh. The royal family was shifted to Shyok palace. It's a nice specimen of the medieval Tibetan architecture involving massive mud-stone walls, wooden balconies, mural paintings, poplar rafters and wooden flooring.

Gurdwara Shri Pathar Sahib is situated about 25 km from Leh. When Guru Nanak Dev ji Maharaj were returning after visiting Tibet around 1515, they rested here for some time and meditated. Indian soldiers do *langar seva* and eat food with the tourists. The visitors have to cover their head under a yellow scarf bearing the *akal takht* symbol. All become one here. It's a message of unity. Tourists from across India and soldiers from different states, regions, castes and classes all sit together on the ground and eat like innocent children. It seems it's managed by the army itself because they take care of all the affairs here. Eating *prasad* here is a very fulfilling experience.

The other place that we visited is Sangam, the confluence of Indus and Zanskar rivers. The Zanskar river carries lots of coquettish energy like *shakti* and the Indus river allows her to have her flirtatious ways and show-off by almost stopping its own flow like Shiva, the stable self. The Indus allowing Zanskar to go rippling across its more stable waters. In fact the Indus waters seem to take a back step to enable the feminine force of Zanskar to surge ahead. Meanwhile massive stony mountains look down at the majestic scene with amusement. Standing at the confluence one can clearly see the green water of the Indus to the left and the brown waters of the Zanskar to the right.

There are buses plying to remote parts of Ladakh from Leh. But one has to be careful about their timing because most of these aren't daily services and operate just two or three days a week. Nowhere else I found the time table painted on a wall at a bus station more useful than here. One can save a lot of money by taking these buses. Bikes are for the young blood. Personal SUVs are for the super-rich. Rented taxis are for the rich. And for the middle class budget travelers the public transport is the safest bet. Moreover, travelling with local Ladakhi people is an added incentive for free if you take a bus. Public transport is a very practical and economic way of exposing one to the local culture. You get a deeper feel of the ground realities.

We take a bus to the Nubra valley. It's a private bus run by an interesting chap named Dorjee. He operates it under a license issued by the government authority. The bus runs twice weekly between Leh and Nubra valley, reaching till a place about 20 km further from Hunder. The jangling, smoke-exhaling vehicle leaves at eight in the morning and reaches the destination in the evening. The return journey is on the next day. A short, strong, agile, athletic man,

Dorjee is a multi-tasker serving as the owner, driver, helper, conductor, fuel man, porter, everything.

An amazing man as we watch him closely during the journey. He is very helpful. He even stops his bus by a little hamlet on the way to inform the passengers who are inside their houses, feeling assured that he won't miss them. I'm sure that he would even wake up some still sleeping person who has asked him to remind that the bus has arrived.

Many local people boarded the bus in Leh for short journeys within the city and easily got down without caring to pay. He doesn't mind such minor issues. He is particularly popular among the lady workers busy in the road-keeping operations on the path. They wave cheerfully at him as they see his rattling, old bus laden with people inside and the roof piled high with luggage and other wares, a bed and sofa set this time that have been firmly tied by his own expert hands.

The road to Nubra valley passes through Khardungla pass about 40 km from Leh. It's the highest motorable road in the world. The construction workers from Bihar, baked by the high altitude sun, are busy almost all along the way. A woman is working with her child tied to her back. They look eagerly at the upcoming bus. They have set up temporary tents along the road, so there is hardly any facility here. To give you a clue to how things are managed in this tough, remote terrain, one worker is cutting another's hair.

It's a busy, noisy, dusty serpentine line across the barren mountains, beaten by a merciless sun and stung by rough winds: the earthmovers and cutters shrieking with effort to gnaw at the stony innards of the lofty mountains; the workers plodding, hacking into the stony sides to leave an imprint of the indomitable spirit of the mankind to reach all points on the earth. But the mountains look too powerful in their barrenness to be daunted by the mankind and their machinery.

Khardungla is the gateway to Nubra and Shyok valleys. After Khardungla pass the road descends to a scenic view. The barren rocks get a slight tinge of green alpine grasses. Nubra river originates from Siachin glacier. (The government plans to start Siachin base camp tourist adventure.) It gurgles like an oasis in the mountainous cold desert. Stunted poplars, willows, bushes and shrubs surround Khardungla village, which is a big hamlet from Ladakhi standards.

As the bus stops for refreshment breaks near little hamlets having a shop or two, I see that even the birds are relaxed like the local people. As I sip tea looking lost in the relaxing wilderness, a black and white Ladakh magpie sits on the branch of a low willow tree by the road, just near the eating point swarmed with the passengers. Unbothered about human intervention, it just sat there for almost ten minutes. It's a lovely sight to see a wild bird sitting so near to you.

Nubra river joins Shyok river, which later on merges with the Indus. As we move on after the break, it becomes even more challenging passage along the mighty and majestic Shyok river. It first follows southeasterly direction through Pangong range; then takes a northwestern turn, almost going parallel to the previous path in reverse direction. In Tibetan its name means 'gravel spreader' which is amply testified by vast stretches of sandy gravel on its broad, intimidating floodplains glistening white like snow under scorching midday sun on the right of the road. It's also mentioned as the river of death due to the havoc caused by it on the silk route trading caravans in ancient times.

We get down at Hunder in the evening. It's famous for the majestic sand dunes running in a broad valley flanked by lofty walls of completely barren dark-brown rocky heights. Here the tourists enjoy rides on double-humped camels walking in a row in the Shyok valley, imitating the famous silk route caravans of the ancient times.

At Hunder we stayed at an ex-soldier's guest house. He had scaled Mount Everest during his army days and now carried the same indomitable spirit in setting up a lovely guest house. The first floor is beautifully done and ready for check-ins. The upper story is still under construction. The mess with classy wooden furniture is as impressive as the officers' mess at an army cantonment. His family assists the cook in making food. The food is delicious. The bedding is clean. It's a nice room. It's like a little oasis among the sand dunes.

The evening breeze is freshened by the swaying branches of poplars, willows, bushes and shrubs. The camels, after a tiring day of ferrying the tourists across the sand dunes, rush to the bushes after their duty is over as the night falls. A lovely clean-watered stream flows through the sparse high-altitude scrub forest nearby.

I have done my research on Ladakh flowers, plants, shrubs and trees. So I'm able to read the traces of life written on stones in the shape of little wild flowers. From May to September, up to an elevation of 3800 m in valleys like Nubra beautiful little flowers welcome you. Purple colored *acomite* is pretty common. Little yellow blooms of a alpine herb named *phulumentok* are the indomitable signs of life among craggy rocks. Then there are flowering shrubs like *khardung* (yellow), Himalaya may apple (white or pink), *chagna* (bright mauve) and a few more.

As I walk along the dwarf scrub growths along the little stream passing near the sand dunes of Hunder, I can spot common juniper (*shukpa*), a shrub with crowned needle-like leaves. How can I forget that fragrant smell that I inhaled in a monastery back at Leh? *Shukpa* has fragrant leaves and bark, which are used by the Buddhists as incense. There are clumps of sea buckthorn as well. It's a dwarf thorny shrub with a woody stem. It's a storehouse of vitamins and medicinal properties. I have ordered online a few packets of Ladakh sea buckthorn tea a few times. It's a strangely elating feeling to stand next to this remote tree in a distant part of India.

On the moist slopes you have *tiktas*, a grass like shrub. On dry rocks and stony slopes there are *kabra* shrubs. All these shrubs are highly medicinal in nature. In the traditional Tibetan system of medicine, these rare hardy plants, flowers and shrubs are used in profusion with great effect. Something that grows in such adverse climatic conditions must be having a very high potential and vitality for life. No wonder they make highly effective medicines.

I met a German woman near Turtuk. She is on a quest to be away from the hassles of professional life back home. There are so many foreigners who have lost their path in the maze of Himalayan spirituality. I feel she is an easy catch to be lost in the exotic Eastern chaos. So I load her with lots of unsolicited advice. I tell her to keep the goal limited, in sight: just aiming to recharge her sagging batteries, go back home and start a new job with new vigor. She was uncomfortable to this truth to begin with. But later she digested the essence of my point.

The Himalaya is a great seducer. It pulls with irresistible charm. It's a great charging port of high frequency energy, no doubt about it. But it's suitable to be there as travelers now and then. Charge your battery, explore yourself and make the most of your potential at a place where you need to be for your own self and your loved ones. I know I have to run away from my old self. But I also know that I have to stop as well. And Ladakh is an endless path. You can tire yourself out, but it won't come to an end. You think you have covered hundreds of miles, but that's nothing on the scale of this limitless playground.

We return to Leh when Dorjee the great comes back for his second weekly trip to Hunder. In the intervening time it was an amazing experience there.

We then plan to go to the Pangong lake. The bus on that route is scheduled for the day after tomorrow. The day in between offers a great opportunity to enjoy HH

Dalai Lama birthday celebrations at Choglamsar about 8 km from Leh city center. It's a Tibetan Buddhist settlement and no wonder it gives a faint smell of how Lhasa must be. There are artisans here who are keeping alive the age-old tradition of handcrafted souvenirs and painted wooden furniture. The place is a heartbeat of Ladakhi and Tibetan traditions.

The great man's birthday celebrations offer a top end, full day festivity for the Buddhists. Family and friends form groups and set up tents in a sprawling ground. You can see people enjoying food and tea on the low tables adorned with Tibetan wood painting involving ornate carvings and spiritual iconography. Everyone is dressed in traditional dresses. They play lovely Tibetan and Ladakhi songs and perform mesmerizing group dancing. The dancers move elegantly in concentric circles. It's a slow movement with poise and grace, gently tapping feet and peacefully waving of limbs. Almost slow poetic movements. Throughout the day they have been enjoying food and tea in their tents with their near and dear ones. An entire day full of being dressed in the best traditional costumes, eating, chatting, dancing and praying. A lovely funfair full of colorful symbolism of spirituality.

Then in the evening there is a lottery ticket result announcement. A woman wins and she can't believe she has won the top prize. She is very shy when she goes to receive the prize. The people shout, laugh and applaud. At a nearby monastery, the boy lamas have toy guns and bows and arrows to play in celebration of the grand occasion. HH Dalai Lama turns 89 this day. Long live the great man because He is almost a lifeline for Tibetan Buddhism.

The Jammu and Kashmir transport bus starts for Pangong lake at four in the morning. Another exciting journey starts. The road ascends to Chang La. It's a lovely weather with slight precipitation on the lower reaches. There are sparse coverings of blue lettuce and peppergrass bushes on the side slopes. White dragonhead enjoy their high altitude seat on the stony slopes. Then the high mountain pass welcomes us with its fluffy spray: snowfall.

Snowfall is a big wonder for the people from the plains. The vehicles halt and the tourists start dancing in the snowfall. And once you start descending from the high mountain pass, beautiful valleys open up with their alpine grasses and wild flowers.

The Ladakhi ecosystem is very relaxed. A tiny chit of black puppy is relaxing in the middle of the road near Durbuk in Tangtse valley. A huge military truck has to halt and honk horn so that the lazy guy clears the road. It doesn't. A smiling *havaldar* with big handlebar moustache gets down, picks up the prince and puts him at a safe distance. Only then the army truck starts on its journey.

The Leh-Pangong road has all the charms to satisfy all of your wanderlust desires. Occasional wild roses smile at you from among the rocks. Tiny yellow dandelions and sea buckthorn (Leh barley) give you an idea that even stones have a heart and they show it through these seasonal blooms. A few stunted willows, poplars, violet-colored Himalayan crane's bill and pink fireweed watch you with curiosity from the side of streams. Purple and white colored spotted heart orchid beautifies the open meadows, moist places and open slopes. There is tiny Himalayan winterfat, a sparse pale grassy shrub by the little streambeds near Durbuk. The stony wastelands also show a softer side as they welcome you with cow's lungwort (*desi* tobacco). Stunted juniper (*shukpa*) is the state tree. Its fragrant leaves and bark provide beautiful moments of perfumed bonhomie at social gatherings and religious ceremonies.

The land of passes has a few offerings in terms of tress: poplars, willows, apricots, walnuts. High altitude meadows with summer blooms of edelweiss and wild roses. The rest is simply imposing barren stone walls, snow-capped peaks, glaciers shining under the sun. And the mankind's eternal quest to reach higher and higher; making roads, repair works, a never-ending job in this tough environment. One can't help marveling at the small, robust Ladakhi women working at the construction sites.

And there we stand on the banks of the multi-colored marvel, a little puddle in the navel of the mighty Himalayas: Pangong lake. It's a work of fluid art by the eternally musing artist. The lake is an open canvas. The surrounding hills are the frame. The brush is made of the sun, the clouds and the sky. The shifting angle of the sun is the hand moving the brush. The swabs of white, grey and dark clouds and the pristine blue lurking through them create a wonderful art of lovely colors on the canvas of the lake waters. Colors mix, flow, merge along the waves. Sit on the bank and you see the colors moving—blue, green, moss green, indigo, grey, purple. A beautiful watery canvas where multiple colors play with the sun, wind, clouds, sky.

We check in at a homestay by the road overlooking the wavy, colorful, heaving bosom of the lake. Just a little row of homestays and the rest comprising mother earth's sunlit yard high in the mountains. It's run by three women: grandmother, daughter-in-law and granddaughter. It's very reasonably priced, just 1500 rupees/night including food. They have a nice little mess hall with carpeted floor, low tables, cushions, chests and little prayer wheels by the seats. You can feel the strong effect of the monastic culture even in the mess room here. Sacred symbols and auspicious motifs have almost as dense existence at homes as they do at monasteries. While we eat, the old woman rolls the prayer wheel and says prayers. 'This is for you guys. She is praying for you so that the food you take is good for you,' her granddaughter tells us while serving the food. That's Buddhism for you, the religion of compassion.

They handle the tourists of all types and inclinations with lots of grace and elegance. After a two-night stay, at the time of leaving I thank them for the nice hospitality. The pretty, young Ladakhi girl softly and shyly says, 'Please come again!' And I say, 'Yes, we will.' One ought to keep one's promises.

It is an otherworldly experience by the lake. Just to be with the lake is a meditative experience. I simply open myself to the icy cold wind and the noisily swashing lake waters. The lake almost a big blue, heaving, rippling temple having a goddess of universal well-being somewhere in its depths. And the moment you accept this fact in totality, a thing or phenomenon will touch you with its essence of divinity. The untamed harmony and solitude percolate deep into my cells. It is a feeling belonging to a new dimension. After a long spell of meditation on the lake shore, with half closed eyes I see my torso as a flaming ball of indigo. A great experience.

I enjoyed lovely walks along the shore. Studied the rare sprouts of vegetation among the alkaline stony barrenness on the stretch between the road and the lake shore for a few kilometers towards the line of actual control (LAC). I could spot a kind of knotweed and cream-colored sprouts, a kind of purslane. If you are an open-hearted wanderlust person, just be there to witness the show, mother nature will surely won't disappoint you. I spot a Himalayan hare among the stones. There is a little colony of brown agile birds that nests in holes dug under small stones. The ground nest is actually a passage under a stone with both ends open. I can see one odd big Himalayan raven and a pair of in-love gulls that leisurely flow over the water. It's very windy most of the time and the waves strike the banks like a mini sea. It's an amazing tapestry of water stretched among high mountains.

The waves crash, the colors change, the wind buffets. The long line of sand and gravel along the shore offers a broad avenue to walk in solitude and find your real footing away from the hustle and bustle of life in the congested plains. During these walks I sit down and meditate now and then. The moment I close my eyes, I can feel that it's a very high energy place. The level of self-peek is totally different.

The lake has its colorful canvas and music that varies through the day. Sometimes I go knee deep in the water, taking a symbolic bath by sprinkling some ice cold drops over my head, bow and pray and taste the salty water as *prasad*.

Some of the tourists who have travelled in the bus with us are staying at the same homestay, the others at the neighboring lodges. One is a very tall Spanish-looking guy from Pune. But good for him that he was balanced by a lack of macho spirit. That makes one more realistic in life. A macho body with macho spirit creates chances of crash landing in pits. There is this girl, a researcher from the JNU, who is travelling solo but has the restlessness and readiness to change her solo status to a partnered travel. The girl is ordinary looking but very high in flirting spirits. She waits for the guys to approach. But they have the alluring Pangong to attend to, so nobody dances around her. The moments here are very precious.

At night most of the tourists are having drinks outside the homestay looking into the wind coming from the lake. She is tipsy and almost falls in the laps of the men around. My brother doesn't drink. A sober guy. I'm a light drinker on very-very special occasions. He proposes a walk in the night on the road circuiting by the side of the lake. All the guys, fifteen to twenty in number, get ready for a walk. The lake is silent. The milky way perfectly clear. The stars so clear and near that you feel like raising your hand and pluck them. But the short, fat, bespectacled man doesn't get up. He is busy with his beer bottle. Slightly cross-eyed, I had observed during the day. 'You guys are from Haryana. Now you are saying that it's just a stroll on the road. Further on you will say let's jump into the lake and try to cross over to the other side. I won't go,' he declares.

The rest of us start. It's pitch dark. There is no running electricity here, just some diesel-set generated power available for a few hours. The nights are pitch dark. Beautiful. We have walked just a couple of hundred meters and it feels like we are in the remotest uninhabited part of the world. No sound, no sight. Just the sky and the stars. My brother then tells them that there is no risk here; no reptiles slithering around. Just this snow leopard sometimes makes it exciting. He is very mischievous at such moments. The word 'snow leopard' drops like a bomb. As we move on and must have walked for another hundred meters or so, we find the group severely depleted in number. Now it's just me, my brother and the two Bangladeshi tourists. The rest have dropped off the walk stealthily, beating any snow leopard in the art, and gone back to the safety of their rooms.

Iftikar is from Bangladesh. He is travelling with his friend. He is in mid fifties. The man is enjoying the trip like a bird set free from the cage. His wife suffered from a rare ailment for almost a quarter century. As her partner he was right there bearing his share of pain and suffering with loving kindness. He gave her the best possible treatment. Then she died. After overcoming the critical phase of mourning the loss, now he is flying freely in Ladakh. I can feel he is a very nice human being who deserves this open joy after a tough personal phase. Joyful, all smiles, making friends, creating group bonhomie, clicking pictures, insisting on sitting on the front seat in the bus—that's Iftikar. On the way up, he had danced with childish joy in the snowfall on the Baralacha pass. Now, in the sympathizing pools of darkness by the lake, it's a gentle talk with the stranger who feels so familiar with his grief and pursuit of happiness after the storm has passed.

We come back to our place after one and a half hours later. All the tourists have gone into their rooms. Only Jishnu is morosely sitting outside on a chair. He had met the Spanish-looking Pune guy on the bus and to save money they had taken a shared room. The Pune guy hasn't returned. Jishnu is very tight on budget and is scared that his room partner will stay with the girl and won't pay half the money he owes for the room charges.

He is a small Keralite; a charmingly dark boy with a flawless white-teethed smile. Well the girl has probably succeeded in changing the solo status of her journey. Girls have an advantage in this manner. In a way, the Pune guy has dumped Jishnu. We have words of consolation with him. He feels that we are friendly guys and breaks his shyness to talk in his broken English and still more devastated Hindi. He stays at his friend's place at Kasol and does some graphic designing for him in return. Presently, he seems to be running around Ladakh like a clueless tiny mouse; understandable because he is around only 25 years in age. On our return to Leh, to help him on his shoe-strung budget, we offer him to stay in our room on a mattress at the rate of 250 rupees/night because this is what he usually pays in a dormitory for a bunk. It makes him very happy.

Back in Leh, Jishnu introduces us to a small eatery in one corner of the bus station compound at the end of a small row of shops. An old Ladakhi lady operates the little tin-shed tea shop. She treats him like her own child. Her tea is fabulous—a big glass, full. The graceful woman looks very happy to serve us Tibetan bread, omelet, noodles or maggi. Her daughter works as a bank clerk in Amritsar. The husband drives a bus on contract for the army. Very soon we also join the league of her sons like Jishnu.

She is our *aunty* now and we become her regular customers. Aunty is graced with a natural, loving smile. She serves us tea like a mother. There is an affectionate touch; not a strictly professional approach to the task. The charges for her servings are cheaper than anywhere else we have seen in Leh.

Jishnu is a quite boy, hardly speaks Hindi. She doesn't understand English. But both of them have developed a mother-son bond with the language of silence. Her glass of tea contains almost double of what others serve in tiny paper cups. Smile and kindness are showered for free. She has visited Delhi and stayed with her daughter in Amritsar for some time. As a tourist, just like any other native of the land, most of whom are saturated with silence and emptiness, she loves crowds and the hustle-bustle of shoulder-rubbing humanity. She also likes lush green trees in the lesser Himalayas and in the plains below. I think they are saturated with the barren emptiness here, which attracts us so forcefully because we are burdened with the crowded strife and chaos at our places in the plains. So it's natural that the crowds of plains seem very interesting to them; and we enjoy the Ladakhi peace and silence.

We enjoy the summertime charms of Leh by visiting more places nearby like Thiksey monastery and Shey palace. We have enough time to feel relaxed, loiter around and experience the deeper layers of Ladakhi culture. So there is no time constraint forcing us to rent a car and go rushing like people usually do while on a short trip. We take a small city bus to Choglamsar and from there the locals tell us that we can get shared vans or jeeps to the monastery and the palace.

We have been waiting for an hour but there is no shared van or jeep today. Finally, a kind gentleman gives us a free lift in his junked van with a luxurious welcome. There are no autos in Leh. Had there been autos, it would have been more congested. But the taxis charge too much for budget travelers. A taxi to and fro from the palace and the monastery charges more than a day's boarding and food costs in Leh.

The gentleman, who has given us a ride, is rich in heart and sits like a king in his junked Maruti van. One sliding door is jammed. One seat at the back is removed and in its place you have jacks, tools and a spare tyre lying on the dusty carpetless floor. We clamber in. The seat is dusty as if sandbags have been ferried on it. A local woman also sneaks in.

The driver is evidently a very kind man. He has to attend a very urgent task at a construction site about one kilometer from Shey palace, so feeling a bit sorry he drops us at this point. When we offer him fare, he says a very firm no and smilingly gives us instructions about the path to the palace from the place where he has dropped us.

Shey palace stands on a hill overlooking the road. It bears toned down ancient Ladakhi luxury embellished with Tibetan architecture. The roofs are made of poplar and willow wood. Starting from one corner of the palace, a craggy ridge reaches to the pointed peak of the neighboring hill. From the sunlit terraces of the palace, one can see the ruins of stonework done in gravel and mud on this peak. The ruined tower somehow still holding its head high. It's an interesting rock-climbing experience to clamber up over the stony ridge to reach the top of the hill bearing the decaying, time-ruined stonework. Long strings of prayer flags are drawn along the way. Most probably it was a religious site used by the royals during their heydays. The cautious climb becomes a pilgrimage. Once you reach the top and enter the roofless tower chamber, you get a feeling of achieving a milestone in your journey.

Coming out of the palace, we take a shortcut along the tiny agricultural fields and poplar and willow groves along the Indus river to reach Thiksey monastery situated on the top of another hill. The place is about 20 km from Leh. It's a tiny replica of Potala palace. There is a separate block, an attached nunnery, for the female renunciates in the 12-storey complex adorned with Buddhist art, little *stupas*, impressive statues, *thankas* and mural paintings. The colorful murals painted with meditative muse; gently painted, weaving majestic tales of symbolism recounting the Buddhist aspect of truth. Done in natural pigments, these much-detailed works open a teasing world of elaborate Buddhist rituals, beliefs and practices. A world of yellow, red, green, blue and gold. A vast ceremonial offering to the ultimate by the human spirit.

The highlight is the 15-meter high statue of *Maitreya* made of clay and copper. It's gold-painted to give it a shiny perfection. In little shrines and alcoves one can see a mesmerizing complexity of murals depicting Tibetan calendars, the wheel of life, thousand armed *Avalokitesvara*, female deities and many other religious symbols. There is a separate temple for an important female deity, Tara. The temple also contains dozens of tiny, alcove-sized shrines for various smaller female deities.

There is an ascending order of floors, the top floors for the high pontiff and the abbots. You feel like rising to a higher dimension as you take the impressive flight of steps from the terraced fronts taking you to the upper floors having marvelous rooms and shrines painted in white, red and ochre. It is clearly visible that it was built as a fort monastery. Standing on the terraced ramparts one can have a beautiful view of the Indus valley below with its semi-sparse green brushstroke among the barren brown of hills.

Ladakh has a unique charm. It's made for purposeless wandering in the open-ended stony charms of mother existence. There is unparalleled solitude and peace. The barren stones more peaceful than lush green forests. Forests are the manifestations of the creative potential in the stony womb. So maybe being in the barren stony embrace of nature makes you feel closer to the source, the emptiness. The source of creation. The stones present a huge truth in their naked, imposing avatar. It's a lovely experience to share this barren serenity and solitude. The people are so warm and gentle, a unique product of this exceptional landscape.

I'm peeling layers after layers of my worldly self in this welcoming wilderness. Ladakh is a travel, a journey, an endless destination for exploring. It's a living entity. As I discover more about it, I discover myself as a sweet byproduct.

Since Leh is our base camp for forays into Ladakhi hinterland, we have built a little circle of acquaintances around the place where we stay. The hotel is located a couple of minutes walk from the bus station. That gives us the choice to loiter around the bus station, enquiring about the buses plying on various routes, whenever we have time. We also go there after our dinner for a digestive stroll. The bus from Delhi arrives around nine at night. And it's a nice sight to see the excited passengers disembarking to feast on these lovely landscapes. We have also made friendly acquaintances with five or six HRTC drivers and conductors who run the buses on this tough route on a rotational basis.

The Muslim guard keeps a vigil inside the compound at night. He has a thin Buddhist friend. Once he pulls the long, low iron-gate on its tiny bearing wheels, it's his kingdom inside the bus station. The guard is lame and keeps a long stick to support his polio-afflicted leg. His Buddhist friend is a wiry man in soiled yellow robes. He is a convert from a poor, low-caste Hindu family. Life is easy for both of them after ten at night once the hustle and bustle stops. They get drunk to a nice degree. During the busy tourist season they make some extra money as well. Tourists ask them to reserve their tickets on the Delhi-Leh and other routes to the tourist destinations in Ladakh. The frequency of buses is very less and there is always a fight for tickets. Since they stay at the station compound itself, they can get a few seats reserved and charge a commission on the tickets. A little enterprise which can be pardoned given the fact that it gives them some scope to get a little high at the end of the day.

There is a *Rajasthani* family, headed by a big-turbaned mustached old man, selling aphrodisiacs. The old man arrives with his family during the summers. At night, we usually find them sprawled on the open floor of the empty high-roofed, open-sided waiting shed. His young daughter-in-law has an infant. She has more privacy. She and her husband need privacy even more, given the product they deal in and must be experimenting on themselves as well. So they have a tiny sleeping tent for the young couple.

The old man has smartly memorized the bus timings to various destinations. If you happen to be lost in semi-darkness looking for the ways and means of increasing your chances of getting a bus tomorrow, he will hark your attention and tell you the timings and the smarter ways of getting an advance ticket. These are very valuable inputs. Of course he would always expect you to reciprocate by buying his vitality-enhancing herbal medicines to make yourself a superhero in the bed.

In these two weeks, we are able to get friendly with a nice group of bus drivers and conductors. These are old-style sturdy buses, lumbering like tanks on high mountain passes. How do they manage to scream and rattle ahead on the world's highest motorable passes? It's wonderful. The drivers are meditative, alert, smoking lots of cigarettes on the way. They know that they have dozens of lives under their care. The slightest mistake and all are gone.

The driver and his conductor have a day off after their arrival from Keylong. Here they drink, eat and take full rest, mustering up strength for the arduous return journey. Early in the morning, they sit in the bus and take advance bookings for the upcoming journey. Sometimes they are mischievous and tell a white tourist that the bus is full, even while there are vacant seats in the bus. They say it's for a reason. In the case of foreigners, it's their duty to get down at a few check-posts and escort the foreigners, holding their passport in their hands, to be verified by the security personnel. They find it an unnecessary hassle which takes much time.

Affectionately known as Sufi, Sandeep Dahiya is a literary luminary from Sonipat, Haryana, whose evocative storytelling bridges the rustic serenity of his Haryanvi village roots with the vibrant rhythm of urban Delhi. Born into a dual world of rural simplicity and city dynamism, he crafted a narrative voice that pulses with poetic grace, spiritual depth and a tender celebration of life's small pleasures.

His academic journey is lengthy and impressive, with master's degrees in multiple subjects, earned through a path from a village school to a small-town college. Initially driven toward a civil services career, a pivotal remark during a Shimla vacation praising his writing prowess redirected his destiny toward literature.

With over a decade of editorial experience at esteemed academic publishers, Sandeep refined a craft that captures the essence of north India's countryside—its hardworking farmers, tranquil landscapes and timeless wisdom. His extensive bibliography features around twenty titles like Footsteps Lost, Faceless Gods, A Half House, Mists on the Moon, Runaway Husbands and Ice Cubes on Desert Sands, spanning fiction, non-fiction, creative non-fiction and poetry.

His writing stands out for its gentle humanism and intricate storytelling, offering a soothing antidote to the chaos of modern life. In a region where agriculture overshadows literature, Sandeep's choice to weave traditional insights into contemporary narratives marks him as a literary outlier. His unique ability to infuse silent spirituality and poetic charm into every page invites readers to pause, reflect and rediscover beauty in the ordinary, cementing his legacy as a storyteller of the soul.

www.ingramcontent.com/pod-product-compliance
Lightning Source LLC
Chambersburg PA
CBHW051138130726
47988CB00005B/1895